# DIVIDING PUBLIC AND PRIVATE

# Dividing Public and Private

## LAW, POLITICS, AND SOCIAL THEORY

Gerald Turkel

PRAEGER

Westport, Connecticut
London

**Library of Congress Cataloging-in-Publication Data**

Turkel, Gerald.
Dividing public and private : law, politics, and social theory / Gerald Turkel.
p. cm.
Includes bibliographical references and index.
ISBN 0-275-94154-X (alk. paper)
1. Social institutions. 2. Law and politics. 3. Sociology—Methodology—History. I. Title.
HM131.T793 1992
301′.01—dc20 92-12105

British Library Cataloguing in Publication Data is available.



Library of Congress Catalog Card Number: 92-12105
ISBN: 0-275-94154-X

First published in 1992

Praeger Publishers, 88 Post Road West, Westport, CT 06881
An imprint of Greenwood Publishing Group, Inc.

Printed in the United States of America

The paper used in this book complies with the Permanent Paper Standard issued by the National Information Standards Organization (Z39.48-1984).

10 9 8 7 6 5 4 3 2 1

**Copyright Acknowledgments**

The author and publisher gratefully acknowledge permission to use the following copyrighted sources.

Arendt, Hannah. *The Human Condition*. Chicago: University of Chicago Press, 1958. Copyright © 1958. Reprinted with permission.

Durkheim, Emile. *The Division of Labor in Society*, translated by George Simpson. New York: The Free Press, 1964. Reprinted with permission of The Free Press, a Division of Macmillan, Inc.

Durkheim, Emile. *The Rules of Sociological Method*, translated by Sarah A. Solovaya and John H. Mueller, edited by George E. G. Catlin. Copyright © 1938, 1966 by George E. G. Catlin.

Durkheim, Emile. *Suicide*, translated by John A. Spaulding and George Simpson. Copyright © 1951, 1979 by The Free Press. Reprinted with permission of The Free Press, a Division of Macmillan, Inc., and of Routledge & Kegan Paul.

Marx, Karl. *Capital*, vol. 1, translated by Ben Fowkes (Penguin Classics, 1990). Copyright © New Left Review, 1976. Translation copyright © Ben Fowkes, 1976. Reproduced by permission of Penguin Books Ltd. and of Random House, Inc.

Marx, Karl. *The Eighteenth Brumare of Louis Bonaparte*. New York: International Publishers, 1963. Reprinted with permission.

Marx, Karl. "The Manifesto of the Communist Party." In *The Marx-Engels Reader*, edited by Robert C. Tucker. New York: Norton, 1978. Reprinted with permission.

Parsons, Talcott. *The Social System*. Copyright © 1951, 1979 by Talcott Parsons. Reprinted with permission of The Free Press, a Division of Macmillan, Inc., and of Routledge & Kegan Paul.

Parsons, Talcott. *The Structure of Social Action*. Copyright © 1937, 1965 by Talcott Parsons. Copyright © 1968 by The Free Press. Reprinted with permission of The Free Press, a Division of Macmillan, Inc.

Sennett, Richard. *The Fall of Public Man*. Copyright © 1974, 1976 by Richard Sennett. Reprinted by permission of Alfred A. Knopf, Inc., and of Faber & Faber Ltd.

To the memory of my father,

Eli Turkel

# Contents


Preface xi

1 Introduction 1

2 Worst Cases: The Social Transformation of the Public/Private Division 17

**Part I Karl Marx**

3 Emancipation and the Public/Private Division 41

4 A Tale of Two Publics 59

**Part II Emile Durkheim**

5 Constructing the Private Sphere through Corporate Holism 81

6 *Suicide*, the Corporate Individual, and Gender 99

7 Dividing Public and Private: Corporatist Law and Politics 111

**Part III Max Weber**

8 Public and Private as Dichotomy: Methodological Condition and Political Dilemma 129

9 Public Rationalities: Discontinuities and Conflicts 147

**Part IV Talcott Parsons**

10 Socializing the Public/Private Division in Action Theory 169

11 The Weakening of Tensions 185

12 Fusion and Societal Autonomy: The Public/Private Division and Adaptive Culture 199

## Part V Conclusion

13 A Social Affirmation of the Public/Private Division 217

Bibliography 239

Index 251

# Preface

In this book, I have sought to provide ways to more fully comprehend relations among our collective and personal conditions of life by focusing on changing divisions among public and private actions, institutions, and meanings. I do this by reworking core themes and concepts in traditions of social thought, paying particular attention to approaches to law and politics. This work is done in the spirit that thinking is itself a political act: reworking, deepening, and clarifying our understanding of the social sources of our identities, our institutions, and our actions renews our principles, our commitments, and our capacities for making our world.

I have benefited greatly in writing this book from the comments of people who have read it in whole or in part in earlier versions. I especially want to thank Richard Appelbaum, Sally Bould, William Chambliss, Paul Colomy, Richard Flacks, Sandra Harding, Christine Harrington, Brinkley Messick, and David Sciulli for helping me clarify and extend my thinking. Many of the ideas presented here were developed through discussions with graduate students in courses that I have taught in social theory and in the sociology of law at the University of Delaware. I hope that these students have learned as much from me as I have from them over the years. Frank Scarpitti, Chairperson of the Department of Sociology and Criminal Justice at the University of Delaware, has provided me with encouragement and support to see this work come to fruition. I thank Linda Keen, Teresa Robeson, and Judy Watson, the office staff in the Department of Sociology and Criminal Justice, for their incredibly efficient and good-natured help in producing the various drafts of this book.

I owe special thanks to Kathleen Doherty Turkel for sharing her insights and thoughts with me on many of the issues presented here. Some of the themes developed in this book came directly out of conversations with her. I am very proud of our children, Eli and Helen, who are the world's leading experts on the public/private division among people under six years of age.

# DIVIDING PUBLIC AND PRIVATE

# CHAPTER 1

# Introduction

> Our status is backed by the solid buildings of the world, while our sense of personal identity often resides in the cracks.
>
> —Irving Goffman (1961: 320)

This book seeks to make the public/private division central to social theory and sociological inquiry. The distinction between private and public realms of experience, of social activity, and of personal identity are fundamental for shaping the everyday understanding and organization of social life. Yet the division has not been paramount in sociological theorizing. Although the public/private division has been a feature of social inquiry, it has not been a focal point for conceptualizing broad issues of social constitution and development. This study seeks to demonstrate that by placing the public/private division at the center of social thought and by reformulating key approaches and concepts through the prism of the public/private distinction, new dimensions are raised for the analysis of authority, legitimacy, law, political participation, and the very meanings of freedom and necessity.

The public/private division is as controversial as it is extensively used in a wide variety of institutional locations and discourses. Historically, the public/private distinction has been fundamental to liberal traditions associated with Thomas Hobbes, John Locke, and Adam Smith. Whatever the differences among these theorists, they affirmed that the legitimacy of authoritative institutions and the state rests on the freedom of private individuals to pursue their interests.[1] A fundamental and highly contentious aspect of the distinction has been the division between the state, based on universalism and full disclosure, and spheres of action based on particular commitments, exclusion, and secrecy. In law, for example, subjecting the distinction to meticulous scrutiny from a variety of perspectives has not led to agreement in evaluations of its importance or its utility. The distinction has been affirmed, on the one hand, as central to legal order, human dignity, and freedom and, on the other hand, as fundamentally outmoded, exhausted, and ritualized.[2] In the analysis of gender, feminists have argued that the oppression of women has been accomplished by relegating women to the private, domestic sphere while men have had the mobility to act in public spheres of production and in the formation of discourses through which the feminine domestic sphere is defined (Taub and Schneider, 1982).

Not only has the liberal formulation of the public/private distinction shaped dominant discourses, but it has also been formative for oppositional movements. Theorists of social movements of the 1960s proclaimed that "the personal is political" and sought, often in Rousseauian terms, to establish communities in which the private orientations and commitments of individuals were meshed authentically with public actions through intensive discussions, participation, and reconstruction of self and immediate communities.[3] Central to contemporary left theory is the idea that the division between public and private is rooted in corporate power, hierarchical patterns of social organization, centralized control of communication, and manipulation. A truly democratic society would more fully integrate public and private institutions, discourses, and identities on principles of participation, equality, and reflection in all social institutions (Mouffe, 1990: 57).

The very pervasiveness and repetitiveness of the public/private dichotomy in different contexts of action indicates the need to make it central for social theory and inquiry. Consider, for example, the increasing technical capacity exercised by medical practitioners to both diagnose and treat fetal defects (Dougherty, 1985: 89–117). Through the 1970s, there was an expansion of methods of prenatal diagnosis including amniocentesis, sonography, and fetoscopy. By the mid-1980s, the ability of medical practicioners to treat fetal defects in utero through drugs and surgery had also developed, although not to the point of treating all fetal conditions that could be diagnosed. A watershed in the medical treatment of fetuses was being realized.

It is no exaggeration to assert that "the bodies of pregnant women are the battleground on which the campaign to define the right to privacy is fought" (Annas, 1989: 329). These new technical capacities have combined with public law and state power in a way that often erodes the autonomy and private decision making of pregnant women. This developing area of medicine has raised the fetus to the status of a medical patient and has, thereby, led to an array of issues that pit rights of the fetus to medical treatment against the rights of the pregnant woman to decide whether the fetus she is carrying should be subjected to medical treatment and her own body subjected to medical intervention to treat the fetus.

Conflicts over these issues have led to new assertions of private rights in the face of extensions of the arenas of state interests. A host of legal arguments have been raised. They range from demands that no medical interventions be allowed without the consent of the mother and that a pregnant woman has an absolute right to make all fetal medical decisions without state interference to the view that the state, under specified conditions, has the obligation to protect fetal life and to require treatment despite the pregnant woman's objections. Yet, the issue has moved beyond the realm of abstraction as state supreme courts, over the objections of pregnant women and their husbands, have required that women have blood transfusions, undergo cesarean sections, take medication, and have their cervixes sutured to prevent miscarriages.

This example is especially pertinent because medicine, resting on technical capabilities and the legitimacy of science, has combined with legal authority, based on a compelling state interest to protect the potential for human life, to shape conflicts involving fetal rights backed by the premier public authority—the state—against a woman's right to privacy. The combined public authority of medicine and law may require a woman to submit to interventions by others in the most intimate of spheres, her own body, for the welfare of another.

The problems raised by developments in fetal medicine show how technological capabilities and scientific legitimacy, combined with court decisions, serve to increase public authority and the power of the state while restricting the private sphere of pregnant women to the point where their bodies are subject to interventions ordered by public authorities. Here court cases initiate political discourses, social movements, and legislation that articulate conflicting approaches to boundaries between public power and personal autonomy. While the direction of expanded public authority and limitations to private freedom are dramatically apparent in this example, other arenas of social action and law demonstrate further institutional aspects of the public/private dichotomy.

In the arena of labor law and labor relations, Karl Klare has shown that the public/private distinction is as pervasive as it is lacking in coherence. Rather than providing clear conceptual distinctions, the public/private division provides "a series of ways of thinking about public and private that are constantly undergoing revision, reformulation, and refinement. . . .The public/private distinction poses as an analytical tool in labor law, but it functions more as a form of political rhetoric used to justify particular results" (1982: 1361). In effect, the public/private distinction combines analysis and legitimacy. Generally, the public/private distinction defines the terrain upon which disputes are conducted, limiting the powers of some parties while expanding the powers of others. Thus, there have been and continue to be conflicts and controversies over whether the employment contract is simply a private contract or has a public interest and is bounded by public policy; the extent to which employees have rights to personal privacy when they are at the workplace, their employer's private property; the extent to which employers have an exclusive right to determine how their capital is used as opposed to interests of the community and their employees; the ways in which labor unions are agencies that fulfill public purposes or are purely private entities.

Beyond these specific areas of controversy, changes in labor legislation since the 1930s have shifted the patterns of power and authority in the relations between labor and management, in large part by redefining their public and private dimensions (1982: 1388–1400). The Norris-LaGuardia Act of 1932 prevented federal courts from issuing labor injunctions that had been used to block union organizing activities and strikes. The act sought to deregulate and, in effect, to privatize relations between employers and employees so that their conflicts could be resolved through private contractual agreements.

Building on this foundation, the National Labor Relations Act of 1935 sought to create a framework of public law in which employees and employers would engage in private bargaining and negotiation to arrive at contractual agreements. Given the greater economic power of employers over employees in contract negotiations, the act sought to enhance the power of employees in reaching private contractual agreements by recognizing a public interest in promoting unions as a form of private power, recognizing the legality of strikes and other self-help measures by employees, defining through public law the obligation of employers to bargain, and instituting the National Labor Relations Board to administer the various provisions of the act. Public power and private freedom were combined so that "public regulation of the workplace was contemporaneously defended and justified on the ground that it would not interfere with *private* determination of working conditions" (1982: 1392).

From the vantage point of the history of labor law since the 1930s, it appears that the combination of public law and private contractual agreements has shifted in both its public and private dimensions. The public dimension has increased as courts have been called on to settle disputes over specific aspects of collective bargaining that were not resolved by the National Labor Relations Board. As a result of further legislation that reflected the experience of World War II, the state has been drawn into the presumed private domain of contract negotiation as mediators and arbritators to make private negotiation work more effectively and, thereby, to prevent strikes and other disruptions of industrial peace. Other legislation, such as the Occupational Safety and Health Act, has led to state regulation of the workplace. Relations within the private contractual dimension have shifted as managerial decisions regarding investment and the scope of the enterprise have become enshrined in collective bargaining agreements along with the pledge of employees not to strike during the term of a contract and the legal obligation of unions to enforce the no-strike pledge.

One lesson that can be drawn from this history is "that 'private ordering' presupposes that public power has established a regime of rules and enforcement agencies, that the 'unregulated' market is a fiction and that private ordering is itself a mode of public regulation" (Klare, 1982: 1415). Although the social relations of authority along with the nature of freedom and compulsion have shifted in the arena of labor law, they have continued to be constructed and legitimated through the private/public division: the public and private dimensions have continually presupposed one another.

The examples of fetal medicine and labor relations point to the pervasiveness of the private/public division and how it shapes power relations, structures conflicts, and defines domains of freedom and allocates responsibility in the authoritative domain of law. Yet, it is also the case that the private/public split shapes personal experiences of authority and is formative for the personal legitimacy that people attribute to their everyday lives. Richard Sennett and Jonathon Cobb, in their study of how white ethnic manual workers mediate their relations in the degrading public sphere of work and in their private households, show how the objective necessity of earning a living is tied to the subjective experience of freedom:

> The working men of Boston almost never voiced resignation in face of the injuries of class. The people we encountered had a powerful, though complicated, sense of mission in their lives: they were determined that, if circumstances of class limited their freedom in comparison to that of educated people, they would *create* freedom for themselves. By that we mean that they were resolved to shape the actions open to them so that, in their own minds, they felt that they

acted from choice rather than necessity. It is not a question of lying about how free you are, existential philosophers have said of such resolves in general, it is a matter of thinking about your circumstances in terms of an end you choose, you want. No matter how much the world has enslaved you, in this way you keep alive your dignity as a man. (1972: 120–121)

The typical experience of the manual workers interviewed by Sennett and Cobb is one of failure to perform for public authorities in the domain of education. This led to a lowered sense of personal worth that was subsequently enhanced when they went to work at menial jobs that afforded them virtually no recognition by authorities in the workplace. Yet this very sense of being demeaned at the hands of public authorities and in the workplace sets the stage for demands and expectations for respect in the private domain of the family.

The degradations in the public sphere of work are grounds for respect on the part of children and wives because these degradations are understood as sacrifices being made for children and wives and should be acknowledged as such by them. These men see themselves as entering the social arena outside of the family to maintain the lives of family members. The typical manual worker "is acting as a free man when he thinks of himself as *choosing* to sacrifice" (1972: 122). Moreover, being subject to harsh authority and degradation outside of the home, when moralized as self-denial and sacrifice for others, is transformed into a resource for legitimating authority in the home. Children and wives not only have an obligation to be respectful but they should also be submissive to the patriarchal authority that is earned through sacrifice. In effect, submission to public authority, interpreted as a willfully chosen sacrifice, confers authority in the private arena of the household.

Yet, in the circumstances of working-class life, the trade-off of submission to public authority for the exercise of private familial authority mediated by a legitimating ideology of self-sacrifice is riddled with conflicts and antagonisms. Most pointedly, the sacrifices made for children serve to defer gratification in a highly dependent way: The benefits of one's sacrifice are to be realized in the future by one's children who, through education and occupational success, are to be economically and socially better off than oneself. Because the purpose of sacrifice is to make the lives of one's children better than one's own, "the father doesn't ask the child to take the parents' lives as a model, but as a warning" (1972: 128). Because sacrifice is oriented toward intergenerational mobility, it provides a condition for conflicts in family relationships and, ultimately, a sense of betrayal.

Children who are the beneficiaries of paternal sacrifice become participants in a world that removes them from the working-class culture of their parents and opens up possibilities for their lives that were unanticipated by their fathers. As a result, fathers feel threatened and even resentful of the attitudes and expectations of their upwardly mobile children. The fathers' unmet demands for respect and expressions of gratitude that follow from their sacrifice may lead to a sense of betrayal and greater distance in relationships with children. "The ungratefulness of a child who has the advantages the father lacked, where the advantages were earned by the father's own sacrifices—this seems to him like ultimate injustice" (1972: 134). Children, on the other hand, resent never having been given the chance to participate in deciding what their fathers would do for them and feel betrayed when they are called on to, in effect, remain submissive and grateful to a father "making a rather cowardly power play" and "who won't stand up for himself" (1972: 134). Thus, the social and psychological forces encapsulated in the legitimating ideology of sacrifice that mediates the public/private split in the form of occupational and familial authority relations tend to generate conflicts over time.

These examples of how the public/private division shapes social order, legitimates authority, and mediates freedom and necessity raise a question for social theory: In both the classic tradition of social theory and in much of current social theory, the public/private division has not been fully or explicitly developed. To be sure, as the following analysis shows, theorists such as Karl Marx, Emile Durkheim, Max Weber, and Talcott Parsons often used the public/private distinction in particular contexts. Yet, they never raised it to full analytic significance. It is, rather, taken for granted in its commonsense understanding without relating it systematically to theoretical concepts. It is used for sociological analysis without being formulated as a core theoretical category.

Sociologists such as C. Wright Mills, Irving Goffman, Arlie Hochschild, Peter Berger, and Daniel Bell have all formulated aspects of the public/private distinction. C. Wright Mills, for example, raised the question of how private troubles become public issues and how the organization of power enables elites to make history through the exercise of public power while the vast majority of people lead private lives removed from the making of history (1956). Irving Goffman, in his analysis of face-to-face interaction, discusses the organization of interaction in back regions that allow for private communication and the preparation of self-presentations and the front in which performances are public (1959). For Goffman, moreover, the private sphere—whether in the back regions of the workplace or in the hidden meanings attributed to small behaviors by the inmates of total institutions—is a location for resistance to publicly organized power (1961). Arlie Hochschild has demonstrated how expression and emotion have become part of the public packaging of commodities, signifying the invasion of commodity logic into private regions of self-expression (1983). She has also analyzed changing relations between domestic and occupational spheres as people and institutions cope with two-job family patterns (1989). Peter Berger et al. have discussed how, under conditions of modernity, freedom is privatized along largely expressive dimensions in the subjective realm of the individual while the public sphere is increasingly rationalized and standardized along instrumental lines (1974). Modernity, moreover, has led to an underinstitutionalization of the private sphere in comparison to the complex and pervasively organized public realm. And Daniel Bell has pointed out the tensions that have emerged in capitalist societies as a result of the disparities that characterize the consumption ethic in the private sphere and the production ethic in the public realm of the economy (1976). Indeed, these tensions and disparities are core contradictions of modernity and industrialism.

Although sociologists have developed important aspects of the public/private division, the distinction has not been systematically formulated through the tradition of social theory.[4] It has not been explicitly developed into broad theoretical frameworks that can serve to analyze both social development and social constitution comprehensively. The absence of such a focal concern is partially explained by the original concerns and objects of inquiry delimited by sociologists. Overwhelmingly, the focus was on new patterns of social organization and orientations toward the world that displaced communal patterns in which public/private relations were both less fully articulated and, where they existed, more subject to unifying rituals, symbols, interpersonal identities, and common worlds.

The core concerns of sociology are with ongoing processes that compel the movement of people and their practical activities out of households and local communities into ever wider public arenas. In these institutional and spatial arrangements, anonymous individuals confront one another as they become dependent on one another for securing their means of life, their safety, and establishing the meanings for their interactions and identities. These processes create new locations of interaction in which people confront one another as strangers and must establish patterns of interaction and codes of meaning that enable them to fulfill their practical activities. Sociology emerged with and attempts to analyze these processes in the wake of its paradigmatic events: the industrial revolution and the democratic revolution (Nisbet, 1966: 21–44). The industrial revolution displaces labor from local communities and the household to factories and the industrial city, changing the nature of property from locally, time-honored conceptions to the vagaries of value in public exchange, and leads to the ever-greater application of technologies to human activities. The democratic revolution raises themes and patterns of action through conceptions of equality, popular sovereignty, and individualism in opposition to fixed statuses, divine right, and corporate identity as it creates citizens and centralized states. These processes continue to shape the realities that people confront on an ever-expanding scale as more and more people are drawn into them.

The social sphere forms the arena of these developments and is the locus of their explanation, understanding, and criticism. It is in the social sphere that people who are relative unknowns to one another are related through abstract rules, technologized spatial configurations, and definitions of competence that are themselves historically emergent social forces. The core problem for social theorists is to define and reformulate the terms of life that are continually undergoing changes in the transition to society in concepts that are themselves socially grounded. Presocial meanings of economic life, politics, individual and family experience, religion, and nature are continually being recast in light of the social grounding of activity and experience.

In this ongoing process of change and knowledge creation, sociology has focused on the locations of interpenetration, of intermingling, and of transition. To a considerable degree, social theory has absorbed aspects of the public/private distinction into all of its leading approaches and concepts without articulating the distinction directly. It conflates divisions between public and private, which are so prominent in law and politics, because its analytic focus is on institutions and discourses that have combined them, often through force that secures inequalities without authentic consent. Its fields of inquiry combine activities and relations that result from transitions from the household to the social sphere, from local to global orientations, from familiarity to anonymity. In a sense, the public/private distinction comes to us from social theory practically deconstructed: Aspects of the distinction have been disassociated, differentiated, and dispersed through various conceptual locations and removed from what is deemed central to inquiry. The public/private distinction is so conceptually broad and diffuse and so detailed and precise in practice that it permeates sociological isssues without being explicitly theorized.

Even though the focus of sociological theory and its conceptual absorption of the public/private distinction are partially explained by its object of inquiry, the consequences of this mode of theorizing have not been attended to adequately. As Alan Wolfe has pointed out, "sociology developed as an alternative to reliance on both the market and the state. It asked the question of whether people can find other ways to tie themselves together than the amoral claim of self-interest or the oppressive use of state power" (1987:96). Sociology locates its domain of knowledge and its vision of reality neither in the privatized sphere of individual gratification or in the public realm of organized state power. Rather, it focuses on and gives analytic independence to persistent structures and patterns of action that are, in large part, located at the intersection of private and public domains and have consequences and characteristics that emerge from that intersection. Mills, Goffman, Hochschild, Berger, and Bell focus on topics of inquiry that combine public and private elements and form concrete problems for investigation. As analytic categories, the public and private dimensions of the issues under analysis are taken for granted as background categories. The emergent consequences of this particular combination of public/private elements are the focal point of inquiry.

The concern of this study is to rethink the public/private division by reformulating classical sociological theory. It seeks to develop the distinction between the public and private realms through the frameworks of classical theory around issues consistent with the concerns of those frameworks: relations among social development, social structure, and social action. The subject matter of this study, the material through which these issues are elaborated, are the social theories of Karl Marx, Emile Durkheim, Max Weber, and Talcott Parsons that have been formative for social theory and social research. The study interprets the work of these theorists through the public/private division to make explicit and to reconstruct the ways in which private and public dimensions are combined in their theories despite the fact that they are not conceptually elaborated in the theories themselves.

One of our purposes, then, is analytic. By reconstructing social theories in terms of the private/public division, we seek to raise a fundamental dimension of social life and individual experience to a level of theoretical consciousness and conceptual clarity that has not been developed despite its general significance and taken-for-granted character. Basic to this approach is that the public/private division cuts across social structure and agency but that it has different relations at the levels of structure and agency. The different ways in which alternative theoretical approaches formulate processes of social development and constitution provide alternative frameworks for analyzing public ordering and its relation to the private sphere. Based on their alternative depictions of social processes, theorists provide different analyses of the relations between public and private realms that are consequential for formulating concepts of autonomy, freedom, and possibilities for human emancipation.

This analytic project provides the grounds for articulating a critical standpoint toward social theory and society. The combination of public and private features in social theory is complex, but it has a general direction: While the private sphere constitutes the primary location of freedom and spontaneity in processes of social development, it becomes increasingly shaped through social processes that determine its range, character, and content. The demands of society foster patterns of public ordering that increasingly incorporate aspects of the private sphere. Through imperatives of public ordering, social processes have increasingly integrated and transformed private relations, experience, and identity through the market and through the state (Wolfe, 1989). While public and private elements of society are joined in a manner that enhances the social determination of aspects of private life through public institutions and discourses, the private sphere continues to be crucial for forming the human capacities that underlie society. It remains fundamental for institutional and individual autonomy, morality, and freedom at the levels of law, politics, and social action.

I consider this attempt to develop a theoretical focus around the public/private distinction to be more than a technical exercise. Since the public/private distinction is so fundamental for common sense legal and political orientations to the world, clarifying the distinction and articulating the implications of alternative views should contribute to more adequate grounds for the formation of research and for practical action.

Social theory has a dual relation to the phenomena that it analyzes. It is primarily part of a scientific enterprise that seeks to explain and predict social phenomena. In its relation to scientific inquiry, social theory views the possibilities for individual action, understanding, and sensibility as fundamentally shaped and constrained by society. The notion that individuals, as members of society, are engaged in both maintaining their lives under circumstances that are constructed through their participation and by wider, historically situated patterns of interaction is central to social theorists as different in other respects as Marx and Parsons. The individual's life chances, comprehension of those life chances, and possibilities for change are viewed by social theory as fundamentally conditioned by the patterns of social interaction and historical social structures that form the boundaries of that individual's world.

This cognitive commitment gives social theory its distinct object of inquiry. Without taking the social as primary and having independent effects, there would be nothing to demarcate social theory from theoretical approaches found in economics, political science, or anthropology. The sociological approach, however, has other consequences: The more the individual and social institutions are analyzed as an element in a determinate set of social relations, the more of a social product the individual's nature must be, including the qualities of autonomy and freedom. This is true despite the fact that individual action and rationality may have independent effects. Society remains the medium, the substance, and material boundaries through which individual action and reason are actualized. Ultimately, social theory grants legitimacy to society as an object of inquiry and as a real, substantial grounding of reason, action, and affect.

No matter how contradictory its elements, society is a grounding for knowledge claims. As such, theory contributes to the view that society can be conceptually ordered and that it is necessary for constituting objects of knowledge. It thereby provides accounts that have the potential for legitimating society and social processes of defining categories like the public/private distinction. Whatever the range of disputes, theoretical discourse secures and affirms society as the grounds for knowledge.

This does not mean that sociology is crudely ideological either scientifically or politically. Social inquiries have varying degrees of distance from the practical interests of individuals, groups, and classes that compose society as well as varying degrees of reflectivity on the forms of association and practical relations through which action is accomplished. Social theories are not an array of apologies for various conflicting social forces. Rather, there are crucial distinctions between vulgar ideologies that merely represent particular interests and scientific theories that provide general and objective frameworks for social analysis despite their social location and underlying standpoints. Yet, the very distance of the theoretical attitude and the very objectivity of the scientific strictures of social theory lend its formulations a legitimating role toward the social as a fundamental ground of knowledge. Objectivity, scientific indifference to particular social interests, and a professional ethic grounded in a concern for truth may serve to support the imagery of order and reality portrayed in social theory.

It is also the case, however, that social theory provides the grounds for reflecting on its conditions of knowledge. For example, social theories objectify features of social life so that authoritative limitations on freedom can be more fully comprehended and subject to criticism. Taken as a discourse, social theory is ideally "coherent, systematic and rationally coordinated" (Savage, 1981: 34). As such, the internal relations among concepts that give concepts their specific meanings can be critically scrutinized and assessed in their internal consistency. These elements, moreover, can be rearranged and reordered, thereby contributing new grounds for knowledge and action. From this analysis, social theory can be taken as a logically constructed image of society, as an expression of society in conceptual form, that can be subjected to further criticism as a legitimating discourse whose affirmed patterns of restraint, freedom, and authority can be explicated, contested, and subjected to reconstruction (Schroyer, 1973: 132–33). In this light, the criticism of social theories opens up the possibility for going beyond its own formulations of society, of socially embedded categories like the public/private distinction, and of the necessary relations between authority and limited freedom.

These reflections on the legitimating role of social theory do not support irrationalism, nihilism, or mindless antiauthoritarianism. Rather, they are rooted in a critical approach to authority, its limits, its constitution, and the pattern of ideas that support it so that authority relations can be more adequately comprehended and, potentially, changed. In addition, it is increasingly clear that scientific theory, and social theory most specifically, combine empirical elements with nonempirical procedures, normative frameworks, and evaluative perspectives. Thomas Kuhn's work in the philosophy of science points out that scientific paradigms have normative features that make them resistant to empirical findings, anomalies, and facts. Indeed, it is questionable whether theories are ever discarded simply because they are empirically disproven (1970). Imre Lakatos, moreover, has argued that theories are crucial in the formation of statements of fact (1970). Jeffrey Alexander has maintained that social theory is shaped by a variety of propositions that range from the empirical to the ideological, and that it distorts social theory to consider it from only one of its dimensions (1980). The criticism of social theory, from the vantage point of all of its dimensions, is itself an aspect of the enterprise of social theory. Social theory, then, has some autonomy and must be approached at its own levels of integrity and complexity. Only in this way can it be adequately understood, criticized, and developed.

Thus, I contend that social theory can be fruitfully reconstructed along the lines of the public/private distinction, that this reconstruction opens new insights into the sociological tradition and provides avenues for developing approaches to sociological analysis. In addition, I seek to demonstrate that the overall direction of social theory has been to increasingly privatize freedom in an ever more pervasive public realm of necessity while maintaining private domains as sources of resistance, innovation, and nondeterminism at the level of social action. This general direction, however, has taken alternative forms. The alternative ways in which core theorists have analyzed the public/private relation is consequential for both social inquiry and practical activity.

In the next chapter, I present perspectives that view the social transformation of the public/private division from concerns rooted in politics as an arena for self-determination of individuals and institutions. This perspective focuses on how the social transformation of the public/private division confuses its core dimensions. Moreover, developing social forces undercut political action, institutional locations that support individual autonomy, and nondeterministic approaches to social life. The logic of the social transformation of the public/private division supports the isolation of the individual in deterministic discourses that trivialize personal freedom while shaping practices of surveillance, hierarchical control, and manipulation.

This political critique of the embeddedness of the public/private division in social change makes rethinking the distinction compelling. The political critique poses a fundamental challenge to social theory: Society is a confusion of public and private relations. Social theory must be reconstructed in ways that overcome that confusion.

In the sections that take up the classical theorists, I demonstrate that there are distinctive approaches to the public/private division. In different ways the public/private division is made into a social category by analyzing how it is transformed through social processes and how it takes on an increasing social content. While the public/private division becomes blurred and its elements are incorporated in social processes and structures, it remains basic for formulating social action.

The sections of the book that focus on Marx, Durkheim, Weber, and Parsons demonstrate this through the works of these theorists. For Marx, the public/private division is at the root of bourgeois ideology and capitalist economic relations. While he criticizes the public/private division as a feature of capitalist domination, he also recognizes both liberatory elements in the division and, most importantly, that the division is a condition for political action that must be confronted and partially maintained in progressive struggles. The power and initiative of working-class movements and individuals are enhanced by infusing the public/private division with democratic participation and increased capacities for production. For Durkheim, the public/private division emerges with social complexity and is bounded by an overall logic of functional relations. He constructs the public/private division from a standpoint of corporate holism that includes policies for social reform. Durkheim's corporatist approach to the public/private division renders scientific knowledge, law, expertise, and hierarchical social locations paramount in relation to private spheres that are zones of individualism, spontaneity, and innovation. For Weber, the radical separation between the private sphere of existential values and the public arenas of rational action is increasingly realized in modernity. A core problem for Weber is the relation of private values and public forms of rational domination that come to characterize social institutions and raise fundamental ethical problems for individual actors. Moreover, disparities and conflicts among the major types of rationality create conceptual spaces for founding alternative patterns of action. For Parsons, the public/private division is a nondeterministic feature of social action that is posed against both statist collectivism and market economism. Elements of the public/private division associated with classical liberalism are increasingly blended through social processes, and there are increasing tendencies for tensions between society and the individual to weaken. Yet the distinction remains vital for establishing individual personality and the formation of values and arenas of choice at the level of individual and collective actors.

While there are tendencies toward totalism in the social transformation of the public/private division, they are countered by reconstituting the division as a feature of autonomy and nondeterminism at the levels of agency and action. The book concludes by relating these themes in social theory to parallels in legal discourse. I maintain that legal discourse and institutions are key locations for mediating the public/private division at the levels of social structure and social action.

## NOTES

1. In this liberal view, the relationship of ownership became the dominant form that defined both the private freedom of the individual and the constraints imposed through interaction in the public sphere. C. B. MacPherson has captured this aspect of liberalism:

> The individual, it was thought, is free inasmuch as he is a proprietor of his person or capacities. The human essence is freedom from dependence on the wills of others, and freedom is a function of possession. Society becomes a lot of free individuals related to each other as proprietors of their own capacities and of what they have acquired by their exercise. Society consists of relations of exchange between proprietors. (1962: 3)

2. See the excellent presentations of alternative perspectives on the public/private distinction, its history, and its use in jurisprudence in the "Symposium on the Public/Private Distinction," *University of Pennsylvania Law Review* 130 (1982). Robert Mnookin (1982: 1429–40) provides an argument for the distinction and Duncan Kennedy argues against it (1982: 1349–57). In feminist legal theory, Nadine Taub and Elizabeth M. Schneider argue that the law has served

to exclude women from the public sphere while, at the same time, providing little in the way of legal protection or control in the private sphere (1983: 117–139).

3. Marshall Berman maintained that the "New Left's lasting cultural achievement—one that may outlive the New Left itself—has been to bring about a return of the repressed, to bring radicalism back to its romantic roots" (1970: x). He analyzes the intellectual sources of authenticity, especially in the writings of Jean Jacques Rousseau, as a relation between self/other and private/public that is deeply problematic—emotionally as well as intellectually—in a corrupting world. See Sara Evans (1980), James Miller (1987), Todd Gitlin (1987), and Richard Flacks (1988) not only for their analyses of the quest for authenticity in the relation between personal life and activism in the 1960s, but also for the way in which these activists have continued this quest by combining historical reflection with autobiography.

4. Joseph Bensman and R. Lillienfeld (1979) develop the public/private distinction from the standpoint of role theory. For example, they state that "the public and private can be conceived of as ways of classifying social roles, the social expectancies and the private exemptions from expectancies placed upon the behavior of individuals in specified social and political situations" (1979: 171). By rendering the distinction into roles, they normalize it and make it appear to be rooted in clear structural relations. It is this framework that must be more adequately formulated. Robert Bellah et al. (1985) have made the relations between the understanding of self and the approach to public life basic to their analysis of American culture. Central to the problematic relation between private identity and public life is the negative quality of American individualism: "The meaning of one's life for most Americans is to become one's own person, almost to give birth to oneself. Much of this process . . . is negative. It involves breaking free from family, community, and inherited" ideas (1985: 82–83).

# CHAPTER 2

## Worst Cases: The Social Transformation of the Public/Private Division

A central theme in social theory is that capacities for individual self-determination and democratic action have become increasingly marginalized by patterns of change associated with advanced Western societies. The blurring of the distinction between public and private spheres of activity transforms politics into administration and reduces individual autonomy to locations of personal intimacy and narrow self-involvement. The widening scope and ever more intensive reproduction of social relations through processes of instrumental control pushes freedom into realms of subjective experience. Extensions of commodity production into processes of self-formation, individual identity, and interaction have privatized the understandings of social life and history, making principled public action less intelligible. These social processes shape a world that is as hierarchical and interdependent as it is subjective, localized, and ephemeral.[1]

In this chapter, I conceptualize these issues from a social transformationist approach to the public/private distinction that is rooted in commitments to autonomy, political action, and the moral equality of individuals.[2] Because it centers on political action and categories of political equality rather than conditions of material and social equality, this approach defies simple classification on liberal/conservative, left/right or other conventional continuums.[3]

Social transformationists maintain that social forces emerging with advanced Western society transform the public/private distinction in directions that undermine the institutional and discursive supports for autonomy, self-determination, and principled political action. This social transformationist approach criticizes social processes and ideologies that limit politics as an arena for ethical development. It historicizes society to analyze the ways in which consensually arrived at collective goals that enhance autonomy and efficacy have been inhibited. By focusing on tendencies that yield worst cases as a baseline for social theorizing, it aims to establish a world that supports the full participation of individuals as equal and self-determining agents in constituting the purposes and organization of society.

The fundamental categories that frame the social transformationist approach to the public/private division are autonomy, plurality, activities, spatial location, language, and ideas. The segregation of different human actors and activities, whether biological reproduction or political decision making, in different spaces, whether open or hidden, has profound consequences for the exercise of human capacities for self-determination. The more activities associated with biological and material necessity enter into public spaces, the greater the likelihood that free action and speech will become privatized, fostering ideas of necessity in public and self-absorbed freedom in intimacy.

Hannah Arendt's work provides the conceptual cornerstone for analyzing the social transformation of the public/private distinction.[4] Formulating relations between the public and private spheres in a broad historical and analytic perspective calls attention to the emergence of society as a distinct form of human activity that has blurred the clear distinction between public and private realms that prevailed in Greek antiquity:

> The distinction between a private and public sphere of life corresponds to the household and political realms, which have existed as distinct entities at least since the rise of the ancient city-state; but the emergence of the social realm, which is neither private nor public, strictly speaking, is a relatively new phenomenon whose origin coincided with the modern age and which found its political form in the nation-state. (1959: 27)

In Greek antiquity, human capacities for political action were preceded by the natural association of the family and household.[5] The household was a private realm, blocked by walls and hidden from the view of outsiders. In it biological and material necessities were met through associations of personal subordination and superordination. The private sphere was a realm of inequality rooted in natural necessity: slaves, women, and children. The very fact that it was oriented to biological survival made it prepolitical. "In ancient feeling the privative trait of privacy, indicated in the word itself, was all-important; it meant literally a state of being deprived of something, and even of the highest and most human of man's capacities" (Arendt, 1959: 35).

The greatest deprivation was the lack of access to the public realm.[6] With no possibility for living a political life, the private individual could not exercise the capacities for speech and action. Political recognition by others was foreclosed.

The polis, on the other hand, was the public realm in which citizens were visible to one another on the basis of their moral equality and the plurality of their standpoints. It was a realm neither of household labor nor philosophical contemplation; it was the realm of action and speech. To have access to the public realm meant to be seen and heard by one's equals in a common world characterized by a plurality of actors and of perspectives. Essentially, it meant going beyond the universal needs of the species that are satisfied by labor and having one's own individuality recognized by others who were also outside of the realm of necessity.

The private realm was organized on the basis of subordination, often accomplished through the exercise of violence. Its members had no place in the world outside the household; their activities were purely life-sustaining and bounded by the necessities of life. The public realm, in contrast, was the realm of freedom, characterized by political discourse, individualism, and mutual recognition. The household was valued because it maintained the conditions necessary for political life. It was the home of the citizen, hidden from view, its inner workings mysterious to the outsiders. It served as the unrevealed, unknown background for political action and speech.

The sharp distinction that existed between private and public life in Greek antiquity and the clear dividing line between them have become "extremely blurred, because we see the body of peoples and political communities in the image of a family whose everyday affairs have to be taken care of by a gigantic, nationwide administration of housekeeping" (1959: 28). As the social realm emerged and developed in the modern epoch, the public and private spheres were transformed.

The emergence and dominance of the labor process in the public sphere changed the nature of public and private life. For what distinguishes modern society from earlier patterns of human life is, on the one hand, the vast growth of the productivity of labor once it is located outside of the private household and personal relations and, on the other hand, the vast increase in the range and extent of consumption that this productivity generates. As labor has become centralized and organized in locations outside the household, its vast productive potential has become unleashed.

Human activity is increasingly constrained and shaped by institutions that have as their orientation production and consumption outside the household. Public life, moreover, increasingly takes on a character and quality of a biological process. The image of public life as a social metabolism in which expanded production and consumption define all human activity becomes increasingly realized.

This process explodes outside of household spheres of competence. It demands the subordination of public activity in the service of economically defined relations. The expansion and increased productivity of socialized labor widens the arena of necessity and penetrates into both public and private spheres of action. The increasing dominance of a social metabolism grounded in production and consumption obliterates the stability of the private household as a secluded background for public activity. Instead, the individual's public life is based on his or her relation to social production which is not fixed by tradition or transcendent principles of authority; it is determined by the production process itself. As both private and public life are incorporated into social processes directly or indirectly determined by production and consumption, the possibility of autonomy and freedom shrink into the realm of intimacy. Autonomy and freedom are increasingly located in the self and its intimate extensions.

In the social realm, matters of necessity that were formerly affairs of the private household, such as making a living and child rearing, become institutionalized in locations that are open to ever-wider scrutiny and control by public authorities. "Society is the form in which the fact of mutual dependence for the sake of nothing else assumes public significance and where the activities connected with sheer survival appear in public" (Arendt, 1959: 43). In other words, society constitutes a realm of necessity in which individuals engage one another publicly to solve the problems of everyday survival.

In Greek antiquity and, indeed, through much of feudalism, the maintenance of the life process through labor was a household matter. But, beginning with the expropriation of land from the peasantry and the expansion of free and public labor markets, the emergence of the social realm has signified the public organization of the life process. Problems of necessity and survival are dealt with in public. Individuals meet on the basis of need, and necessity is experienced publicly. Work becomes a public activity that intertwines individual, household, and collective survival.

Politics as well becomes bounded by concerns for material and biological reproduction. In early market societies, these concerns were expressed in the politics of social interest groups; in more advanced societies, they are expressed more fully through the growth of administrative bureaucracies that articulate and manage social needs. Increasingly, politics moves away from free action and toward administrative organization. In this sense, the public realm—in both its economic and political aspects—is increasingly determined by social needs for production and consumption. Accordingly, the public sphere increasingly becomes characterized by calculations of necessity that are administratively determed. It is the realm necessary for the fulfillment of needs determined by the social life process.

As the public realm becomes more oriented toward material and biological necessities, the private sphere becomes a realm of spontaneous individual expression and freedom. With the emergence of society, choice in consumption, intimate relations, and mobility, the autonomous construction of individual biography and pleasure in small things became ideals of freedom (Arendt, 1959: 35–36). As life has become more socialized, that is, more organized by imperatives of sheer survival, the private, and, eventually, the most intimate realms of life are experienced as free expressions of the individual. As social dependence grows, freedom becomes more privatized, hidden, and distanced from public action.

Society, then, is more than a movement of freedom from the public to the private sphere and a movement of survival needs from the private to the public sphere. Rather, the social represents a transformation of the relations on which these categories are based. The public sphere is transformed into an all encompassing social realm characterized by labor, administration, and managerial imperatives while the private sphere becomes a realm of intimacy and subjective freedom. As a result of the emergence of needs into the administrative arena of the modern nation-state, problems of organization, efficiency, resource allocation, and social interests dominate public concern. The political realm as an arena of mutual recognition among equals fades as officials, experts, managers, and leaders of social interest groups come to monopolize political life. The realms of private life and personal intimacy become the location of free expression and autonomy as public action and speech are mediated by social imperatives and concomitant patterns of power and ideology.

For Arendt, these social processes are basic to the emergence of totalitarianism, not only in its specific manifestations in National Socialism and Stalinism but also as a more general tendency of social development. Changes in class structure, social organization, and the nation-state have been driven by capital accumulation, isolating individuals in their private interests, and generating forces that overwhelm individual capacities for principled public action rooted in the recognition of others as moral agents.

Production and consumption, once they dominate life outside of the household, erode sources of stability for individual identity and shared meanings on which political action must be based. Imperialism, a form of global expansion of economic and administrative power, "was born when the ruling class in capitalist production came up against national limits to economic expansion" (1951: 126). For the bourgeoisie, who had generally been satisfied with economic power and had not exercised direct political rule, politics became necessary for continued economic expansion. Imperialism fused private interests in profitable investment with an expansive foreign policy.

The nation-state, as a set of public institutions legitimated through principles that sought to establish consent, declined as a result of imperialism. Instead, imperatives of military power, bureaucratic authority that was first practiced abroad and then brought home for political rule, and racist forms of nationalism came to dominate public institutions. These changes combine massive disparities in wealth, hierarchical patterns of authority, and administrative discourses that stifle politics as an arena of moral equality and ethical action. Moreover, dependence on capitalist expansion generated massive and extreme dislocations of people who demanded strong leaders to push for further expansionist policies (1951: 150).

The bourgeoisie is a virtual vanguard of privatism and privatized politics. The bourgeoisie, whatever form of government they have been under, have tended to be "essentially private persons" (1951: 138). Their personal concerns with moneymaking, however, confronted political structures that blocked the continued realization of their private interests. They were led to shape a political sphere that would conform to the expansionism that their private concerns required.

This is true not only for bourgeois interests but also for their everyday economic orientations. The competitive, acquisitive, and self-centered orientation of the bourgeoisie "produced apathy and even hostility toward public life" (1951: 313). These aspects of the bourgeois approach to life combined with the cynicism and hypocrisy engendered when public virtues are suspected of concealing private interests "are very useful for those forms of dictatorship in which a 'strong man' takes upon himself the troublesome responsibility for the conduct of public affairs" (1951: 313–15). Moreover, the "competitive structures" and "concomitant loneliness of the individual" combined with severe economic dislocations, such as rampant inflation and depression, to generate the isolated individuals who are the mass base for totalitarianism (1951: 317). The indifference of the bourgeoisie to public life becomes, under conditions of economic crisis, a mass phenomenon. Indeed,

> the bourgeoisie's political philosophy was always "totalitarian"; it always assumed an identity of politics, economics and society, in which political institutions served only as the facade for private interests. The bourgeoisie's double standard, its differentiation between public and private life, were a concession to the nation-state which had desperately tried to keep the two spheres apart. (1951: 336)

The relationships among bourgeois sensibilities, privatism, and internalization of administrative power are posed very concretely in Arendt's portrayal of Adolph Eichmann. He is a displaced person whose bourgeois origins heightened his needs for authority, careerism, and the exercise of administrative power. His emersion in the Nazi movement and his incorporation of official language into his identity demonstrate a fusion of public administration and private orientations in directions that make the recognition of others impossible (1965: 32).

Eichmann's careerism infused societal totalism into his personal motivations. His career and the bureaucratic positions that he occupied were not only his sole source of identity but also a reference: All of his actions were understood in terms of their meaning for his personal success. The structures of authority in which he participated took a totally privatized meaning through the filter of careerism. Career was a framework for understanding the world and actions within it through their significance for personal advancement and prestige. Careerism is a way of appropriating events in thought and memory that enhance their personal meaning to the exclusion of the actual consequences that they have for others.

Eichmann expressed everything in cliches and official language, reinforcing his isolation from interpersonal involvement and fostering privatized significance. He was outside of the language of everyday life in which communication with others depends to some degree on taking their points of view; rather he stated that "officialize is my only language" (1965: 49). Careerism fused his private interests to bureaucratic administration by internalizing the public language of officialdom. This blocked interaction with others and rendered them into objects to be acted on.

Eichmann's world denied intersubjectivity. His patterns of lying and self-deception, his belief that he could find peace with former enemies, his equating of his own suffering with that of concentration camp inmates, and his sentimental attachment to victims that he personally knew point to an outlook that is as self-referential as it is imbued with the isolated experience of routine, adminstrative power. He exemplifies a type of isolation, a quality of self-involvement, and inflated self-importance that is possible only in the socially constituted world of administrative power. Even thought becomes embedded in this process. "The longer one listened to him, the more obvious it became that his inability to speak was closely connected with his inability to *think*, namely, to think from the standpoint of somebody else" (1965: 49).

Although totalitarian outcomes are a limiting case of the social transformation of the public/private division, it is an underlying tendency of modern social structure. The progressive aspects of social development appear to be accompanied by tendencies toward the withering of the public sphere, the collapse of individual integrity, and a loss of capacities for principled action.

Social development leads to a heightened orientation toward the private sphere as a primary source of meaning, motivation, and individual freedom. While the private sphere can become the location of spontaneity and freedom as a result of expanding social processes, it also becomes increasingly technologized, psychologized, and focused through careerism. The public sphere is increasingly characterized by the collectivization of needs through administration, commodification, and managerial decision making. Power is transformed into hierarchical authority rather than emerging from collective will formation. This makes the private sphere into an individualized, socially dependent location that is fully incorporated into the very processes that shape it. Mundane politics take on the character of consumer choice as behavior based on impulse and preference displaces relations that foster reasoned action.

The social transformation of the public/private distinction has direct effects on forms of public interaction and the patterns through which people and issues are represented.[7] With regard to the political public sphere, Jürgen Habermas argues that the liberal public sphere is increasingly massified. While the modern public political sphere has been dominated by the representation of economic interests, these interests tend to increase with democratization and tend to be formulated through an increasing variety of elites. The representation of interests becomes increasingly distanced from its sources in the actions of people and becomes increasingly mediated (Habermas, 1989).

As the public sphere becomes defined in terms of necessity, patterns of legitimate authority and relations of social control are increasingly supported by technological and scientific discourses. Jürgen Habermas has argued that, as these social processes develop, the "mass loyalty" that bolsters support for the social system is created through "rewards for *privatized needs*" (1986: 112). Because rewards are related to subjective preferences grounded in privatized needs, the social system is much less likely to be interpreted through political discourses based on principles of collective action. Rather, legitimating the social system on the basis of privatized needs goes along with a "technocratic justification" of social organization. All practical questions are rendered into technical terms consistent with the expansion of production and consumption. The most positivist versions of science that focus on the prediction of outcomes by exercising technical control over conditions becomes the grounds for justifying the technocratic orientations toward production that supports society.

In the early stages of capitalist development, a public sphere emerged that provided the locations, media, and languages through which a plurality of actors could form public opinions (Habermas, 1989). It was initially located in representative political institutions distinct from state administration, and it was elaborated in the nineteenth century through a variety of newspapers and other forums. The bourgeois public sphere was in its heyday when competitive market relations were dominant, property ownership was required for the franchise, and state administration was financially dependent on representative bodies. Mass democracy and economic concentration have weakened these aspects of the public sphere that served as the conditions for public opinion formation. These processes have been increasingly absorbed into administration and have become more organized around interests in administrative state programs.

These changes in the political sphere parallel and are shaped by underlying changes in the patterns of interaction that constitute public order. Richard Sennett's focus on changes in public interaction that emerged during the transition from the eighteenth century through the nineteenth century raises crucial features of the transformation of everyday arenas of interaction (1977). His analysis extends issues about the origins and transformation of the bourgeois public sphere by Habermas to arenas of face-to-face interaction.

Changes in codes of interaction, the organization of cities as spatial locations for interaction, and changes in self-orientation and self-presentation that developed with industrial capitalism and consumerism had profound effects on the division between public and private spheres of life and on relations in public. Just as social life has become increasingly characterized by withdrawal into a self that revolves around privatized interests and intimacy, politics has tended to become an arena for emotionally charged affirmations of collective identity rather than a sphere of speech and principled action.

In the eighteenth century, the capital cities of London and Paris had influxes of population. The era of mercantile capitalism was at its high point, court society was declining, and the bourgeoisie was emerging. The movement of people to capital cities, the social transformations engendered by economic change and shifting class relations posed a major problem of public order: With the breakdown of court society—in which public order was based on fixed rank and interpersonal knowledge—how was a public realm to be constituted among strangers? How could a public order be established among people who did not know one another?

The problem of public order was largely solved through impersonal codes of conduct that distanced public interaction from personal life. In part, this took the form of dress codes. People dressed in a manner appropriate to their social and occupational status so that they could be socially recognizable and locatable. The body in public was impersonalized through the use of costumes, wigs, and facial makeup. The idea was not to reveal one's private self in public dress, not to use dress as an expression of the self, but, rather, to treat the body as an object of decoration. Public appearance was both highly playful and distanced from personal meanings. Clothes did not so much reveal the private self as make it irrelevant. Although the artifice of clothing was related to public rank and social position, it was not taken as an expression of the self but, rather, as formative for public order.

While the artifice of clothing served to differentiate social members in public, speech cut across social rank. As in the case of clothing, speech was not viewed as personally expressive and revealing, but as having significance solely in public action. The meaningfulness of public speech was seen as self-contained in its moment of expression rather than expressive of the inner experience of the speaker. Speech created a public reality rather than expressing or symbolizing underlying personal identities.

The importance of both dress and speech as impersonal mediums is exemplified by their use in public settings. In the theater, for example, actors wore street clothes that bore no resemblance to the dramatic roles they were playing. Instead of a concern with symbolism that was revealing of an underlying reality, or expressing the actors' real emotions, theatrical productions were taken on their own terms. The idea was to create self-contained expression that was a presentation of emotion rather than something symbolic of a greater reality. Indeed, there was less of a clear-cut differentiation between the theater and the street than there was continuity. Theaters were lighted, the audience spoke to one another as well as to the performers, often demanding that performers repeat lines that were particularly funny or moving. There was a great deal of movement in and out of the theater. The theater and the street mutually conditioned one another as realms of public interaction built on the same conventions. In the theater as in the street, codes of interaction enabled people to arouse "each other's feelings without having to attempt to define themselves to each other, a definition the material conditions of life would have made difficult, frustrating, and probably fruitless" (1977: 64).

A similar impersonality reigned in the coffeehouse. The coffeehouse was primarily a center of public information in which patrons read newspapers and conversed with one another. The conventions of the coffeehouse, moreover, facilitated a free flow of public communication and sharing of information. In the coffeehouse, "distinctions of rank were temporarily suspended; anyone sitting in the coffeehouse had a right to talk to anyone else, to enter into any conversation, whether he knew the other person or not, whether he was bidden to speak or not. It was bad form even to touch on the social origins of other persons when talking to them in the coffeehouse, because the free flow of talk might then be impeded" (1977: 81). By breaking down social distinction, speech fostered spontaneous expression. Ideas, emotions, and information were transmitted without the aim of revealing the character of the speakers. Speech created an immediately shared world in which all could participate.

The impersonal codes of conduct of the eighteenth century facilitated the spontaneity of individuals in public. Through a set of conventional rules, individuals were able to act apart from their personal lives. Because public speech and action were not taken as revealing of the private self, the ability to act in public without having to reflect on what that action symbolized about the self reduced inhibitions, giving public life a lively quality. Public activity, taken as a reality in itself rather than as a symbolic rendering of one's inner life, had its own vitality and meaning.

While the public realm was constituted on the basis of impersonal codes, so the private realm of the bourgeois household and family was not thought of primarily in personal terms. To be sure, the family was a realm of intimacy and private expression. It was a location for both the greater laxity, less convention, and more individualized action. Nonetheless, it was not bounded solely by personal meaning. The freedom of private life resided primarily in the character of the home as a refuge from the convention and complexity of the artificial public world. Most importantly, it was a realm of natural as opposed to social expression:

> The line drawn between public and private was essentially one on which the claims of civility—epitomized by cosmopolitan public behavior—were balanced against the claims of nature—epitomized by the family. They saw these

claims in conflict, and the complexity of their vision lay in that they refused to prefer the one over the other, but held the two in a state of equilibrium. Behaving with strangers in an emotionally satisfying way and yet remaining aloof from them was seen by the mid-eighteenth century as the means by which the human animal was transformed into a social being. The capacities for parenthood and deep friendship were seen in turn to be natural potentials, rather than human creations; while man made himself in public, he realized his nature in the private realm, above all in his experience within the family (1977: 18–19).

The private sphere, as a realm of natural propensities and feelings, was seen as having a universal character. Feelings and sensibilities associated with private life were thought of as having a spontaneity that was both intimate, close, and particular as well as general to humanity. The private self was ordered, not by individual will and determination, but by human capacities that transcended the individual as a member of society. Against the conventional world of public life, the private sphere allowed for natural relations of dependency between parents and children. These relations were viewed as fulfilling natural potentials rather than as contrived acts of personality.

Just as the public world created self-distance through artifice and speech, so in the private sphere the expression of feeling and emotion were not taken as expressions of the individual's unique personality. Since public and private expressions did not demand immediate self-reflection, they facilitated spontaneity. The relative impersonality of both the public and private realms enhanced the active affirmation of a shared world.

These patterns changed during the nineteenth century. In the nineteenth century the individual's representation of emotion and information, in both public and private settings, is overlayered by the fear of self-disclosure. The sources of this transformation, and the effect it had on public and private life is to be found in the major social consequences of the industrial revolution.[8]

Two developments in the capital cities of London and Paris had particularly striking effects on the public realm and led to its relative decline. First, as population in these urban centers drastically increased, people became increasingly segregated in areas of the city according to their social class. Now it was not only the case that individuals were strangers to one another—whole sections of the city became unknown to people who did not live in them. The effect was to induce fear of the unknown, both unknown individuals and unknown sections of the city that they happened to be traveling through, especially for the more mobile middle class and upper-middle class.

Second, the industrial revolution generated mass produced goods in huge quantities and standardized varieties. The flood of goods, both domestically produced and imported, was sold increasingly in centralized locations, most notably in department stores, where prices were fixed and where they were displayed amid exotic imagery. These changes in production and distribution of goods disoriented people, making them unsure of themselves and not knowing what to expect. Moreover, the promise of consumerism was a promise of self-expression. Through discriminate consumption, there was a possibility of creating a self that was differentiated from others.

These changes in demography and patterns of distribution yielded a public culture characterized by silence, observation, and self-involvement. The fear of others, of strangers in public, oriented people to view one another's appearance as potential sources of information. Looking at others, in a way that did not draw attention to one's self, induced silence and rigidity in public interaction. People became spectators of one another, distanced by an observatory orientation. The public realm was reduced from something shared and interacted through to an instrument for individual action. Moving from place to place, attending to the latest in objects of consumption being displayed, and focusing on the appearance of others became the norm of public life.

The notion that people are revealed through their dress and demeanor, that appearances tell something about individual character, had the effect of standardizing clothing. No one wanted to be seen as distinctive, as different in a world where drawing attention to one's self might create a situation of danger. Thus, aside from the effect of mass production on standardized clothing, there was also a belief in the value of standardization. To appear like everyone else meant safety in anonymity.

Yet this concern with blending into the crowd did not detract from mutual observation. If anything, observation had to be closer and more careful. For while differences in individuals were not revealed in gross differences in appearance, they were revealed, or potentially could be revealed, in details. Observation became more detailed as the appearance of people became differentiated by details rather than by major differences in dress.

The use of the public realm as an observatory of others was heightened by the scientization and secularization of culture. The scientific ideal of objectivity—that knowledge could be most fruitfully gained by close, detached observation—became standard not only for the physical and biological sciences but also for the social sciences. The ideal of study as an observation of the facts and the classification of organisms, objects, and people by the way they differed in appearance became the dominant method of inquiry, certainly in France and Great Britain. Scientific detachment took on the quality of spectatorship—of looking carefully, finding similarities and differences, and making close observations, independent of subjective value, the grounds of the factual. Indeed, science itself became characterized as a method in which underlying causes and relationships became available through detached observation. The distance between the scientist and the object of observation was defined increasingly in methods of observation and classification as the result of close observation. Explanations were to be found in causes that were immediately viable and detectable to observation. No metaphysical infrastructure had to be inferred: what was seen was what was to be believed.

The secularization of culture supported close observation. In its social implications, secularization meant there was no reality beyond the here and now. The real was no longer ethereal, metaphysical, or transcendent in the theological sense, but, rather, the real and the rational were revealed in appearance. The meaningfulness and significance of the world was imminent within it rather than in some transcendent realm of faith or philosophical speculation. To know the world, to understand fundamental reality, one had to see the world and observe it.

In this way, science and secular culture supported the passive observation in the public world of strangers and commodities. All focused on the belief in the observation of others, of biological and physical reality and, of great importance, of the self.

The notion that one could know oneself, not through a shared public world of conventions and language or through the natural propensities that were enacted in the private household, but, rather, through an examination of one's personality became increasingly dominant. The idea emerged that each individual was a unique personality that developed over time and was subject to willful determination through the self-creation of appearances and activity. This generated a belief in the self as a realm of introspection and as a representational field had immense consequences on public and private action.

The idea that appearance represents personality heightened fears of self-disclosure in public and supported the concerns about self-control. The presentation of the self as something willful restricted the possibility of spontaneity and enhanced self-reflective aspects of action and speech. All activity became calculated from the perspective of inferences drawn by others. Formality, silence, and attention to the details of appearance and speech were the means through which action in public could be safely presented.

In the mid- to late nineteenth century the theater became silent and dark. The audience became a relatively disassociated group of spectators, sitting in silence, watching the details of a performance without intervening in it. Indeed, the attitude of the audience changed. Instead of viewing theatrical productions as events, they were increasingly thought of as symbolic of the reality they were representing. Concerns with realism in costuming, setting, and with the personality of performers as the central feature of acting, exemplified the attitude of silent observation and the belief that meaning could be derived from detached observation.

These social and cultural transformations had a major impact on the private realm of the family.[9] The family was both the ground for a competitive market society and a sanctuary from it. As Alvin W. Gouldner pointed out, "the middle-class concern to extend or defend property was always motivated, in important part, by the viability of the middle-class family, by the bourgeois' felt obligations to it, and by his concern to protect and advantage 'his' family" (1976: 203). The strains of public life, and especially individualized economic activity, can be seen, in part, as a defensive effort to secure material life for those to whom one was morally bound. At the same time that the family provided an altruistic ground for economic activity, it also served as a realm of domination in which the subordination of wives and children, as well as private consumption, provided relief from public and economic life. The relief from struggles over competitive advantage, of self-presentation, and calculating rationality that was provided in family relations served to restore the capacity for activity in broader arenas of social life.

Yet, the very importance of the family as a refuge tended to make it ritualized and formal (Poster, 1978; Sennett, 1977). As public life came to be seen as an exertion of willful personality and as something personally created, the possibility of naturalism in private life declined. Moreover, the fear of disorder and catastrophe in public life heightened the need for stability in the private domain of the family. Far from being an arena of expressivity, the private family tended to become increasingly rigid and codified. The ideal of the Victorian bourgeois family as orderly, calm, and rigidly formalized served as a refuge from social chaos. Thus, even the sanctuary of the private family, as it increasingly became seen as an arena for personality rather than nature, did not reduce strains imposed by participation in the wider social world. Rather, these strains required yet greater willful control both in public and private life.

As a consequence of the heightened focus on ever-deeper aspects of the personality as a source of meaning and the cloistered atmosphere of the bourgeois family, patterns of reference shift from public action to personal identity. Action, which rests on codes, necessary fictions, and expressions of common beliefs that cut across personal sources of meaning, engages people in issues and collective passions that are distanced and apart from the self. Action engages people in the pursuit of ends guided by meanings that are publicly presented and collectively held. Identity, on the other hand, holds the private self as a source of meaning. Events are viewed as expressions of individualized states that are revealed through behavioral manifestations and personal feelings. The public world becomes a location through which authenticity of feeling and demands for personal relevance can be realized. The culture tends toward privatized self-absorption and concerns with the manifestations of a bottomless and unknown subjective interior. The public sphere is reduced to moments of interaction through which people reveal themselves to one another, attempting to authenticate their personal feelings and self-images.

In effect, the public sphere is a means for manifesting personal meanings. Public spaces, rather than locations for collective action, become places where the individual experiences "isolation in the midst of visibility" (Sennett, 1977: 12–14). Most significantly, public space is increasingly deadened; it is transformed into grids for the movement of individuals by private motor vehicles. Public space becomes subordinated to the free movement of individuals who are isolated yet visible to one another in their pursuit of private ends. The very ecology of urban space forces people into deeper spheres of intimacy for their meanings and purposes.

To be sure, the privatization and intensification of meaning can be viewed as functional for instrumental rationality that characterizes the public realm. As the "technological economy makes more and more social relations opaque to the individual" and "the institutional fabric as a whole tends toward incomprehensibility," so the private sphere and personalized meanings "compensate for the discontents brought about by the large structures of modern society" (Berger et al., 1974: 182–86). Yet the private sphere is underinstitutionalized and overintensified. It is itself determined by wider social forces. The concern with self and personalized meaning takes on a life of its own. It becomes the zone of subjective experience in the interpenetration of private and public arenas.

The personalization of private and public spheres of life, of taking private and public realms of interaction as fields for observation of the self and others, has had major effects on political action and political legitimacy. The basis of political legitimacy has been dislocated from the concerns for a common world that goes beyond what is immediately felt to more discontinuous, fleeting, and personally limited orientations. Politics, like other public activities, becomes a spectacle to be observed or ignored. And, most importantly, what is observed is the image of the politician who is judged less on programs than on expressions of emotion, personality, morality, and private resources. The identity of the politician, and whether that identity fosters collective identity, comes to replace more impersonal sources of political cohesion, such as class interest. Political struggle loses its contextual location in history, social structure, and culture and becomes, instead, a realm of personal interaction mediated by collective affirmation or denigration. Politics, as an arena for the collective determination of the conditions of life, is reduced to a realm of interpersonal disclosure and identity formation limited to immediate persons.

The psychological direction of the social transformation of the public/private division is toward narcissistic self-involvement. Narcissism is a kind of "self-absorption which prevents one from understanding what belongs within the domain of the self and self-ratification and what belongs outside of it" (Sennett, 1977: 8). It is a condition in which the boundaries between personal identity and objects in the world, including other people, are obliterated in such a way that everything is either incorporated in the self or experienced as an extention of the self.

Rooted in the fears, aggressive impulses, and love of earliest infant dependency, narcissism emerges when the emotions associated with separation from parental nurturing are unresolved. Parental nurturing becomes private, exclusive, intense, and sexual in the bourgeois family (Poster, 1978: 166–78). As a result, the narcissist comes to experience "dependence on the vicarious warmth of others combined with a fear of dependence, a sense of inner emptiness, boundless repressed rage, and unsatisfied oral cravings" (Lasch, 1979: 74). The preoccupation with attachment to and flight from dependency provide the emotional grounds for an attentive anxiety toward the self that leads to "pseudo-self insight, calculating seductiveness, nervous, self-deprecating humor" (1979: 74). Most pointedly, infantile rage and desires for wholeness are combined with fears of rage and desire. These lead to fantasies of personal autonomy, omipotence, power, wealth, beauty, and continuing youth. The narcissist "sees the world as a mirror of himself and has no interest in external events except as they throw back a reflection of his own image" (1979: 96).

A narcissistic society gives prominence to and provides a structure of support for narcissistic traits (1979: 23). As the necessities of production, consumption, and reproduction move from the private realm to public arenas with social development, there is an ever-greater dependency by individuals on anonymous public organizations and experts for securing and stabilizing the means of life. Restraints on the individual in situations of authority become ever more internalized and the individual becomes defensive against both desires and the rage generated by defenses against desire. Thus, narcissism comes to characterize the psychological dependence on others as that dependence becomes publicly ordered through social institutions. Material dependency becomes fused with needs for approval and recognition. Contemporary patterns of bureaucratic work and careerism, the saturation of everyday life with media images that come to verify experience, and the prevalence of therapeutic ideologies that provide templates of normal personal development enhance tendencies toward dependence on others for validation and intensive self-scrutiny. Directions toward narcissistic privatism, which make restricted personal meaning the sole grounds for orientation toward the world, are psychological tendencies deeply intertwined with the emergence of society as a field of public dependency for private life: "Dependence on these intricate, supremely sophisticated life-support systems, and more generally on externally provided goods and services, recreates some of the infantile feelings of helplessness" (Lasch, 1984: 34).

Survivalist ideologies are the fundamental expression of the combination of privatism, heightened to the point of nacissism, and collective interdependence for the necessities of life. A pervasive sense of crisis in everyday activities trivializes history and the actual threats faced by humanity. Yet the belief that daily life is a "succession of emergencies" is also a psychological defense against real global threats. "When the grim rhetoric of survivalism invades everyday life, it simultaneously intensifies and relieves the fear of disaster" (Lasch, 1984: 61). By preparing psychologically for the worst possible outcomes, there is a feeling of relief when these outcomes are avoided. To be sure, the "focus on manageable private stresses rather than public disasters" tends to preclude efforts to confront the sources of collective threats through political action (1984: 65). This ideology, however, heightens the salience of the personal sphere where the boundaries of experience do not exceed the capacities for private action.

Survivalist ideologies, moreover, have affinities with a sense of victimization. The notion that individuals are victims of crushing social forces not only lends the moral superiority of suffering to actual oppression, harms, and indignities but also transforms struggles against these forces into fights for survival. Identities based on victimization tend toward particularism and expressive politics rather than public and rational projects that open up collective action that raises universal demands. Oppression is totalized, particularized, and reduced to survivalist themes. This truncates discourse to particularistic demands and personal narratives.

Associated with survivalism and victimization are apocalyptic visions of nuclear extinction or environmental catastrophies that will leave a remnant of humanity to build a new world (1984: 83). While religious versions of survivalism predict an end of the world in which an elect will be triumphant and will spiritually transcend the fireball that is to come, secular versions span the gamut. Privatized, antipolitical solutions view fallout shelters and self-sufficiency in ethically charged terms of personal self-responsibility; space colonization is envisioned as a fresh start for humanity (1984: 85). All are characterized by a realism regarding the virtual inevitability of mass destruction and the need to minimize attachments to others.

In contrast to apocalyptic survivalism is a more mundane, everyday survivalism. Here the hope is to maintain a private sphere as a way of securing immediate life. Everyday survivalism has continuity "with a sense of place, loyalty to immediate surroundings and their associations" (1984: 91); it also minimizes feelings and attachments by subordinating everything to struggles for the satisfactions of momentary needs and comforts. Heroism is devalued in favor of small happinesses; historical time and collective action are devalued in favor of getting through one day at a time; full-fledged resistance is devalued in favor of psychological withdrawal and detachment; and sacrifices for collective goods are devalued in favor of personal safety. Because no future is envisioned beyond the self, there is no sense that one is participating in making a world in which others will live. Ideologies based on survivalist ethics and privatized sensibilities support and reproduce the public sphere as a totalizing process that, in turn, engenders survivalist outlooks.

With the emergence of modern society, frameworks for political action have been shaped by institutional processes that enhance the significance of the private lives of individuals over a world held in common. Throughout the modern epoch, the terms of private and public life stand juxtaposed to one another in a general direction: The meanings attached to private life become both increasingly salient for individual identity and activity as well as increasingly distant from a shared public realm. At the same time, the significance attributed to private life has served as the basis for affirming the political order. Beliefs that support relations of power and authority tend to become increasingly privatized. Everyday activity gains significance from the personalized contexts of spiritual fulfillment, familial relations, and occupational life and friendships.

Activity has purely personal significance. Political efforts to affect the conditions under which everyday life is conducted—which would require the active constitution of social power on the basis on moral equality, ethical codes, and broad-based identities—are severely limited as a result of the personally bounded meaning attributed to action. Instead, the conditions through which everyday life are publicly ordered are taken for granted as strategic and instrumental boundaries for maintaining and enhancing private life. The public realm, as an arena for participatory political life and collective action, all but disappears. It shrinks in a manner that heightens the significance of personal life: spiritual fulfillment, careers, private property, and intimate relations overly personalize political action. The private sphere, moreover, is reduced to meanings that are increasingly self-referential and narcissistic. Boundaries between the self and the outside world and, ultimately, survivalist ethics formulate dependence on society in ways that mimic biological necessity and instrumentalize public action.

The tendency toward heightened privatism is not primarily psychological; rather, it is part of the structural merging of private and public spheres of life into a social metabolism that transforms all terms of action, including the individual. The expanding social arena is the public location of privatized action. It becomes the taken-for-granted grounds of self-maintenance. The absorption with private life yields a politics of silence and acquiescence when issues are not rendered meaningful in the most personal terms.

## NOTES

1. These themes have been central to writers who have formulated divergent critical frameworks. Herbert Marcuse (1964) argued that individual autonomy and consciousness are so manipulated by systems of production and consumerism that the possibilities of independent thought and action are virtually obliterated for all strata and classes except those who are at the extreme margins of the system. Michel Foucault (1977; 1980), on the other hand, argued that the individual and individual consciousness must be seen as part of emerging systems of power that serves as a locus of surveillance. Both of these approaches, one from the standpoint of consciousness and the other from the standpoint of the microtechniques of power, agree on the decline of autonomy and political space in patterns of modern society. Pertinent here is Orlando Patterson's (1982) analysis of the difference between slaves and nonslaves. Among these differences are the slaves' "alienation from all ties of natality and in their lack of honor and publicly recognized repute" (1982: 26). Slavery is constituted in part through the lack of visibility in free public arenas.

2. Autonomy is used here to stand for relations that enable individuals and/or institutions to have capacities for self-constitution and self-determination. Autonomy is a type of relation; it is not synonymous with individuals and/or

institutions being isolated from one another. The underpinnings of the public/private division in notions of autonomy and, most particularly, political autonomy, are developed by Christian Bay (1970; 1981) and in a book of essays edited by John Christman (1989). The notion that the public/private division is at the core of legal autonomy, and, indeed, the autonomy of institutions and their relations to individual autonomy is a core theme of this book. For a contemporary discussion of issues of legal autonomy in light of autopoietic theory see the collection of essays edited by Gunther Teubner (1988).

3. This does not mean that politics should be decoupled from social policy. Rather, social policies should be formulated more from the standpoint of political action, political personhood, and citizenship. This is consistent with approaches formulated by William Julius Wilson (1987) and Theda Skocpol (1990) that argue for a policy mix that emphasizes universal needs rather than aiming at problems of specifically disadvantaged groups.

4. See Elizabeth Young-Bruehl (1982) for the definitive intellectual biography of Hannah Arendt. Also see collected essays on Arendt's work in Melvin Hill (1979) and in a special issue of *Social Research* (1977). Arendt's method of conceptual analysis shares the view of sociologists that the status of outsider and conditions of marginality are valued critical standpoints. Yet her focus was on the political insights that could be gained from these standpoints, especially regarding categories of citizenship, statelessness, and political action. See Nancy Hartsock (1985) for a discussion of how feminist theorists have both criticized and appropriated Arendt's analysis of the public/private split and power.

5. Jürgen Habermas also roots his vision of politics in Aristotelian ethics, distinguishing among politics as the "good and just life," "techne" as skilled work that produces lasting artifacts, and labor which produces for immediate survival (1973: 42). He does not develop these distinctions through the public/private division as elaborately as in Arendt's writings.

6. There are parallels to writers who dealt with issues of conformity in the 1950s. Christopher Bryant (1978: 71) points out, for example, that David Riesman et al. (1950) viewed privatization as "privacy without autonomy." Although Riesman did not focus fully on the political implications of privatization, Shils (1956) was more troubled by it.

7. Norbert Elias demonstrates that the emergence of patterns of etiquette and detailed control of everyday social interaction through the internalization of manners emerges with courtly society (1978). Here people who were strangers had to engage in face-to-face interactions with one another in a public place.

8. See E. J. Hobsbawm's *The Age of Capital: 1848–1875* (1979) for an overview of this historical transition. Hobsbawm analyzes the fundamental transformations that were occurring in patterns of production and social life. He relates this to changes in private life, especially in the emergence of the bourgeois household, and to changes in patterns of public representation in art and literature.

9. Hobsbawm states that "the home was the quintessential bourgeois world, for in it, and only in it, could the contradictions and conflicts within his society

be forgotten or artificially eliminated. Here and here alone the bourgeois and even more the petty bourgeois family could maintain the illusion of a harmonious, hierarchic happiness" (1979: 254). Witold Rybcynski's *Home: A Short History of an Idea* (1986) demonstrates how the subdivision and specialization of spaces within the bourgeois home during the nineteenth century went along with the formation of deeper notions of privacy and conventional ideas of family.

# Part I

## KARL MARX

# CHAPTER 3

## Emancipation and the Public/Private Division

Alternative interpretations of Marx's theory have been raised through the public/private distinction. Hannah Arendt criticized Marx's political economy for collapsing the public sphere of politics into the social metabolism of production and consumption (1959: 71–95). Marx carried the analysis of society initiated by classical political economy to its logical conclusion: Once the forces of production are socialized, the control and appropriation of wealth through private ownership becomes anachronistic; the movement of production into the public sphere ultimately requires a public form of property. By analyzing Marx's political economy as a culmination of classical liberalism, Arendt criticizes his politics, debunking his originality and revolutionary claims. Marx's vision of political emancipation is severely limited because of his virtual reduction of humanity to a laboring animal without distinct political and cultural dimensions. For Arendt, the public emancipation of the labor process may, indeed, lead to a form of life characterized by less toil and enhanced consumption. Yet the domination of people by labor and consumption erodes the formation of a public sphere based on moral autonomy, individuation, and collective self-determination.

Theorists identified with neo-Marxism have views similar to Arendt's. Critical theorists such as Albrecht Wellmer (1971) and Jürgen Habermas (1971) have argued that the positivist strain in Marx's theory results from the centrality of the labor process and instrumental rationality in his analysis of society. They argue that communicative and symbolic dimensions must be coupled with Marxian political economy to adequately formulate political and policy issues. Steven Seidman, making the claim that Marx's theory can be fully appreciated through its associations with liberalism and European sociological theory, faults Marx for failing to "harmonize the dual ideals of autonomy and human wholeness" because of his "reduction of humans to a tool-making animal" (1983: 138). These features of Marx's theory, it is alleged, support technocratic control of the public sphere. Isaac Balbus argues that the antistatist vision of the contemporary socialist left must be partially founded on a rejection of Marx's vision of communism as an "apolitical society" where neutral administration of production replaces conflicts based on class (1982: 114).

Other theorists, however, argue that Marx's theory of politics is not overly determined by the needs of labor and consumption because labor and consumption are simultaneously political and economic categories.[1] They maintain that Marxian theory seeks to overcome those conditions of economic domination that depoliticize and privatize experience to enable people to participate in consciously shaping collective actions through public participation. From this perspective, Marx provided a core theoretical standpoint for democratic socialist movements seeking to establish the participation of self-conscious members of the working class in the public spheres of culture and politics (Flacks and Turkel, 1978; Harrington, 1972: 41–90; Harrington, 1989: 1–59). Richard Sennett, for example, has characterized Marx as a supporter of cosmopolitanism, urbanism, and a rich public life. Indeed, for Sennett, Marx is a "champion" of public man (1977: 252).

These alternative interpretations are more fully joined by analyzing Marx's theoretical approach in a way that makes the public/private distinction pivotal. In this chapter, I discuss the public/private division in Marx's early writings through *The German Ideology*. In these writings, Marx analyzed the public/private division as formative for experience, political activity, and power differentials that shape everyday life. He is most concerned with formulating a method of inquiry that captures the radical separation of public discourses and private life under the forces of dissociation that shape industrial capitalism: alienated labor, the division of labor, and private property. Critically reconstructing the public/private distinction is both a topic and a resource for overcoming categories of action and knowledge that were basic for establishing the social forms of labor, politics, and knowledge that dissociated people from one another and thwart collective action.

For Marx, the social transformation of human life creates new conditions for knowledge and for emancipatory action. Knowledge of these conditions can be initially established by criticizing the public/private division in its most consistent and theoretically rigorous statements in philosophy and political economy. This critical approach not only shows the limits of speculative and abstract knowledge but also prepares the way for socially grounded knowledge and the analysis of concrete events.

Marx argued that the philosophical approach to the public/private distinction could not justify the internal relations of its concepts because it could not adequately comprehend the emerging social conditions that formed the ground of public/private relations. In addition, Marx went beyond philosophical discourse by criticizing the public/private distinction in political economy. Here again, Marx argued that political economy, while more rooted than philosophy in social relations, did not adequately account for the internal relations of its categories because it could not adequately formulate the social relations for the public/private distinction. He criticized the public/private distinctions in politics and in law as ideologies that mystify sources of power, initiative, dissociation, and exploitation in bourgeois social relations.

In criticizing these approaches, Marx establishes labor as the key social category. Labor, as it emerged in the public sphere through the commodity form, becomes the ground for the public/private division. Through struggles over patterns of labor control, the public/private division is elaborated through law and politics.

We see this demonstrated in the next chapter by contrasting the ways in which Marx conceptualized the public/private distinction as both a topic and a resource for studying particular instances of politics and law creation, most prominently in his analysis of laws limiting the working day in Great Britain and in the coming to power of Louis Bonaparte. Even though Marx's engagement with the public/private distinction in philosophy and political economy has an abstract, monological character, his analysis of particular events of state formation and lawmaking maintains that the public/private division supports democratic politics.

Marx's early critique of the public/private division in Hegelian philosophy and in political economy emphasizes the disparity between public discourses of freedom and equality and the conditions of action in private life. Marx argues that the concepts of public freedom in philosophy and political economy are as lacking in material foundations as they are universal in their claims to equality. Most pointedly, the equality and freedom that they posit in the public sphere are ideological. They establish social, religious, and material distinctions in the form of private rights that actually secure conditions of inequality and conflict in everyday life. While political and legal representations of freedom and equality claim to be reasonable and have laudable utopian elements, they are frameworks for establishing and enhancing private power and domination.

Central to Marx's critique is a search for the social grounds of concepts. The speculative bases for philosophical categories are themselves privatized: They are founded on subjective experience and mystify freedom. Marx went beyond this by both historicizing and materializing Georg Hegel's dialectical approach. He focuses on how Hegel's analysis of relationships among public and private arenas distorts the practical and intellectual transformations through which human capacities have evolved. For Marx, the categories of private and public activity are necessary for forming the bourgeois epoch. Moreover, they generate conditions for overcoming mystification, oppression, and alienation.

Marx argued that the universal, abstract categories of the public sphere posited by German idealism are not adequately grounded in the actual conditions that make social life and the forms through which it is conducted possible. Rather, idealist categories are rooted in a speculative and contemplative approach to theorizing that removes them from actual social practices, rendering them inadequate for analytic purposes. The inadequacy of this idealized public sphere is demonstrated by the tendency to deduce those forms of social life closest to the private sphere, such as the family, from the most universal categories. The private sphere and the realms of everyday action are made into aspects of an abstract logic of social and political constitution.

Hegel inverts the family and civil society and the state so that the state appears as a subject of action while the family and civil society become "unreal objective elements of the idea with a changed significance" (1978a: 16). This is accomplished by "mystically" making the state into a predicate with an "independent existence"; the family and civil society are conceptualized as results of state action (1978a: 17–18). In effect, the most abstracted form of public action in presented as an independent subject that generates the more private forms of social action.

In opposition, Marx maintains that the "family and civil society are, actually, the driving force of the state rather than being merely produced by the idea of the state" (1978a: 17). Instead of being determined by a speculative logic that locates necessity within relations among ideas, "the fact is that the state issues from the multitude in their existence as members of families and as members of civil society" (1978a: 17). Indeed, it is from this social reality rather than from speculative thought that the family and civil society can be correctly understood as the natural basis of the state. Individuals, in their actual relations with one another in the private sphere of the family and in civil society are the true grounds on which forms of public life and, most notably, the state, are based.

By inverting the relationship between the extended sphere of everyday action rooted in the private realm of the family and the state, Marx establishes the grounds for delimiting democracy. Democracy, in contrast to monarchy, is the only source of sovereignty and political order that can be understood on its own terms. While monarchy rests, at least in part, on some theological or transcendental grounds, democracy is self-grounding. It is located in the actual activity of people engaged in ruling themselves through their everyday actions rooted in social relations that develop out of the private sphere. Because democracy is based on actual activities of self-ruling people, it does not require an abstracted, transendental origin; through democracy, people can recognize that "it is not the constitution which creates the people but the people who create the constitution" (1978a: 20). In this light, bureaucratic ideologies of the state rooted in specialized knowledge of technical legal norms that mystify the state can be challenged. Politics, rooted in the actual activity of people engaged in social relations, represents a sphere of public freedom since it is generated from intended patterns of action rather than dictated from trancendental or logical necessity.

Democracy locates the sources of politics and the state in the actual activities of people and, therefore, represents a major departure for the self-grounding of human activity; nonetheless, democratically based constitutions may distort the realities of social life because of the nature of the relations of private life and civil society. The character of these relations may generate distant and abstracted forms of politics and the state precisely because the private sphere and civil society block patterns of mutual recognition and activity that would make truly democratic politics possible. As Marx points out, "the abstraction of the *state as such* belongs only to modern times, because the abstraction of private life belongs only to modern times" (1978a: 22). The separation of life into public and private realms emerges with modern society and can only be directed in liberatory directions by transforming the practices on which they are based. This is, in part, a theoretical problem that requires new standpoints for knowledge. To more adequately analyze both the relations between the private sphere and the state generally and the potential for the true realization of democracy more particularly, it is necessary to analyze the relations of the private sphere and to more specifically formulate the relationship of the state to the private sphere.

Two initial directions for furthering this analysis are presented in "On the Jewish Question." First, Marx argues that the public sphere delineated by the political state under modern conditions is both partial and illusory (1978b: 35–42). Although the political state depicts a realm of public freedom grounded in equality, the communal character of the individual as citizen, and oriented toward the development of the human species as a whole, it is completely split off from the actual conditions of people's everyday lives. In large part this is the case because the political state affirms rights based on an individualism that abstracts supposedly universal features from the material conditions of life and postulates them as legal and political categories. This eventuates in the "division of man into *public person* and *private person*" so that in the conduct of social life, the individual "acts simply as a *private individual*, treats other men as means, degrades himself to the role of a mere means, and becomes the plaything of alien powers" (1978b: 33–34). In effect, the modern political state purges the material content and actual activity out of private individualism and social interaction, idealizing them in political and legal categories that are as universal as they are lacking in concrete determination.

Because of this abstract universalism, law and politics take on a peculiar character: Legal categories that provide for political freedom lack any worldly depiction of private life. At the same time, they affirm the distinctions and inequalities found in the private sphere and in civil society on the basis of private rights. With regard to religion, for example, "man emancipates himself *politically* from religion by expelling it from the sphere of public law to that of private law" (1978b: 35). Although the state does not recognize any particular religion as a public religion, it affirms the right to religious belief as a private matter. With regard to property, the state does not publicly mandate any particular distribution of property at the level of public law, but makes property and its unequal distribution in civil society a matter of private rights. All of the actual determinations of private life and civil society that are abstracted out of the political state and public law reemerge more forcefully in the apparently depoliticized private sphere and civil society. The determinants of the actual conditions of life appear as private individuals making choices and interacting with one another.

This pattern of political emancipation developed because the political revolution against feudalism dissolved feudal relationships into the fundamental features of civil society and affirmed these fundamental features as universal rights. Most importantly, the political state affirms the rights of "egoistic man . . . an individual separated from the community, withdrawn into himself, wholly preoccupied with his private interest and acting in accordance with his private caprice" (1978b: 43). While this dissolution takes the form of political emancipation, the actual elements that make up civil society and the private individual who is the actor in civil society are left unchanged. Indeed, they are affirmed as natural relations to be preserved through the state.

Because political emancipation generates an abstract public sphere of freedom in the form of individual rights while perpetuating the egoism and inequality of the private sphere, it cannot fulfill aspirations for human emancipation. For Marx, human emancipation is only possible when there is a unity between the private individual and the political individual. This unity must be accomplished in the everyday activities of people in such a way that social powers, including their private relationships, are integrated and organized as political powers. True political emancipation and democracy can only be fully realized when the conditions that shape private life are transformed in an emancipatory direction.

Marx's critique of German idealism and the liberal state shows that their lack of grounding and that their distortions of the actual conditions of life result in speculative concepts. Thus, Hegel's theory of the state inverts the actual relationship between private and public aspects of social constitution. For Marx, the ideal of a politically emancipated public sphere must realize human emancipation on the basis of the actual conditions of the private individual and civil society. Yet, Marx's own analysis, although directed toward the material relations that shape the private sphere, is speculative and grounded in philosophical opposition. It constitutes the beginnings of his search for an adequate analysis of the relations of the private and public spheres.

Grounded in arguments about the limits of political emancipation and in his view that full emancipation requires a transformation of the conditions that shape the private individual in civil society, Marx increasingly focuses on the forms of activities that encapsulate the private individual in egoism and that generate the conditions that make the public spheres of law and the state affirmations of egoistic privatism. In this light, *The Economic and Philosophical Manuscripts of 1844*, although still speculative and lacking in directly applicable empirical concepts, ground the analysis of the private individual and civil society at a deeper level of social relations by focusing on the commodification of labor as the source of alienation.

Alienated labor is the core relationship through which the private lives, productive activity, and patterns of public action for the vast majority of people are recreated. It is through alienated labor that people participate in producing the social relations that dominate them, generating indifference to communal needs and social development. Alienated labor divorces work from democratic forms of decision making, making work a matter of privatized necessity rather a sphere of public freedom and individual fullfilment. It depletes the material conditions of private life for the overwhelming majority of people, and shapes social and individual orientations in directions of egoism, privatized needs and possessiveness. Alienated labor is an active relationship to the world that distorts the relationship between productive powers and potentials for emancipation. People recreate the social forms that deplete their private material conditions while enhancing the most privatized orientations toward the world.

The commodification of labor, and the public discourses and institutions that facilitate it, are the conditions for its alienation. The worker's private existence depends on the sale of his labor as if it were any other commodity to be sold in the public market. The social character of this dependence means that "the worker has to struggle not only for his physical means of subsistence; he has to struggle to get work, i.e., the possibility, the means to perform his activity" (1964: 66–67). As a commodity, the capabilities and individual talents of the worker must conform to the requirements of the market; individual talents and knowledge are sacrificed to the tasks defined in the labor market. Dependence on the market depletes the worker both spiritually and physically so that he becomes "an abstract activity and a belly" (1964: 68). The private life of the worker in both its material and spiritual dimensions is conditioned by his or her public definition as a resource for commodity production, as an object, as a thing.

Alienated labor connects the worker's private life to wider social relations and material conditions. In selling and expending labor to earn a wage to maintain private existence, the worker is engaged in a social process that both produces commodities for sale on the market and produces himself as a public object in the form of a commodity (1964: 107). Indeed, to the extent to which workers are engaged in an increasing process of commodity production, they are also engaged in deepening and extending their labor as a commodity. Thus, the products of labor come to have "an independent power" over the worker since his productive activity is the condition through which his products become ever more external to him and serve to enhance the conditions that render his productive activity into an external commodity (1964: 108). The alienation of labor makes the world of things created by the worker a public arena that is the condition for maintaining his ever more dependent private existence.

Alienation from the product is one of the modes through which the worker becomes removed as a subject of action from the wider, public consequences of his productive activity. Indifference to the product, except as a salable object that serves immediate private needs for wages, estranges the worker's productive activity and consciousness from the construction of the human community as a whole and from participating in freely constructing a collective future. As a result of this structured indifference to the product, the worker's relation to the public determination of collective purposes is one of privatized, individual necessity as a result of his structured indifference to his product. Moreover, members of society become estranged from one another since their objective form of interaction—through commodities—is based on indifference and immediate private necessity. The public sphere in the form of a political economy, as calculable relations among the products of labor, is a material expression of privatized needs felt by the multitude of individuals.

Alienation from the product and its consequences for the public sphere are directly related to subjective depletion of labor as an estranged activity. Because labor is itself an object of sale, a commodity, it becomes as dissociated from the worker as the product. Work becomes a situated activity where the worker "does not affirm but denies himself" both mentally and physically (1964: 110). Since the activity of labor does not satisfy a need in and of itself but is, rather, a mere means of maintaining individual survival, the worker "only feels himself outside of his work, and in his work he feels outside himself. He is at home when he is not working, and when he is working he is not at home" (1964: 110). The only avenue left open for the experience of freedom for the worker is in the most privatized and intimate relations, indeed, "in his animal functions—eating, drinking, procreating, or at most in his dwelling and in dressing up" (1964: 110).

Alienated labor, beyond shaping the material pattern of public and private life for the majority of people, is also the relational ground for knowledge. Most pointedly, political economy is a dominant form of public discourse that provides the scientific categories shaping privatized sensibilities cognitively. By analyzing the categories of political economy from the ground of alienated labor, Marx gets to the bottom of their taken-for-granted character in privatized orientations of commodity relations.

In a manner similar to his critique of German idealism, Marx argues that political economy is neither grounded in the actual conditions that are the basis for its categories nor does it adequately conceptualize the active relationships that its categories formally express. By positing the categories of private property, exchange, labor, profit, and rent as fundamental premises without fully attending to the actual human activity that gives rise to them and without grounding them in the social relations that actively produce them, they take on the character of rarefied analytic concepts. Thus, Marx argues that political economy "expresses in general, abstract formulas the *material* process through which private property actually passes, and these formulas it then takes for *laws*" (1964: 106). Abstractions predominate, distorting the actual activities on which they are concretely based.

Marx, then, views the estrangement of the worker from laboring activity as pivotal for understanding the public discourse of wage labor, contracts, and private property. When the worker's productive activity is alienated from the worker through the commodity form, wages, the payment for labor as a commodity, and the capitalist, the owner of labor as a commodity, fully emerge as the categories through which production is publicly organized. In addition, modern forms of rent and profit, which presuppose an indifference to land and products except through their value in exchange, fully emerge when social relations are commodified on the basis of wage labor. The isolation of the worker from his product and from the process of its production through the wage system is the primal relationship that makes all the other categories of political economy possible because it depersonalizes and, thereby, frees products from their immediate relationship to their producer. The external, public representation of labor takes on an existence independent of the internal, personal relationships of its production and use.

The core legal category that both presupposes alienated labor and heightens its complex pattern of dissociation is private property. Private property is not only "the result, the necessary consequence, of *alienated labor*, of the external relation of the worker to nature and to himself," it is also the form and process of alienated labor, it is its "means and product" (1964: 116–117). Private property is the public presentation of the external results of alienated labor, of the separation of the person from the product, in the legal form of its appropriation.

Private property, moreover, is the point of active contradiction between alienated labor and its product; just as labor is the condition for the appropriation of objects that are produced for private ownership, so private ownership is the condition for labor as a commodity that is excluded from the product it creates. Private property, in the form of capital, is the relation through which labor is removed from the worker in a manner that serves to make the organization, the productive process, and the product of labor come to dominate labor as a power of itself. The more productive labor is, the greater is the capital it generates and, thereby, the greater is the condition for its further domination and estrangement.

Through its expression as private property, alienated labor enhances egoistic orientations and sensibilities. Manifested as private property, alienated labor produces man as a commodity not only in his relations in public through production and the market but, also, "as a *mentally* and physically dehumanized being. . . . Its product is the *self-conscious and self-acting commodity*" (1964: 121). In large part, this results from the material conditions of the private life of working-class people documented by Frederich Engels in *The Condition of the English Working Class* (1968): the cramped housing, the lack of sanitation, the poor diet, the fetid air, the over-crowded neighborhoods, the inadequate clothing, and the absence of adequate health care. Moreover, as Marx pointed out, these miserable conditions of private life require that those with "inactive, extravagant wealth" engage their "own unbridled extravagance and ceaseless, unproductive consumption" so that labor will be employed at subsistence levels for the production of luxury goods (1964: 156). The private consumption of luxury goods by the wealthy is the objective condition for the subsistence wages of the mass of workers.

Class differences in private consumption patterns are both a result and a condition of alienated labor and private property. Yet there are also common threads of privatism that cut across class differences and that go beyond class patterns of consumption. Alienated labor and private property lead to a generalized estrangement of the senses that equates appropriation of objects with the sheer possession of them. Marx states that "an object is truly *ours* only when we have it—when it exists for us as capital, or when it is directly possessed, eaten, drunk, worn, inhabited, etc." (1964: 139). The immediate experience of life, the very sensations that we have of the world, are determined through privatized appropriation and egoistic possessiveness. Thus, alienation of labor and private property shape the senses by determining the activities of production and consumption. Although class differences affect the range and content of objects of experience that deprive working people of sense experiences relative to the experiences available to the rich, it is nonetheless the case that the form of sensation—its egoism and possessiveness—is generalized for humanity as a whole. The senses are the result of "a labor of the entire history of the world down to the present" (1964: 141). Rather than the senses being either a residual category of social processes or so primary that they are autonomous from social processes, as much sociological theory suggests, Marx argues that the senses are a social category. They mediate the distinctions between public processes of production and distribution and private processes of consumption. The privatization of the senses is inherent in the alienation of labor and private property.

Privatizing the senses through egoistic possessiveness transforms human needs. Dependent on market relations, individuals are driven to create new needs in other people so that they can sell something to them and, in turn, gain the income to satisfy their own market-driven needs. People struggle with one another to make one another dependent on one another for their gratifications. While this generates an ever more sophisticated pattern of needs and private consumption, it also reduces social interaction to dependency and mutual huckstering. Salability, of one's powers and the objects that one owns, by becoming the dominant orientation of the private individual, determines the nature of private experience and social interaction.

The complex of these relations finds its ultimate manifestation, both in the interior experience of the private individual and in the sphere of public representation, in money. Because all needs in a market society based on alienated labor and on private property are mediated through money, individuals calculate private desires, needs, and power through money. Money becomes the fundamental need of each individual because it is the means through which all other needs are satisfied. Money becomes the abstract and necessary medium through which the private individual fulfills needs regardless of particular powers and abilities. Money, moreover, takes on an objective, public reality as the social relations and private orientations that support it expand. Through its power to mediate exchange, money takes on both symbolic and real powers of private individuals, their needs, and their patterns of interaction in consumption, public interaction and, ultimately, in the most private reaches of their senses and personal awareness.

Marx, then, conceptualized alienated labor as the active ground for the public/private split. From the most private needs of the individual to the most abstract level of public symbols, alienated labor is central to the formation of the contradictory relations that make up the totality of capitalist society. Alienated labor is the active premise for developing a theoretical approach that is self-grounded and, therefore, adequate for analyzing the elaboration of the public/private distinction in capitalist society.

Despite this important departure, the conceptualization of alienated labor in *The Manuscripts* is a speculative, critical philosophical approach to theorizing. While *The Manuscripts* goes beyond the opposition between "what private individuals actually do in civil society" and the "public arena of the emancipated political state," alienated labor and its foundational role for the categories of private and public life lack historical content and worldly definition. It is still in the bounds of philosophical discourse. Most importantly, there is an absence of a historical grounding of the material formation of different aspects of the public/private split and their contradictory relations.

The "materialist conception of history" articulated in *The German Ideology* is an important advance over critical philosophy for analyzing the public/private division as social categories. The resolution of contradictions through the radicalization of consciousness does not go much beyond a privatized, subjective experience of emancipation. The subjective experience of emancipation may leave social relations unchanged or may even accommodate people to domination. For this reason, Marx advocates a public form of knowledge established through observations of the objective connections among social and political structures as they evolve with patterns of production. Knowledge must not be limited to the common sense or philosophical views on individualism but, rather, on how "definite individuals" are engaged in "the life process," that is, how "they operate, produce materially, and hence as they work under definite material limits, presuppositions and conditions independent of their will" (1970: 46).

A more generalized historical analysis of the processes through which the public/private distinction shapes social action and is reproduced must be based on the fundamental conditions that make the life process possible (1970: 48–52). First, and analytically most important, is that human beings are distinguished from other species in that they produce their means of immediate survival and their material conditions of life. Indeed, individuals must engage in production "daily and hourly . . . merely to sustain human life." Second, in the process of producing the material means of survival, individuals produce new needs. In effect, the act of producing and satisfying survival needs generates needs that go beyond the most immediate needs of survival. Third, in producing their material life, human beings produce new life; they "propagate their kind" through the family, the first social relationship which becomes increasingly subordinate to other social relations as the material relations of production become developed. Fourth, the production of human life always involves a double relationship that combines natural and social aspects: the production and satisfaction of natural needs is accomplished through social relationships that entail cooperation among individuals. These natural and social aspects are combined in the practical activity of production and are virtually indistinguishable in ongoing activity.

Concrete analysis must take into account an array of factors in relating sociopolitical developments to production. The physical organization of a society, its population, its pattern of interaction, its geological and climatic location, its division of labor, and its development of productive forces must all be included in analyzing the material relations among people and the development of their needs through production. These conditions and the relations among them are primary and have analytic priority over ideal elements of social constitution, whether religious, political, or scientific.

While these factors are associated with the public/private distinction, Marx focused on the division of labor. The division "determines the relations of individuals to one another with reference to the material, instrument, and product of labor" (1970: 43). The division of labor dissociates individuals and activities, forming new locations for particular individuals and new patterns of interaction. The division of labor develops in ways that separate individuals from one another, reestablishing their relationships through property forms defined through legal discourses and maintained through state power. Forms of property have their sources in patterns of production, technology, distribution, and, most importantly, the social relationship of labor to the means of production.

The significance of the division of labor for the development of the public/private distinction is demonstrated by the forms of ownership through which the division of labor has been practically organized and through which production has been accomplished historically. The first form of property is tribal ownership. This collective pattern of ownership is based on the common ancestry of community members and is maintained through an elementary division of labor involving little more than an extension of the "natural division of labor" found in the family (1970: 43–44). The control of labor through household slavery is an important aspect of this form of property. A second form of property is ancient communal property combined with state ownership. This pattern emerges with the union of tribes and the formation of more complex political organization. It is characterized by a high degree of communal ownership under political control. Private property appears here, first as movable and then as unmovable objects. This pattern also involves the development of class relations and distinctions in property that follow from the development of the division of labor. Differences between industrial and maritime property as well as antagonisms between town and country begin to emerge. Major differences in property relations are reflected in the distinction between citizen and slave due to the preponderance of communal property that is state owned. Feudal or estate property, which emerged with the breakdown of the political organization of the Roman empire, rests on a sparse population engaged in agricultural production. It is characterized by a hierarchical structure of landownership and a small peasantry that is enserfed. In addition, industrial and commercial property located in cities is corporative in nature, reflecting craft control of production.

In large part, tribal ownership, state communal property and associated forms of private property, and feudal land ownership and corporative property reflect society's limited productive capacity and dependence on instruments of production that are given by nature. Even though the labor that goes into production may be characterized by a high degree of skill and craft knowledge, both the conditions of production and the means of production—energy sources, raw materials, and tools—are predominantly natural and not socially produced. These forms of property, then, rest on productive capacities that are directly restricted by nature. Individuals related to one another through a division of labor that rests on natural instruments of production and concomitantly restricted forms of property are in natural social relations: family, kinship, tribe, and symbolic identifications with the natural environment. Because of these limited productive and social relations, the possibilities for the division between the private and public sphere are themselves very limited. The individual's sphere is circumscribed by communal and natural bonds, precluding an elaborate distinction between the private and public spheres.

When the division of labor develops to the point where the instruments of production are socially produced, these restrictions are reduced. New patterns of production, property, and social relations emerge that are conducive for forming distinctions between public and private spheres. With the formation of urban centers, the movement of labor from rural areas to cities in the search for work in ever-increasing concentrations of population and the resulting spread of political administration, the social grounds for increased exchange relations and enhanced production through the growth of commerce and manufacturing are established. Individuals who entered into urban centers, propertyless and separate from one another, constituted a socially and economically deprived source of labor: "The rabble of these towns was devoid of any power, composed as it was of individuals strange to one another who had entered separately, and who stood unorganized over against an organized power, armed for war, and jealously watching over them" (1970: 70). The formation of a mass labor force was a central condition for the pattern of labor organization that allowed for the accumulation of wealth in the form of capital and in establishing wage labor. The dissociation and powerlessness of workers was a primary condition for the growth in the social power of production.

This malleable labor force provided the condition for the privatized appropriation of the products of labor by those employing labor through the wage system and for the more thorough development of production and private property. The separation of labor from the instruments of production, the hallmark of modern private property, was both a condition and a result of the separation of town and country, the separation of industry from commerce and the growing separation of the worker from arenas where decisions about production were made.

The division of labor and the growth of the social power of production as private property manifest public/private distinctions. First, private property is elaborated as the legally and politically constituted form through which social production is publicly defined and accomplished. Second, private property shapes the bonds of interdependence and differential powers through which people act contractually. The division of labor and the distinctions that it creates take on the character of natural facticity. Each individual is forced to maintain a particular pattern of productive activity "from which he cannot escape" if he is to survive (1970: 53). Third, the unequal distribution of society's product is determined by location in the process of production and by the ownership of private property. In effect, private property establishes unequal patterns of private consumption. Fourth, within each individual there is a separation between personal life and public life that is determined by the particular conditions of labor that the individual faces (1970: 83). The division of labor generates the public/private distinction not only by separating individuals materially but also by separating the activities of the individual.

The public/private distinction shapes the institutional and discursive relations that give rise to active social classes. Since individuals are separated from one another and are related to one another outside of their private relations through commodity relations, they tend to be "on hostile terms with each other as competitors" (1970: 82). The structural separation of individuals from one another and their competitive conflicts are partially overcome when individuals with similar interests rooted in similar locations in the division of labor and property relations come into conflict with other groups that have differing interests. In the face of these conflicts, classes are formed by individuals to carry on common battles against other classes. These classes are active associations based on structually rooted divisions that are collective agents of conflict. Nevertheless, because classes are alliances based ultimately on the separation of individuals along competitive lines, they tend to be short-term, shifting alliances.

The sporadic organization of separated individuals oriented toward private interests into active classes gives rise to enduring public institutions that shape intellectual, political, and legal activity. Most importantly, individual distinctions rooted in the process of production and in property ownership determine which individuals and classes have the array of resources for engaging fully in public life and ruling society. Thus, Marx argues that there is a coincidence between the capacity to exercise rule over society through the state, law, and ideas, on the one hand, and, on the other hand, control of the material means of production through the private ownership of the means of production: "The class which is the ruling *material* force of society is at the same time its ruling *intellectual* force" (1970: 64). Similarly, the state is the political form through which members of the ruling class exercise their common interests and civil law represents the interests of private property in its legal form.

To be sure, this is not to say that the ruling class is either homogenous or completely unified. Indeed, factions of the ruling class and its individual members are separated from one another by their private interests and specific locations in the process of production. Most important for elaborating the public sphere, the ruling class is itself characterized by a "division of mental and material labor" (1970: 65). These separations within the ruling class generate a "partial potential for opposition and hostility" among its factions and individual members (1970: 65). In addition, the fact that the private lives and social locations of ruling-class intellectuals, politicians, and legal representatives are divorced from the actual participation in and control over material production shapes the form of their activity and ideational products.

Because the private lives and activities of these factions of the ruling class are removed from the sphere of material labor, they tend to locate their ideas and practices within thought and abstract concepts rather than within the actual conditions of production that are the grounds of their own private material conditions. Privatism is an assumption for theorizing. For this reason, they tend to generate universalistic conceptions of history, the state, and law that represent society as a whole in ideas that are independent from actual conditions of material production and the labor process. This gives rise to the appearance that society is controlled and ruled by ideas rather than ideas being the representation of material activity in thought. It is the division of the ruling class through mental and material labor that gives rise, for example, to the "illusion that law is based on the will, and indeed on the will divorced from its real basis—on *free will*. Similarly, justice is in its turn reduced to the actual laws" (1970: 80). While other individuals and members of social classes, including those in the ruling class, may be passive and receptive to these ideas and the public forms that they shape and support, it is nonetheless the case that these ideas are partial and distorted representations of both class relations and social processes rooted in the private and social locations of their producers.

Marx went beyond speculative and idealist conceptions by analyzing the ways in which alienated labor, the division of labor, and private property shape the development of the public/private division. He did not dismiss speculative thought and political economy but, rather, argued that they were lacking in internal coherence and social grounding. He analyzed the social forces that grounded the public/private distinction as a condition of life and as conditions for thought and action. By framing these issues in a materialist conception of history, the focus is shifted to empirically researchable, historically created constraints and forms of action that condition the private lives of individuals and their public forms of interaction rather than their subjective significance that is reflected in abstract and philosophical categories. Indeed, the theory advanced in *The German Ideology* enabled Marx to account for and to analyze these ideas critically as publicly dominant ideologies that represent the privatized and partial social locations of their producers. Knowledge claims about the public/private division are central to a critical science project that seeks to explain its own development and emancipation from unnecessary social constraints.

## NOTES

1. A core text that represents this point of view is Herbert Marcuse's *Reason and Revolution* (1941) which maintains that there is a continuity in Marx's writings from his early philosophical work to his political economy. The focus on emancipatory action that includes philosophical critique is an underlying aspect of Marx's analytic categories. This focus on the political character of Marx's economic analysis is stressed by Martin Nicolaus in his introduction to the *Grundrisse* (1973), by Bertell Ollman (1971), and by Roslyn Wallach Bologh (1979). Each of these scholars focuses on the self-forming, active nature of humanity that infuses Marx's concept formation. Richard Appelbaum (1978) demonstrates that activism and struggle are basic not only to Marx's concept formation but also to his approach to scientific explanation.

# CHAPTER 4

## A Tale of Two Publics

The public/private distinction plays more than a critical role in Marx's programmatic writings on politics and in his analysis of specific events. It is conceptualized concretely through class relations and institutional practices, especially in the public arenas of politics and law.[1] The public/private distinction defines relationships among material, organizational, symbolic, and intellectual conditions of conflict and change in social formations. It is used to analyze changing frameworks for political action and social reform within dominant bourgeois institutions.

Focusing on the public/private division opens new perspectives on Marx's approach to politics. Disputes about Marxian political theory have hinged around alternative interpretations of the relationships among capitalism and the state. Instrumental theories have viewed the state as dominated by members of the capitalist class who realize their interests through state policies and law (Domhoff, 1990; Miliband, 1969). Structural theories look at systemic and formal relations between capitalism as an economic system and as a political system to determine the functional relations between these two relatively autonomous systems (Poulantzas, 1973; Balbus, 1977). Other approaches have analyzed the functional relation of the state to capitalism as largely shaped by class struggles (Wright, 1978) and, more critically, from a standpoint of state autonomy and state managerialism (Block, 1987: 81–96).[2] From the vantage point of the public/private division, the focus is more on legal and state institutions as arenas for mobilization and action through which political, cultural, and economic purposes of working-class movements can be realized.[3]

This chapter conceptualizes these aspects of the public/private distinction in Marx's writings by first reconstructing the *Communist Manifesto*. The *Manifesto* schematically presents the formation of a working-class public sphere and the relations that underlie it as central to human emancipation and autonomy. Based on this interpretation of the *Manifesto*, we present Marx's analyses of the coming to power of Louis Bonaparte in the 1850s and of the creation of legislation limiting the working day in Great Britain. These analyses are used as contrasting case studies that elaborate on the approach of the *Manifesto*. The coming to power of Louis Bonaparte demonstrates the regression of public arenas of action in establishing a dictatorship, while the formation of legislation limiting the working day demonstrates the establishment of a progressive public sphere.

The *Manifesto* conceptualizes social classes, through their struggles with one another, as either progressive agents of social revolution or regressive agents of the status quo and social decay. The historic role of social classes depends on their relations to society's productive capacities within the boundaries of particular historical epochs and under specifiable circumstances. Progessive classes extend the power of productive forces in creating wealth, establish conditions for enhancing the material and social conditions of private life, and extend participation and collective decision making by creating public institutions. Regressive classes restrict productive capacities, undermine the material and social conditions of private life, and restrict participation in public arenas of decision making.

Marx extolled the bourgeoisie as a progressive class. In its victory over feudal classes, the bourgeoisie opened a new historical epoch that reconstituted the spheres of public interaction and of the private individual on a vastly more dynamic, interdependent and wider scale than had ever been known before in history. Of primary importance, the bourgeoisie revolutionized production into a global, interdependent public sphere. The intensification of the division of labor enhanced by industrial production and the use of machinery and steam power generated "industrial armies" that were led into "an immense development of commerce, navigation and communication" by the bourgeoisie (1978c: 474–75). The cheap prices of commodities brought about by capitalist industrialization intensified international trade through the global movement of resources, commodities and, indeed, industry itself (1978c: 476). The ushering in of a "universal interdependence of nations" created new wants on a global scale and created conditions for a generalized public realm through the emergence of a world literature and world history.

By fostering a "cosmopolitan character to production and consumption," the bourgeoisie created a global public sphere of production, exchange, and culture that undermined restricted patterns of local life (1978c: 476). The growth of industrial cities and towns forced strangers into mutual dependency with one another and provided opportunities for broader understandings of the world, ending "the idiocy of rural life" (1978c: 477). The spread of an ethic of equality fostered by market relations and the maintenance of the private sphere through the rationality of exchange value located individuals subjectively in social processes as never before in history. Moreover, conditions of public action were created through the centralization of state power, the consolidation of the population, the concentration of property, and the application of science and technology to production. Capacities for controlling nature and for humanity's self-determination transformed the sense of the possible.

Yet, just as the case with earlier forms of society, capitalism has tendencies toward crises at the levels of providing for the material needs of private individuals and maintaining public institutions. These tendencies mark its historic limits and open possibilities for either new patterns of productive growth or for decay. Rather than signaling the culmination of human development, capitalism, like slave society and feudalism that preceded it, reaches a stage in its development where its contradictory characteristics become ever more apparent and disruptive for the continuity of social life.

In its early stages, capitalist relations are defined through legal and economic categories that privatize orientations toward action: property, exchange, money, and profit. These generate ever-greater forces of production—technology, skilled workers, control over natural resources and means of communication—reinforcing the social relations of production, increasing production, and extending the public sphere. Indeed, capitalism displays its most progressive character and its highest degree of rationality when its social relations are conducive to increased production and a more developed public arena founded on privatized rationality. As capitalism becomes more established and more mature, however, there is an increased tendency for its social relations to come into conflict with and to contradict the very forces of production that they generated. In effect, capitalist forms of organization and social action increasingly block rather than facilitate the forces of production and public life.

Under mature conditions of capitalism, "the history of industry and commerce is but the history of the revolt of modern productive forces against modern conditions of production, against the property relations that are the conditions for the existence of the bourgeoisie and its rule" (1978c: 478). A new pattern of irrationality emerges in

> the epidemic of overproduction. Society suddenly finds itself put back into a state of momentary barbarism; it appears as if a famine, a universal war of devastation had cut off the supply of every means of subsistence; industry and commerce seem to be destroyed; and why? Because there is too much civilization, too much industry, too much commerce. The productive forces at the disposal of society no longer tend to further the development of bourgeois property; on the contrary, they have become too powerful for these conditions, by which they are fettered, and so soon as they overcome these fetters, they bring disorder into the whole of bourgeois society, endanger the existence of bourgeois property. The conditions of bourgeois society are too narrow to comprise the wealth created by them (1978c: 478).

The "epidemic of overproduction" does not lead to an automatic breakdown of capitalism because it can be resolved by extending bourgeois orientations and public institutions. One regressive alternative resolution is that the business failures, unemployment, underutilization of resources, and declining wages, which are the immediate result of such a crisis, may lead to a more prolonged and deeper destruction of society's productive forces. In effect, capitalist social relations are maintained by weakening society's capacities to produce and, consequently, lead to both a general depletion of the material resources available to private individuals and to a contraction and consolidation of the bourgeois public sphere. On the other hand, crises may be resolved progressively by expanding markets and by reinvigorating productive forces. This alternative leads to both an expansion of the material conditions available to private individuals as well as to an expansive renewal of the public sphere. Yet, progressive resolutions, since they incorporate more individuals and regions into capitalist relations, set the stage for wider crises in the future. While there is no automatic breakdown of capitalism, the underlying contradiction between the social relations and productive forces is a continual source of crises, threatening the material underpinnings of private life and the stability of the public sphere.

Despite the force of capitalist crises, the dynamic of the material development of capitalism does not contain the sources of ideas and activism that transform society in any fundamental way. While this dynamic provides the material conditions for such a transformation, the transformation itself is a political project rooted in the contradictory lines of capitalist development and patterns of public interaction.

The systemic crises of capitalism are, to a large degree, the result of unintended consequences of privatized orientations and public institutions that support these orientations. To transform the system, new orientations toward action and public institutions that seek progressive, collective resolutions of crises must emerge. For Marx, the working class plays a historic role in forming these progressive orientations and institutions.

Fundamental to the transformation of capitalism is the creation of a public sphere by the working class. Through its atagonistic relations to bourgeois institutions, the working class enhances its organizational and discursive capacities to the point where it can initiate and carry out its own projects. Ultimately, it develops the intellectual and organizational capacities to overcome capitalist social relations in democratic and collective directions that transform the political economy. Marx ties the development of the working class as a social movement to the development of a working class public sphere that provides the collective framework for realizing human capacities beyond the bourgeois epoch.

The conditions of capitalist production and social relations established on these conditions have contradictory effects on workers. While these relations increasingly change individual workers into a homogenous commodity that is "exposed to all the vicissitudes of competition, to all the fluctuations of the market," they also create new patterns of association among workers (1978c: 479). As capitalist production develops, workers are increasingly located in factory systems where the labor process is dominated by machines. Taking on the character of military organization, the production process tends to require fewer skills from individual workers, simplifies and routinizes their activities, and diminishes the importance of their individual characterisitics, including physical strength related to age and sex. Ultimately, workers are aggregated through patterns of discipline and organization that renders their activity into a mass of undifferentiated labor that becomes "an appendage of the machine" (1978c: 479). The logic of capitalist production atomizes and privatizes workers.

On the other hand, the conditions of life faced by individual workers become increasingly equalized and public. The lives of individual workers are consolidated both at the workplace and in the crowded conditions of working-class districts in industrial cities. As a result, workers become increasingly visible to one another in the rounds of their daily lives. They live under conditions that facilitate mutual recognition and communication on a scale unimaginable under earlier forms of production. In addition, wages tend to become increasingly uniform and tend to provide for subsistence levels of consumption. The similarity of wages leads to similarities in life-style which heightens patterns of mutual recognition and the sense of a shared fate. These conditions are formative for a public sphere rooted in the commonalities of working-class life. The formation of this public sphere, moreover, takes on its direction from workers' resistance to the demands of capitalist production and from their struggles against the bourgeoisie.

Resistance and collective power are shaped in interpersonal relations of work and shared living conditions, moving from privatized forms of resistance to public action. Marx places great stress on the development of ever-wider forms of collective resistance and ever more public forms of self-determination by workers as they create their own organizations and culture. Initially, resistance to the discipline and routine of capitalist production takes the form of individual, privatized acts of rebellion, such as industrial sabotage, to gain some control over the conditions of labor. Increasingly, the social situations of workers both in their aggregatated condition in factories and in their urban districts leads to more collective resistance. Collective action within individual factories sets the stage for organization across trades and specific localities. The working class becomes organized into trade unions that go beyond attacking individual capitalist enterprises and machinery to unified demands for higher wages, job security, and better working conditions. Ultimately, the working class is organized as an "ever-expanding union" that extends itself to the boundaries of the movement of capital in both the national and international arenas (1978c: 481). These developments lead to the formation of working-class political parties that struggle for democratization. They raise political demands in the form of statutes, such as health and safety legislation, that cannot be realized through economic struggles. In effect, the basic conditions of life under capitalism leads workers to organize and to participate in public arenas of capitalist society.

These directions toward public action are deeply affected by relationships internal to the working class, relationships with the bourgeoisie, and capitalist crises. There are numerous differences within the working class including ethnicity, age, gender, and sectors of production. These differences make the formation of a cohesive working-class movement and a unified public representation difficult to achieve, especially since these differences are often exploited by the bourgeoisie in its effort to weaken the collective power of workers. Yet sectors of the bourgeoisie often seek out the help of the organized working class in its own struggles against foreign capital and the domestic bourgeoisie hostile to industrial capital. Moreover, as a result of capitalist crises, individual members of the bourgeoisie "sink" to the working class and "enlightened elements of the bourgeoisie" join the working class during periods of crisis (1978c: 481). The working class is infused with members of the bourgeoisie that bring theoretical, cultural, and organizational resources to working-class movements and politics. Thus, the development of the working class and its participation in public life are enhanced both by the growth of working-class leadership and culture that emerges through its self-organization as well as by the movement of people with bourgeois origins into the working class.

As the working class becomes more cohesive, powerful, and increasingly engaged in public life, it develops capacities to effectively rule society. These capacities emerge, as we have seen, through its internal development and through its relationship with the bourgeoisie. The effectiveness of the working class is, moreover, largely determined by situations of capitalist crises. As crises grow in scope and intensity, the everyday lives of increasingly large numbers of people are disrupted. The dominance of the bourgeoisie in public life can be effectively challenged by working-class movements, political parties, and public demands. The working class becomes a "movement of the immense majority" whose "competence to rule" expands in the face of ever greater crises (1978c: 481). The coming together of the working class as an agency of social change and the growing intensity of capitalist crises leads to a progressive transformation of capitalism.

There is one further element in Marx's theory of transformation. The working class must develop a set of ideas and a framework for analyzing the constitution of public life that is grounded in working-class experience and that formulates a radical alternative to the bourgeois knowledge and institutions. To facilitate and define a working class public, activists and intellectuals emerge who offer a distinctively working-class analysis and program that unifies the working class by universalizing its outlook and public presentation.

Marx refers to these activists and intellectuals as the "Communists" (1978c: 483–84). The Communists are "the most advanced and most resolute section of the working-class parties in every country" who, because of their backgrounds and experiences, are able to understand the general conditions faced by the working-class as a whole and to construct theoretical frameworks and general projects in broad geographical and historical terms (1978c: 484). The Communists constitute the most cosmopolitan, intellectually forward elements of the working-class movement. Their purpose is to establish an international working-class public sphere that is grounded in the "common interests of the entire proletariat, independent of nationality" and to integrate local working-class movements and struggles into working class as a whole (1978c: 483–84). Through these efforts, public forums and public identities may be established through the interaction of diverse working-class movements and parties. They can direct their powers toward the "overthrow of bourgeois supremacy" and become politically dominant.

Grounded in the diversity of working-class conditions and striving to articulate issues for the working class as a whole, the principles and demands formulated by the Communists seek to express the movement of the working class in the most general and historical terms. Most pointedly, the Communists seek to generate a public discourse and framework for the activities of the working class that are rooted in the realities of working-class life and that overcomes the bourgeois interpretation of these realities that have dominated public discourse and have segregated and privatized experience and action.

Analytically, the overcoming of privatized power in the form of private property is fundamental to the interests of the working class. Indeed, Marx states that "the theory of the Communists may be summed up in the single sentence: Abolition of private property" (1978c: 484). In the bourgeois epoch, private property has been transformed from the private holdings of small peasants and artisans to a form of property that facilitates the private appropriation of the labor of masses of workers and that continually requires "a new supply of wage-labor for fresh exploitation" (1978c: 485). Bourgeois private property rests on a continued socialization of the production process that allows for the exercise of individual power over the majority of people who produce material wealth. While the contradictory character of the relationship of private property to socialized production is manifested during periods of economic crisis, the full public recognition of this antagonism and the possibility of overcoming it can only be realized when property is analyzed in light of its social conditions.

Capitalist property has the widest public significance because it is a social rather than a personal power. More positively, the conversion of capitalist private property into "common property, into the property of all members of society" would both expand the capacity of society to produce beyond the confines of capitalist social relations and allow for the expansion of personal appropriation at the most private locations "for the maintenance and reproduction of human life, and that leaves no surplus wherewith to command the labor of others" (1978c: 485). In effect, by converting capitalist private property into a common ownership of the means of production, the actual appropriation and use of socially produced wealth in the private sphere would expand. The common ownership of the means of production does not abolish the private sphere or personal appropriation but, rather, enhances the private sphere and personal appropriation. A more public pattern of productive relations is established enhancing the socialized nature of production that capitalism helped to generate.

Just as bourgeois private property must be transformed into a new form of common property that allows for public action and an enriched private life, so other partial social relations that characterize capitalism require changes to reflect the interdependent nature of socialized production. The grounds for the exploitation of women in bourgeois marriage for the purpose of transmitting private property generationally and allowing for their privatized domination are exploded along with the transformation of productive property. Similarly, the growth of international commerce and, most especially, the movement of workers across national borders, erodes the grounds of nationalism and the nation-state. Indeed, the development of the working class as an international movement generates a worldwide public sphere by hastening the decline of nationalism and the creation of a worldwide culture and polity.

With the transformation of bourgeois property, the family and political organization, social life can be opened to collective determination through wider patterns of public participation by the majority of productive individuals. As capital loses its mystified, independent power to create dependencies for maintaining everyday life for the vast majority of people, a public arena is opened up that is forward looking and that is shaped by the recognition of commonality rather than privatized ownership of past labor for the domination of present labor (1978c: 347). The "political supremacy" of the working class sets the stage for democratically increasing "the total of productive forces as rapidly as possible" and for widening and enhancing the scope of civilization (1978c: 352).

As we stated earlier, the *Manifesto* presents, in schematic form, central directions in Marx's approach to concrete issues. Marx proposed that the increasingly contradictory relationship between private property and productive forces sets the stage for either regressive or progressive changes in production and public life. At the progressive pole, Marx proposed the emergence of theoretically sophisticated working-class movements. These movements change the social relations of production in directions that enhance the development of productive forces through democratically organized public forms of action, especially in the political and legal arenas.

Since the *Manifesto* is schematic, we now turn to two contrasting case studies that elaborate the claims of the *Manifesto* concretely. These case studies demonstrate the complexity of class, ideology, public symbolism, and institutional contexts for the analysis of public action. Moreover, the contrast between the coming to power of Louis Bonaparte as emperor shows regression of the public sphere under conditions of class antagonism, while the creation of laws regulating the working day in Great Britain demonstrates progressive change, class alliances, and an expansion of public participation.

Although the *Manifesto* presents a logic of development that leads to the emergence of the working class as the vast majority of the population that creates new public forms for the exercise of social power in emancipatory directions, *The Eighteenth Brumaire* is a concrete analysis of a failed revolution that leads to the general decline of public life, not only for the working class, but for all social classes. This failure of progressive change has a historical trajectory and developmental logic that is the reverse of both the French Revolution of 1789 and the framework of the *Manifesto.*

Marx analyzes many aspects of public action from 1848 to 1852, including the importance of the dramatic presentation of social movements and political personages on the public stage in the language, clothing, and symbolism of past greatness as a way of creating the appearance of a decisive historical moment that engulfs people in collective action. For example, the activists and movements in 1848 model themselves after the French revolutionary period from 1789 to 1815 as a way of presenting themselves as publicly recognizable figures with historically decisive missions. Yet, in contrast to this public presentation, the direction of 1848 is regressive and despotic rather than progressive and democratic.

The initial impulse for the Revolution of 1848 was the overthrow of the bourgeois monarchy of Louis Phillipe and the creation of a republican form of government. In opposition to the monarchy, there was considerable unity across social classes, including significant parts of the army and the National Guard. With the successful overthrow of Louis Phillipe, however, the social base and political unity that was successful in opposition increasingly disintegrated. The capacity and collective will to exercise public power withered.

A major reason for this decline was the order in which social classes and their political leaderships entered into public action. In the French Revolution of 1789, the landed classes initiated the challenge to the monarchy; they were followed by the bourgeoisie and the working class. As conservative classes played out their roles, they first sought alliances with and then were displaced by more liberal and progressive classes. Thus, the democratic direction of the revolution built up over time. More progressive classes entered the public arena after the more conservative classes had expended themselves and had, sometimes inadvertently, created new public forums and greater public awareness about issues.

In 1848, this direction was reversed. The working-class movement and bourgeois elements in the republican movement split into social republicans and straight republicans after Louis Phillipe's abdication. The social republicans demanded greater public intervention in the economy and were successful in setting up national workshops for unemployed laborers; the straight republicans limited their goals to a democratic form of government and a liberalized economy. This led to a range of conflicts in the Constituent Assembly. Working-class Paris was pitted against the straight republicans and the rural peasantry. By June, there were massive riots in Paris that led to more than ten thousand deaths and the imprisoning of more than eleven thousand people, including the most advanced leaders of the working class. Early on, the working class had fully expended itself and was "removed from the public stage" (1963: 23–24). In addition, the leadership of the working class suffered from an "illusion" about the capacities of the working class to realize its goals. The capacity of the working class to forge a "modern revolution . . . was in most singular contradiction to everything that, with the material available, with the degree of education attained by the masses, under the given circumstances and relations, could be immediately realized in practice" (1963: 22). The working class's entrance into the public arena was as ill-timed as it was romantic.

Despite its weakness and virtual destruction, the working-class movement provided a source of negative public symbolism for the formation of conservative forces. The party of Order presented itself in opposition to the anarchic forces of socialism and communism. Differences among the demands of divergent bourgeois classes and for reform were cast in absolute terms as conservative and reactionary elements became more visible and vocal: "Every demand of the simplest bourgeois financial reform, of the most ordinary liberalism, of the most formal republicanism, of the most shallow democracy, is simultaneously castigated as 'an attempt on society' and stigmatized as 'Socialism' " (1963: 25).

This polarization reflected the lack of unity within the bourgeoisie. The most visible faction of the bourgeoisie was the republicans who included no more than "bourgeois writers, lawyers, officers and officials" that had some public influence but no material base in society (1963: 25). The "mass of the bourgeoisie" had monarchist sympathies either in the legitimist direction if they were large landowners or in the Orleanist direction if they owned large industrial or financial interests. As such, they were easily swayed to support the party of Order when "socialism" was used to characterize republicanism and when they felt that their property was threatened (1963: 36–39). The petite bourgeoisie, which supported social democracy and first formed an alliance with the working class, was politically indecisive. At crucial times they allied themselves with the republican bourgeoisie and, often, with the party of Order.

The tendency, then, was toward ever more restricted class alliances and ever more restricted openings for participation in public life for progressive social movements. After the alliance of the working class and the petit bourgeoisie expended itself, petit bourgeois democrats increasingly allied themselves with the republican bourgeoisie. As the republican bourgeoisie demonstrated its inability and unwillingness to exercise power, elements of it became allied with the party of Order. In Marx's words, "the revolution moves in a descending line" (1963: 42).

Moreover, the failure of leadership across classes was reflected in and enhanced by the decline of parliament as a public forum and a source of power. The decline of parliament as a public body had many sources. As pointed out, it lost democratic legitimacy by expelling its most progressive members. This was enhanced by the fact that Bonaparte, often distant and aloof from controversy, claimed that while parliament was at best representative of local interests, he was elected by the nation as a whole and, therefore, spoke for the interests of the nation as a whole rather than for specific regional and class interests. In addition, Bonaparte consolidated his personal control over state power through the control of ministries, finance, and the armed forces at opportune times when parliament was weakest. Moreover, parliament, as it increasingly became under the control of privileged classes, became ever more dependent on the president and the army in its extraparliamentary confrontations with the working class. Thus, public power shifted to the personal and administrative executive branch and away from the public forum of the parliament as the class base that dominated parliament became more restricted.

Marx argued that, in large part, the restriction of public power and the decline of deliberative bodies was conditioned by efforts of the bourgeoisie to maintain its social and private power. The bourgeoisie could not exercise rule directly without mediation of a monarch or an emperor or a powerful executive in a parliamentary manner because all the underlying social conflicts would become public through parliamentary rule, especially the conflict of capital and labor. Parliament itself was attacked as "socialistic" because parliamentary rights and liberties could, and at times were, turned against the bourgeoisie. In effect,

> the bourgeoisie confesses that its own interests dictate that it should be delivered from *its own rule* . . . that in order to preserve its social power, its political power

must be broken; that the individual bourgeois can continue to exploit other classes and to enjoy undisturbed property, family, religion and order only on condition that their class be condemned along with the other classes to like political nullity. (1963: 67)

While working-class movements rushed into political action and sought to expand the public sphere prematurely, the bourgeoisie played a decidedly different role. Although initially supporting a full-fledged republican form of government, the bourgeoisie continually retreated from its commitments to a democratic public sphere as its interests were threatened. Ultimately, as its private interests came into conflict with its convictions about an open public sphere, its commitments to democraticizing the public order declined to the point of accepting the authoritarianism of executive power over the public deliberations of parliament. The bourgeoisie acted "out of sheer egoism, which makes the ordinary bourgeois always inclined to sacrifice the general interest of his class for this or that private motive" (1963: 90). While the working class was unable to exercise public power at this juncture of history, the bourgeoisie had reached a point in its development where the social relations that supported its private interests required its retreat from public life and its support of authoritarianism.

For diametrically opposed reasons, then, neither the working class nor the bourgeoisie was positioned to constitute public order. Yet, Bonaparte required a mass base to support his efforts to dominate politics and public symbolism. This mass base was forged from the most disorganized and privatized segments of French society: the lumpenproletariat and elements of the peasantry.

The lumpenproletariat— made up of the "whole indefinite disintegrated mass" of French society including displaced elements of the bourgeoisie, members of the underworld, "discharged soldiers and discharged jailbirds"—was organized into the Society of December 10 by Bonaparte, largely with the use of state finances (1963: 75). Without any stable social location or productive relationship to society, "this scum, offal, refuse of all classes" was constituted as Bonaparte's private army, police force, and entourage. The extreme precariousness of their individual private lives made them open to being organized by and identifying with Bonaparte to serve the "higher powers" of "cigars, champagne, cold poultry and garlic sausage" (1963: 77). While Bonaparte ultimately organized the army on the model of the Society of December 10, the society played an important role in his early control of public symbolism and state power:

On his journeys the detachments of this society packing the railways had to improvise a public for him, stage public enthusiasm, roar *vive l'Empereur*, insult and thrash republicans, of course, under the protection of the police. On his return journeys to Paris they had to form the advance guard, forestall counter-demonstrations or disperse them. (1963: 76–77)

Along with this public appearance of support by the lumpenproletariat, he had an electoral base in the small-holding peasantry. The small-holding peasantry is a mass of individual peasant families that produce for their individual consumption in isolation from one another and, because of their poverty and lack of means of communication, from society generally. "Their field of production, the small holding, admits of no division of labor in its cultivation, no application of science and, therefore, no diversity of development, no variety of talent, no wealth of social relationships" (1963: 123). Because they are so radically separated from one another, they cannot act coherently for their own interests despite the fact that they do have class interests hostile to the economic and cultural interests of other classes. In addition, as a result of their historic relation to the army, they are infused with a nationalism that rests on the glorification of the state. For these reasons, they are prone to support an authoritarian state that severely restricts participation in public life (1963: 124). Beyond this, the small-holding peasantry was most taken with the symbolism surrounding the name "Napoleon" and his vision of a strong, glorious, and centralized state power. Thus, even in those rural areas where peasants recognized that their mortgage payments and other indebtedness to the bourgeoisie was a reason for forming alliances with the working class to the point of occasionally participating in revolts, they supported Bonaparte in elections and saw in him the symbol of the nation and the army.

The creation of an authoritarian public sphere was rooted in the most privatized interests of the bourgeoisie, the organization of the lumpenproletariat into a secret society and the backward, privatized condition of the small-holding peasantry. It was accomplished through the collapse of parliament, which had constituted a deliberative public authority that reflected the diversity of French society, and its replacement by the personal symbolism, nationalism, and executive power of Bonaparte first as president and, finally, as emperor. Politically constituted class power dissolved, largely in egoistic and privatized directions, and with it the possibility of a democratic public sphere.

While Louis Bonaparte's rise to power demonstrates the collapse of progressive forces in the formation of a democratic public sphere, the formation of the legal regulation of the working day in Great Britain exemplifies how diverse class interests are mobilized for both reconstituting the private lives of working people and democratizing the public sphere. Marx's analysis shows the importance of the private/public distinction for progressive change.

The problem of the working day is rooted in the social transformation of economic activity. It emerges most fully when the economy is fully dominated by production for exchange rather than production for use. When labor is used to produce a "more or less confined set of needs," there is no economic imperative to maximally utilize labor in the production process (1977: 345). When, however, production is organized toward exchange and labor itself becomes a commodity, each capitalist seeks to buy labor at the cheapest price and to extend the working day as long as possible to produce the greatest surplus. Here struggles over the working day emerge with the capitalist, as the purchaser of capital, seeking to extend the working day as long as possible and the worker, as seller of labor power, who seeks to limit the working day to a "particular normal length" (1977: 344). These antagonisms, which take the typical form of private rights at odds with one another, tend to become public issues and political conflicts. Because equal rights are in conflict, ultimately force decides the outcome. The struggle over the limits of the working day becomes a political and legal struggle, "a struggle between collective capital, i.e., the class of capitalists, and collective labor, i.e., the working class" (1977: 344).

Although the fight over the working day originates in bourgeois relations among private individuals and seeks its resolution within state structures that are "ruled by capitalist and landlord," it emerges as a public issue because it affects the condition of society as a whole (1977: 348). The length of the working day has significance for the state that goes beyond the interests of particular capitalists:

> The limiting of factory labor was dictated by the same necessity as forced the manuring of English fields with guano. The same blind desire for profit that in the one case exhausted the soil had in the other case seized hold of the vital force of the nation at its roots. Periodical epidemics speak as clearly to this point as the diminished military standing of height in France and Germany. (1977: 348)

Capitalists confronting one another in competitive circumstances face pressures to not take the health and life of the worker into account, especially since fresh supplies of labor are available both from rural areas and from foreign countries. Yet, the length of the working day has collective significance as a health issue and as a military issue for each nation. Consequently, it emerges as a public issue out of the confines of the conflicting private rights of capitalists and workers. In addition, by citing the *Report of the Committee on the Baking Trade in Ireland for 1861*, Marx demonstrates that the length of the working day is a public issue because it poses a threat to the moral and social reproduction of workers through the bourgeois patriarchal family:

> Any constant work beyond 12 hours a day encroaches on the domestic and private life of the working man, and so leads to disastrous moral results, interfering with each man's home, and the discharge of his family duties as a son, a brother, a husband, a father. That work beyond 12 hours has a tendency to undermine the health of the working man, and so leads to premature old age and death, to the great injury of families of working men, thus deprived of the head of the family when most required. (1977: 362)

The private conditions of working-class life are changed into a public issue as a result of collective interests in limiting the working day. Yet, as Marx points out in his discussion of the history of legislation dealing with the working day, the effort did not always focus around limiting the working day. During the formative stages of capitalism "the force of sheer economic relations to secure a sufficient quantity of surplus labor" were not yet developed and it was necessary to lengthen the working day through legislation and the application of state power (1977: 382). From the fourteenth century through much of the eighteenth and early nineteenth centuries, legislation tended to actually increase the working day and to shorten the time allowed workers for meals. Thus, while legislation in 1496 limited the working day to ten hours, the limitation to the working day was entended to twelve hours by 1833. This coincided with legislation that extended the time during which workers could be employed, including children and young persons, from earlier in the morning to later at night. Marx points out that a fourteen-hour day with two hours per day for meals and a six-day workweek had been considered to be an ideal and a just punishment for paupers in the eighteenth century, became the dominant reality in the early nineteenth century (1977: 389).

By the early nineteenth century, the working day and hours of work had been so extended that "every boundary set by morality and nature, age and sex, day and night, was broken down" (1977: 390). The factory system had succeeded in homogenizing the productive activity of workers to such an extent that their time was virtually under the complete control of the labor process. They had lost any distinctive demarcations between private time and time devoted to working. Legislation passed between 1802 and

1833, in part as a result of working-class resistance, did little more than codify an extention of limits to the working day. Even these limits were not adhered to since "parliament . . . was shrewd enough not to vote one penny for their compulsory implementation, for the necessary official personnel, etc." (1977: 390).

With the march of industrial capitalism and the spread of the factory system, however, a progressive coalition was emerging that, among other things, formed the basis for enhancing the private terms of life for workers by limiting their exploitation through limits on the working day and democratizing public life. Marx analyzed this in terms of public activism by workers, divisions within the bourgeoisie and between the bourgeoisie and large landowners, and compelling national interests recognized by bourgeois political leaders. By 1838 factory workers

> had made the Ten Hours Bill their economic, as they had made the Charter (universal male suffrage) their political, election cry. Some of the manufacturers, even, who had run their factories in conformity with the Act of 1833, overwhelmed parliament with representations on the immoral "competition" of their "false brethren," who were able to break the law because of their greater impudence or their more fortunate local circumstances. Moreover, however much the individual manufacturer might like to give free reign to his old lust for gain, the spokesmen and political leaders of the manufacturing class ordered a change in attitude and in language toward the workers. They had started their campaign to repeal the Corn Laws, and they needed the workers to help them to victory! They promised, therefore, not only that the loaf of bread would be twice its size, but also that the Ten Hours Bill would be enacted in the free trade millenium. . . . And finally the Tories, threatened in their most sacred interest, the rent of land, thundered with philanthropic indignation against the "nefarious practices" of their foes. (1977: 393)

At this stage of social development, the extension of economic liberalism combined with political democratization to yield fuller participation of the working class in public life and the enactment of progressive legislation regarding the working day. The Factory Act of 1844 regulated the working day and limited the number of hours for women over eighteen years of age. Marx deemed this to be progressive because "for the first time it was found necessary for the labor of adults to be controlled directly and officially by legislation" (1977: 394). The Act of 1847 limited the working day of young persons and women to eleven hours and further mandated that the working day for these categories of workers be lowered to ten hours by 1848. In addition, these acts extended legislation to areas of employment that had not been previously covered and limited the times of day during which work could be performed.

To be sure, elements of the capitalist class used their considerable power over public institutions and their private rights to organize the workplace to particularize and block the implementation of these laws. Factory inspectors were attacked in the press, wages were lowered, young persons and women were fired, adult males were made to work night shifts, and workers were forced to take their meals at home. The British reaction to the June insurrection of workers in France in 1848 led to the imprisonment of leaders of the Chartist movement and "shattered the self-confidence of the English working class" (1977: 396). When litigation was initiated against violators of the law, it was typically the case that the courts were stacked against workers since "in these tribunals the manufacturers sat in judgement of themselves" (1977: 398). By 1850, the Court of Exchequer rendered decisions that had the effect of nullifying many of the provisions of recent Factory Acts.

These attacks, however, generated their own public reactions. There was considerable resistance by workers who held public meetings and engaged in an array of protest activities. Segments of the clergy, factory inspectors, and politicians voiced their support for the factory legislation. Among manufacturers themselves there was considerable support for revising the factory legislation to overcome the lack of uniformity in law across localities and to put them on an equal footing with other manufacterers. Ultimately, there was a new wave of factory legislation beginning in 1850 that more clearly limited the working day, allowed for meal times and determined the hours during which work had to take place. Overall, manufacturers accepted and even supported this legislation. "The capitalists' power of resistance gradually weakened, while at the same time the working class's power of attack grew with the number of its allies in those social layers not directly interested in the question" (1977: 408–9). Of great significance, the victories won for limiting the working day became generalized to other nations and took on an international character.

For Marx, the successful struggle to limit the working day had major ramifications. It went "hand in hand with the physical and moral regeneration of the factory worker" (1977: 408–9). The increased health and vitality brought about by limits to the working day, moreover, was "preliminary and necessary for further emancipation and improvement" (1977: 415). The public definition of the working day through legislation and the collective efforts to bring it about enabled workers to exercise rights over their time, rights that characteristically took the form of private rights. There was a clearer definition of the amount of time and the periods during which workers were contractually obligated to expend their labor for their employers. On the other hand, there was a more defined amount and period of time that could be privately controlled by workers themselves for their own recreation and development. "Time for education, for intellectual development, for the fulfillment of social functions, for social intercourse, for the free play of his body and his mind" (1977: 375).

It was Marx's view that the formation of the progressive public sphere through the organized efforts of working people tied the private sphere to the public sphere in novel directions. Increasing private rights of workers to control their time would generate conditions both for the enhancement of workers' private lives and, also, for their fuller enlightenment and participation in public life. Even though the limitation of the working day did not overcome the realm of necessity, the realm that had entered the public sphere through the increased social nature of economic life under capitalism, it nonetheless served to open up the possibilities of fulfillment and freedom through both the worker's development as a private individual and as an actor in the public spheres of politics and culture.

## NOTES

1. Alan Hunt's (1985) reformulation of Marxist analyses of law argues that the concept of ideology must be established at the level of concrete analysis. The direction that I seek to establish through the public/private distinction partially supports this view; however, it is also analytically necessary to maintain the integrity of critique at the levels of philosophy and political economy and to maintain a critical approach within concrete analysis. Alan Stone's (1985) reconstruction of the base/superstructure approach is valuable in this regard. Also important is Ellen Wood's (1981) analysis of the separation of the economic and the political under capitalism.

2. Fred Block relies on a Weberian formulation of the state that is "not reducible to class power" (1987: 84). Yet Block's characterization of Max Weber's definition of power as "the monopoly over the means of violence" is mistaken because it neglects the crucial dimension of legitimacy.

3. This approach stresses the importance of concrete historical studies and the analysis of actual conflicts that establish new forms of action and participation. See William Chambliss (1979), Steven Spitzer (1983), and E. P. Thompson (1975; 1978).

# Part II

# EMILE DURKHEIM

# CHAPTER 5

# Constructing the Private Sphere through Corporate Holism

Emile Durkheim, like Karl Marx, approached the public/private distinction by initially criticizing political economy and liberal individualism. He opposed assumptions that autonomous individuals pursuing private interests through a utilitarian calculus of maximizing private happiness could provide adequate grounds for comprehending the social foundations of the private/public division. For Durkheim, both political economy and utilitarian liberalism lacked adequate grounds in the organization and underlying patterns of association through which society is constituted. Because they deal with the effects of social development rather than underlying causes, their approaches to the public/private distinction take the very categories that require sociological analysis for granted.

While opposing the view that the actions of discrete individuals oriented toward private ends is the proper starting point for social analysis, Durkheim also criticized Marx's approach to the public/private distinction as overly economistic.[1] Marx limited the content of the public/private distinction to material factors that could not adequately account for socially rooted sources of restraint on private wants and action; Marx's approach was a continuation of the liberal and utilitarian individualism's self-referential, egoistic rationality that did not afford moral authority to the state or sufficiently account for the moral role of the family. Also, Marxian socialism had heightened tendencies toward a conflict-ridden public sphere due to its principle of class struggle.

Durkheim's approach to the social transformation of the public/private division is distinctive. It is rooted in an evolutionary perspective that sought to harmonize the strains of industrial society and integrate the public and private spheres through scientifically grounded reforms.[2] Rooted in positivist epistemologies, he sought to establish expert knowledge and policy making that would coordinate society through a public discourse formed through overarching political, legal, educational, and financial institutions. His evolutionary approach also sought to create and inculcate shared beliefs that would replace theology and popular religion as sources of cohesion in the private sphere.

Just as the working-class movement and revolutionary socialism are basic to Marx's formulation of the public/private division, corporatism is central to Durkheim's evolutionary approach.[3] While critical evaluations of Durkheim have sought to characterize his political standpoint as conservative (Nisbet, 1966), liberal reformist (Giddens, 1986) or mildly socialist (Gouldner, 1962), these evaluations tend to be based on Durkheim's political views toward moral authority, individual rights, or inheritance. Durkheim formulated these views, however, through a framework that unified his commitments as a political thinker and a social scientist (Kaufman-Osborn, 1986: 639). His approach to sociological method, the role of theoretical concepts in problem formation and his approach to the division between public and private spheres of social life are founded on a corporatist commitment.[4]

Durkheim analyzed the public/private division as emerging with social developments that necessitated corporatist constraints that harmonized divergent aspects of social life, shaping the individual toward collective rather than privatized norms.[5] In the face of industrial society's tendencies toward privatized dissociation, Durkheim articulated an approach to the public/private division that includes such corporatist themes as hierarchies of knowledge, the centrality of national political organization and the administrative state, occupational associations, education for social discipline and collective values, and scientifically informed social policies articulated through laws that strive to coordinate a differentiating social order to overcome conflict, privatism, and egoism.

From Durkheim's corporatist approach, the public/private division emerges as a central, highly problematic condition for formulating methods of sociological inquiry, social development, law, the state, social pathologies, and gender. His corporatist approach provides a holistic framework for analyzing the development of the public/private distinction in a direction that subordinates elements of social life associated with the private sphere to a hierarchical public sphere founded on collective, functional rationality.

Overall for Durkheim, the public/private division is embedded in sociohistorical developments that combine progressive and pathological tendencies. The public/private division is a normal feature of social development: The structural and cognitive sources that give rise to it differentiate spheres of human activity from one another, generate the grounds for specialized knowledges, and establish the organizational and ethical grounds for the individual as a moral agent. The public/private division emerges as a progressive pattern of social organization. It provides the structural and intellectual grounds for individual responsibility, scientifically based discourse, and rationally legitimated hierarchy through law and other public discourses.

Yet the public/private division is also pivotal for moral and organizational pathologies. Modern social pathologies have a dual form. On the one hand, they are manifested as privatized dislocations and dissociations that appear as spiritual, philosophical, and existential crises at the level of the individual. They are also expressed through patterns of social disorganization that generate pathologies at the levels of the individual and social processes. This duality is rooted in the problematic relationship between the private individual, emerging as a self-referential entity, and a public sphere that results from the interrelations of atomized individuals. Most importantly, the morality of the private individual tends to become less autonomous and less reflective the more social conditions foster egoism, self-referential thought, and a rationality of private ends. Ultimately, accumulated pathologies create potentials for social crises that require public action based on scientific knowledge implemented through law.

To rationally formulate a social morality that can guide social reconstruction, the public/private distinction must first be adequately formulated for scientific inquiry. Only a scientific approach to knowledge can capture the reality of the human condition in modern society. The organization and pattern of association of social life undermine speculative epistemologies. For Durkheim, an adequate approach to the social transformation of the public/private distinction must be based on a strict sociological analysis. The sociological approach must establish itself through a critique of other approaches. It must provide concepts and a method for analyzing how the public/private distinction emerges from social development and from collective forms of association. A sociological analysis of the public/private distinction can provide a rationally redeemable public morality that encompasses the private sphere.

Durkheim's critique is based on a fundamental opposition to concepts rooted in individualism, the practical necessities of private life and commonsense understandings of social issues.[6] Adequate knowledge about society cannot be rooted in casual observation, self-referential thinking, or the necessities of private life. These approaches are fundamentally flawed in their analysis of the public/private dimensions of social life because they are unable to conceptualize their sources in social development and constitutions that are independent of subjective experience. Because they lack collectively rooted concepts and methodological discipline, they tend toward abstraction.

From these flawed perspectives, knowledge rests on what is immediately observable by individual actors engaged in practical activity. By making instances of practical activity the observational basis for principles of social order, commonsense understandings of social life are elevated to the status of scientific facts. The realism imposed by the private necessities of everyday life—which are already constituted through practical categories of individualism, exchange, private morality, and property—are rendered into concepts. As they are theorized, these practical orientations and frameworks gain consistency and abstract applicability. Yet they do not go beyond reflecting private necessities of everyday life in thought. Rather than explaining categories of social life by demonstrating how they arose or how they constitute a scheme of justification by the ends they serve, they are abstractly elevated to theoretical discourse: Everyday life is translated into a more formalized language.

Establishing the public/private division on the grounds of individualized and partial knowledge rooted in private necessity is inadequate for sociological inquiry. It distorts the organizational, historical, and associational sources of the distinction that constitute its social content. Providing grounds in social relations for the conceptual demarcations between the private individual and public order is fundamental for analyzing the public/private distinction sociologically. Reducing either the individual to a manifestation of society or rendering society as an object projected from purely individual propensities erases their distinct properties and their relation to one another.

Moreover, privatized and individualistic approaches to the public/private distinction rooted in private life lead to reductionism. The individual's practical rationality for satisfying routine private desires leads to either a biological or sociological reductionism. To the extent that scientific explanations demand a relational ground for analyzing phenomena objectively, individual rationality and private necessities are ultimately accounted for either on the basis of biological, genetic programming that is manifested as a subjective sense of rational calculation, or the rationality of the private individual is derived from the social environment itself and is reflected in the individual's subjective reasoning. In either case, the autonomy of the private individual is reduced to a function either of a biological process or the social environment. In either case, private individualism loses its developmental character and its complex foundations in hierarchical public order.

Similarly, starting with individual rationality and private necessity renders the public sphere into a reflex of determinate causes with little independent properties. If public order is taken to be a result of actions among individuals, it is essential that public order be viewed as an outcome of individual actions that complement one another. Here we are faced with either imposing an "identity of interests" on the totality of individual actions and interpreting them as if they are complementary, or the public order is a culmination of biologically programmed propensities that are manifested at the level of the individual but reflect the social whole. The outcome, again, is to reduce spheres of public and private life to underlying egoistic or biological causes.

Attempts at reconciling the private individual and public sphere through individual rationality and private necessity undermine their distinctive features, the causes that give rise to them, and the relation among them. The subjectivity of the individual is no longer rooted in hidden private necessities, spiritualism, or moral freedom. If subjective rationality is determined either through biological programming or the structure of environmental conditions, then the individual's private thought loses its inherent independence from its biological and social conditions. The public sphere also loses its moral distinctness and becomes an expression of prior necessity. By formulating the private individual and public order as mere reflections of an underlying reality, distinctions between the realms of public and private life lose salience and are collapsed either into a total biological or sociological formula.

Durkheim's corporatist approach seeks to overcome these tendencies. Durkheim combines scientific and moral discourse in accounting for and explaining the public and private realms. While Durkheim's corporatism is partially grounded in biology, he nevertheless attempts to overcome the reduction of private and public relations by drawing an analytic analogy between the unity of the biological organism and society as a moral whole that, under a variety of pressures, undergoes a process of developmental division. Patterns of social organization condition, limit, and give shape to morality. This process leads to the emergence of the individual and particular social locations, generating specialized moral functions for the social whole and for the private individual. The split between private social locations and the overall public order are functionally related through a process of hierarchical differentiation, yielding a public morality that overarches the moral autonomy of the private individual. The public and private spheres have emergent properties that cannot be understood solely in the conditions that give rise to them. They have independence because of their respective internal relations and their hierarchical relations to one another as moral constraints.

In the development and constitution of social morality, a hierarchical distinction emerges between public and private realms and institutions. The more distant the determinants of the public sphere are from differentiated everyday life necessities of private individuals, the greater becomes their objective character. Elements of public order are increasingly transformed from shared sentiments through which individuals order their activities to more formal, rule governed, and externally locatable constraints. This process leads to the development of a personally significant world that is radically distinguishable from a shared reality. It also generates an overall rule-governed corporate whole that integrates the diverse social processes through knowledge that is itself constituted through rules and imbued with a theoretical attitude toward social wholism rather than fragmented concerns.

*The Rules of Sociological Method* seeks to establish this knowledge. It is a veritable corporatist manifesto for formulating the social grounds of knowledge and for articulating an approach to the social relations that give the public/private distinction its discursive and institutional force. In *The Rules*, Durkheim combines a political rhetoric for legitimating sociology as an academic discipline with a vision of the norms for the internal regulation of its knowledge claims. The corporatist direction of *The Rules* is manifested in the rule-governed character of social facticity and scientific inquiry, the power and morality of the collective over the individual, the inadequacy of common sense and privately located knowledge, the general tendency to formulate social deviance as pathological, and the strategic relation of sociological knowledge to social policy through complementary, functionally legitimated relations.

Durkheim's corporatist approach to the scientific study of society relies thoroughly on publicly open procedures and facts. Asserting that a range of social facts are distinct from private sensation, experience, and "mental activity," Durkheim eschews introspection as an adequate method of inquiry in favor of dispassionate and disciplined observation, comparison, and causal reasoning (1964a: xliii). Maintaining that the sociologist must abandon speculation and metaphysics, Durkheim calls for suspending common sense understanding of social life so that the sociologist can be immersed "in the presence of facts whose laws are as unsuspected as were those of life before the era of biology" (1964a: xlv). Methods and publicly justifiable rules formulated by the scientific community must replace subjective, immediately practical approaches to knowledge.

Central for sociology as a discipline and for establishing the social grounds of knowledge is the distinctive character of social facts: "They consist of ways of acting, thinking and feeling external to the individual, and endowed with a power of coercion, by which they control him" (1964a: 3). The focus of inquiry is directed outside of the subjective, private sphere and into the collective realm. The truth of society is in the outer relations of public life rather than the privatized interior that is marginalized as an object of sociological inquiry.

To be sure, social facts have great diversity because they consist of a wide range of representations and actions—from legal and moral regulations, religion, and financial systems to art, literature, and occupational groups. In addition, social facts include such relatively ephemeral phenomena as collective emotions and crowd behavior that lack full-scale organization and historical longevity. Despite this diversity, social facts have a common core: They are neither biological nor psychological because they are rooted in objective, externally coercive, and constraining forces that emerge through the association of individuals with one another; they represent the collective constraints of social interaction over the individual. Transmitted through such enduring structures as education, law, family, religion, and science, social facts have a force and an objective character. They fashion an obligatory, collective construction of expectations that goes beyond the private individual's experience and scope of action. They are distinct from the general characterisitics that individuals may share because they result from the combined actions and associations of individuals that do not appear directly in individual consciousness or interaction.

Social facts have an independence from the private sensations and motives of individuals. They have distinct public forms that indicate their roles in social life. They are not only rooted in associations that are publicly significant but also manifested through such public representations as law, religious codes, dress, and literary works. Social facts also appear through statistics that represent rates of birth, marriage, suicide, and crime in a manner that enables their social aspects to be separated from individual cases. The statistical computation of rates "contains all the individual cases indiscriminately, the individual circumstances which may have had a share in the production of the phenomenon are neutralized and, consequently, do not contribute to its determination" (1964a: 8). Statistical data and their analysis enable the abstraction of a social content from repetitious actions and behaviors that emerge from specific associations, opening them to sociological explanation. In principle, these facts cannot be known by individuals rooted in private necessity or through speculative thought. They must be gathered, analyzed, and presented by administrative and scientific institutions that constitute social knowledge through corporate organizational principles.

The degree of longevity, repetitiveness, and centrality of patterns of association for stabilizing society as a corporate whole determine the form of their public representation as social facts. Law and political organization, which are fundamental to the maintenance of hierarchical public order, are crystallized into representations that enable them to be communicated discursively as explicit codes (1964a: 12). Indeed, the dense patterns of specialized communication underlying law and political organization form the grounds of legal and political action that define the relatively permanent features of social life for individual actors. By contrast, statistical representations indicate repetitive actions that are more variable, less permanent, and less articulated through public patterns of communication. The malleability and lesser continuity of these patterns of association render their public representation nondiscursive and in greater need of explication.

The adequate analysis of facts is tied to methodological expertise rooted in corporate holism. Just as the nature of social facts and the form of public representations are determined by the degree to which they are central to the maintenance of public order, so the construction of social facts as phenomena requires strict objectivity and distance from those variations in everyday ideas of social order that shape the practical activity of private individuals. Because of the natural tendency that people have to project their subjectively held ideas of society on the world and to view the world as "simply the embodiment of the ideas we hold concerning society, the state, justice, etc.," much of sociology "has dealt more or less exclusively with concepts and not with things" (1964a: 17–18). What are generally taken to be laws of social organization and social development are often no more than the subjective and speculative image of reality that connects ideas to one another. Instead of observing social facts that represent the associations through which public order is constituted, social analysis has been characterized by idealistic reflection and speculation rooted in private experience. Thus, political economy has as its initial premise the subjective goal of acquiring wealth without any factual grounds for its premise. "Consequently, the subject matter of economics, so defined, comprises not the realities given to immediate observation but merely conjectures that are the product of pure intellect" (1964a: 24).

Because a scientific approach requires the consideration of "social phenomenon in themselves as distinct from the consciously formed representations of them in the mind," the study of society from the vantage point of private and subjective goals should be rejected in favor of analyzing "them objectively as external things" (1964a: 28). Social facts are independent of private consciousness and must be approached without preconceptions but, rather, through definitions that capture their external characteristics, collective character, and public significance. Deviance from moral rules, for example, is best analyzed in light of observable "widespread repressive sanction, that is, a condemnation by public opinion that punishes all violations of the precept" (1964a: 41). Crime should be defined in terms of punishment because this is the most apparent and public approach that detaches it from subjective evaluation and opens up directions for objectively based inquiry. Definitions formed on the basis of collectively enforced sanctions reveal the public importance of crime and other patterns of deviance rather than the individual aspect's acts. Instead of focusing on individual acts, we are directed to study social facts in their collective and public aspects.

While the definition of a distinct realm of facticity is central to developing knowledge grounded in social processes, it is also necessary to develop explanatory frameworks in manifestly social terms. Sociological explanations should be based on the premise that "society represents a specific reality which has its own characteristics" (1964a: 102). As we pointed out, Durkheim viewed social reality as emerging from persistent patterns of association among individuals and, "since it infinitely surpasses the individual in time as well as in space, it is in a position to impose upon him ways of acting and thinking which it has consecrated with its prestige" (1964a: 102).

Grounded in the recognition that social facts have their basis in an emergent reality, frameworks for the explanation of asocial facts must not proceed at biological or psychological levels. Rather, a framework must be established so that social facts can be explained at their own level of emergence: Social facts should be used to explain social facts since it is social facts that cause social effects (1964a: 110–14). In developing sociological knowledge, the proper application of this explanatory framework is through comparative studies. Societies at similar stages of development are to be systematically compared to one another to determine patterns of social causation. While, to be sure, each society has some unique features that result from its particular history, valid comparisons can be drawn that serve to establish social causes for social effects. In this way, the range of actual societies subjected to rigorous comparative analysis provides the grounds for social knowledge. Based on these relations of facts and rules of explanation, sociology becomes a scientific consciousness of corporate society. It is constructed through professionally disinterested, rule-governed procedures that place the collective power of the hierarchical scientific community over the private sensibilities and partial knowledges of individual practitioners. Through its methodological rules, sociology codifies a public knowledge of society based on impersonal social facts and comparative explanations of social phenomena.

Alongside this objective and public grounding of social knowledge, there is also for Durkheim an animating public purpose: social health. While sociology is constructed along scientific lines, it also can serve the broad public purpose of providing a clinical knowledge of social pathology, social health, and policy recommendations for enhancing the well-being of society as a whole. Through the comparative analysis of social facts, sociology can formulate average rates of social facts, such as crime and suicide, and determine the consequences of divergences from these average rates for societies at the same stage of development. Through this analysis, factually based definitions of normal and pathological social conditions can be formulated. Sociology, similar to all "sciences of life," strives to "define and explain the normal state and to distinguish it from its opposite," not through utopian visions based on speculative ideals, but, rather, by analyzing its object of inquiry (1964a: 74). The sociologist contributes to society's health while sustaining a corporate ordering of social life through patterns of knowledge formation that rest on administratively based observation and data collection that are potentially usable by policy institutions for law creation.

As we have seen, *The Rules of Sociological Method* formulates the public/private distinction through facts that have their sources in administrative processes of data collection and hierarchical discourses such as religion and law. This approach defines the public and private spheres through corporatist institutional practices that are central to social organization and policy making. In a similar way, Durkheim's typology of social order in *The Division of Labor in Society* conceptualizes the public/private distinction from the vantage point of social holism founded on alternative patterns of association that generate alternative patterns of moral integration. While *The Rules* provides the social grounding of the public/private distinction primarily in the scientific norms for rendering data from organizational sources into facts, *The Division of Labor* provides a typology of the public/private distinction rooted in corporatist holism.

Durkheim's typology of social order is formulated on alternative models of moral solidarity. A major dimension of these types of social order and the moral solidarity that underlies them is the relationship between private and public spheres of conduct. Summarily stated, mechanical solidarity is characterized by the identity of public and private spheres, organic solidarity is characterized by a balanced differentiation of private and public spheres held together by a corporatist state and intermediary institutions such as the occupational association, and anomie points to a pathological condition in which social disorganization generates egoistic orientations and a breakdown of social controls and hierarchy.

The first type, a mechanical solidarity society, is characterized by a relatively low division of labor, similarity among social members, and repressive law. Most fundamental, the moral cohesiveness of mechanical solidarity has its basis in the absence of major distinctions between private and public realms (1964b: 174–81). Under these conditions, social members participate in the constitution of a world that is grounded in common experience and activity. Social order, given the low differentiation of social functions and low differentiation of individualized outlooks, is held together by the likeness of social members and a correspondingly high level of participation in group life.

In its most ideal form, mechanical solidarity is a type of social morality that is anchored in a high degree of interaction among all members of a society. When the total number of social members is small enough for persistent face-to-face interactions, and when the practical tasks that members perform are mutually understandable because of shared knowledge and skills, there is a high degree of participation in a common consciousness. The effect of this is to bind members to one another through a shared and taken-for-granted range of practical activities. Virtually all of social life is mutually observable and understandable, thereby reducing the possible locations for the emergence of privatized sources of action, both at a material and cognitive level.

This participation in a world of shared activity tends to yield a consensus around public notions of "right and wrong" that is both deeply affective and taken for granted. Resemblances among social members that are reinforced through common knowledge and practical face-to-face activity enhance the vitality and pervasiveness of shared moral rules of conduct that are deeply embedded in common orientations and activities. Just as the practical activities of everyday life for each social member express that which is commonly shared by all members, so the moral rules that govern everyday life are equally expressive of a shared common life. Because these deeply shared sources of action are persistently reinforced in interaction, breaches in this consensual morality tend to be equally deep, penetrating, traumatic, and give rise to repressive law. This is true for the community as a whole, because of the visibility of offenses and the violation of taken-for-granted expectations, and for the offender as well, because of deep cognitive and emotional dependence on other community members.

In his analysis of the sources of the transition of society from mechanical to organic solidarity, Durkheim places a great deal of emphasis on causes that are, at least in principle, observable. Rejecting the idea that social complexity has its basis in increasing private experiences of happiness among individuals and in actions oriented toward greater happiness, Durkheim argues that it is the transformation of the moral basis of society itself—which is itself induced by essentially material and associational causes—that yields complexity and differentiation in social forms, as well as a change toward restitutive law. "The division of labor varies," wrote Durkheim, "in direct ratio with the volume and density of societies, and, if it progresses in a continuous manner in the course of social development, it is because societies become regularly denser and generally more voluminous" (1964b: 262). As a result of the growth of population, the coming together of diverse social groups into a single society, and the absence of the possibility of direct communication of all social members that follows from these conditions, the moral basis of social order undergoes a process of differentiation. It is, thus, the "growth and condensation" of societies that "necessitate a greater division of labor."

An underlying analogy that Durkheim uses to elaborate on the sources of the division of labor is drawn from Darwin's evolutionary theory. Just as varieties of animal species emerge when resources become scarce through the development of specialized needs that lead to coexistence rather than a struggle for survival, so different occupations emerge in human society that pursue different objects. "The soldier seeks military glory, the priest moral authority, the statesman power, the businessman riches, and the scholar scientific reknown. Each can attain his end without preventing the others from attaining theirs" (1964b: 266).

In effect, Durkheim's theory of social development rests on a corporatist translation of biological, organismic unity and societal survival. Society is a complex of organs that is maintained in a metabolic unity through regulations that are incorporated in hierarchically related moralities. While the species that Durkheim refers to in his analogy to Darwin adapt to specific environmental niches through a process of specialized differentiation that enables them to live in a precarious harmony since they do not depend on the exact same resources for the fulfillment of their physiological needs as do other species, each society undergoes a similar process of internal differentiation so that social members can be contained within a moral unity in the face of population pressures and the narrowing of specific social milieux. The hierarchical coupling of moral integrity and survival with biological integrity and survival enables Durkheim to explain the division of labor on primarily moral grounds rather than on either biological or economic grounds.

Indeed, fundamental to Durkheim's theory is that the differentiation characteristic of organic solidarity is grounded primarily in socially based morality rather than economic causes. Rather than serving primarily to increase production—and with it the material basis for higher levels of private happiness through consumption—the main cause of the division of labor is the functional need for corporatist organization of social life that both grounds the individual in social relations that generate morality and provides a unified order for this multiplicity of contexts.

The emergence of the private individual, and more generally, private spheres of activity, is one aspect of social evolution within relations of greater complexity in the development of social organization. Basically, as population expands and becomes more compressed, shared experience and consensus among all social members becomes less likely; more particularized and privatized moral contexts emerge. These, being ever more specialized, form particularized social locations generating a multiplicity of contexts of interaction, norms, and knowledge.

In considering Durkheim's theory from the perspective of the public/private division, we are led to unravel how the two major features of social order, that is, the division of social labor and the law, are formative both for the private individual and public life. Most particularly, the manner in which these two features determine the relation between private and public experience is most salient.

As I pointed out, Durkheim attempted to explain the emergence of the division of labor on social grounds rather than on the basis of any goal that individuals or groups may have toward greater possibilities of happiness through consumption. Given this grounding, it is problematic why the main direction of moral differentiation and privatization should be along occupational lines rather than along more symbolic directions such as common religious beliefs. If the basis of social differentiation is moral differentiation, why does development proceed along occupational lines?

Durkheim offers two related explanations to this question. First, the concentration of small groups into a larger social order is often predicated on the fact that previously segregated groups had distinctive social relations that were associated with specialized patterns of production and consumption. The incorporation of small groups into a wider social order accentuates tendencies toward specialization through processes of economic exchange of products and services. The condensation of society often heightens tendencies toward occupational differentiation already present in rudimentary form in the groups that form organic solidarity. This also reinforces methodological strictures about the uniqueness of societies that result from their specific histories.

Second, and more decisive, is the fact that the very pressures of complex societies and the competitive struggle in which individuals are located generate new and greater needs among the population. "It is thus that the peasant," writes Durkheim, "whose work is less exhausting than that of the workman in cities can bear a poorer sustenance" (1964b: 272). Beyond increasing material needs, the effect of complex social life on the nervous system and mental life of people creates the need for new services and diversions that enable individuals to restore themselves and recreate the capacities to engage in social processes. In addition, the development of intellectual life generated by participation in complex societies leads to needs for new insights and literary and scientific products for its satisfaction. Thus, from Durkheim's perspective, economic advances are the indirect effect of social needs that follow from social differentiation.

These tendencies in economic development enhance the growth of individuality and private spheres of experience. The location of people in specific milieux not only leads to specialized knowledge and norms regulating work but also to more specific patterns of consumption. While it is questionable whether this leads to greater happiness among people, it does serve to further differentiate social locations, disassociating the experiences of groups from one another and privatizing individual orientations.

In addition to the division of labor leading to the emergence of private spheres of activity and the economic developments that accompany it, there are secondary causes toward privatism that Durkheim points out. First, the division of labor enhances social mobility, in both geographical and social directions. This, in no small part, leads to the formation of an individualized sense of biography and heightens the private significance of social life. Second, the division of labor tends to remove people from traditional family contexts in which older people have authority and claim veneration. The movement of young people into cities, at least partially cut off from their families of origin, leads to a potential for inventiveness in social life. No longer encapsulated within the authority of family and venerable old people, the segregation of youth in cities serves to both heighten the sense of personal anxiety regarding how life should be lived and make the individual more dependent on his or her own initiatives. Finally, the growth of a complex division of labor leads to a decline in the importance of hereditary factors in determining individual activity. The force of biological determinism declines in shaping individual life as life becomes more socialized along complex social encounters, practical knowledge, and skills. Again, this serves to enhance the role of the individual consciousness in social life.

Mechanical and organic solidarities are normal, cohesive, and coherent social types. While mechanical solidarity is stabilized through the interpenetration of public and private spheres based on the likeness of social members and participation in common activities, organic solidarity fosters a corporate holism based on hierarchical unity of differentiated functions and privatized individualism. Durkheim also presents a third type that he classifies as abnormal and which is a tendency within complex society. This type of society, anomic society, is characterized by a dominance of privatized values and orientations that emerge with the collapse of public order. It leads to crisis tendencies at both the levels of moral integration and organization.

Central to the anomic division of labor is the idea that the distinction between private and public spheres progresses without functional integration. As in physiological disorders such as cancer, there is growth and differentiation that does not contribute to the overall functioning of the organism, and, indeed, has debilitating and destructive effects. In considering the causes of anomie, Durkheim placed great stress on changes internal to society. When private gain supplants social use as the main source of economic organization and activity, the functional and moral relations of society are disrupted. Instead of society being held together by a mutually supporting occupational division of labor and the individual being controlled by occupational associations, privatized orientations prevail. Limitless profitability, market relations, and short-term contracts become the main sources of social bonding. Most importantly, the industrial division of labor disrupts social solidarity and harmony:

> As the market extends, great industry appears. But it results in changing the relations between employer and employee. The great strain upon the nervous system and the contagious influence of great agglomerations increase the need of the latter. Machines replace men; manufacturing replaces hand work. The worker is regimated, separated from his family throughout the day. He always lives apart from his employer, etc. These new conditions of industrial life naturally demand a new organization, but as these changes have been accomplished with extreme rapidity, the interests in conflict have not yet had time to be equilibrated. (Durkheim, 1964b: 370)

The thrust of Durkheim's analysis is clear. The extension and dominance of society by economic institutions and values erodes the moral foundation of the private sphere and public order. The pervasive tendency to define activity from the perspective of economic advantage, the loss of stable occupational locations and skills among workers, and the dislocations that these tendencies generate have the combined effects of disrupting the functional integration of society and atomizing individuals. The anomic division of labor has detrimental effects on the harmony of social order and, most directly, on the character of the public realm, the state, and law, and the private realm of the individual.

The anomic division of labor stands in stark contrast to both mechanical and organic solidarity as a formulation of the relationship between private and public life. Under mechanical solidarity, private and public dimensions of experience are fused in a common world and morality. Under organic solidarity, the two spheres are differentiated but held together through functional, hierarchical relations. Under anomic conditions, the public realm in the form of the state and law, tends toward arbitrary coercion and the private realm becomes a sphere of chaos and disorientation. As a pathology of social life, anomie signals the lack of derivation of public and private dimensions from corporate holism. The consequence is the dissolution of coherent and stable realms of private experience and public life.

Participation in the anomic division of labor renders it impossible for the individual to regulate both public and private dimensions of life. Anomie locates the individual in a social situation that violates the expectations that interaction is based on, isolating the individual from persistent ties with others that serve as the grounding for moral constraints that limit and direct action. It ultimately leads to a state where normlessness is the norm (Mestrovic, 1988). In this situation, the individual is thrown further back on privatized motives. This has such severity that Durkheim considered it to be a central social pathology and the central cause of suicide in modern society.

## NOTES

1. According to Tom Bottomore, "Durkheim was a convinced opponent of Marxism, and any kind of socialism which went beyond the idea of gradual social reform within the limits of a capitalist economy, even though he conceded some merit to Marx's theory as a major attempt to construct a social science" (1981: 902). This view seems well founded not only by inference from

Durkheim's major writings, but more particularly from his reviews and commentaries (1982).

2. Studies of social complexity and legal development that have sought to assess Durkheim's theory empirically have claimed to partially invalidate it (Schwartz and Miller, 1964; Schwartz, 1965; Spitzer, 1975; Wimberly, 1973). I have critically examined these studies (Turkel, 1979) and found them wanting methodologically, in agreement with Udy (1965) and Baxi (1974). Beyond methodological issues, however, it should be recognized that evolutionism is part of a critical effort to theorize processes of change that may lead to emancipatory projects (Teubner, 1983). The question of evolutionism in Durkheim's theory has long been contentious. Robert Merton (1934) considered Durkheim's typology as ideal types for comparative research. For Anthony Giddens (1972), Durkheim's evolutionary sociological approach stands in opposition to revolutionary political change as a way of realizing development (1972: 38).

3. The intellectual background for Durkheim's corporatism is amply presented in a two-part study by J.E.S. Hayward (1960; 1960). Steven Lukes presents the centrality of corporatism for Durkheim's vision of the future of social organization (1973: 538–46).

4. Timothy Kaufman-Osborne states that corporatism is "the site upon which Durkheim's theory and practice merge, [and it] constitutes the institutional medium through which scientific rationality achieves its rightful standing as the creator of collective reality" (1986: 640). Dominick LaCapra argues that corporatism was "an integral component of his perspective from which he applied his general ideas of social normality to the problem of structural change in modern society. Essential to this vision of modern social normality was a triangular model of the state, the corporative group, and the individual, existing in a dialectical balance" (1972: 211).

5. See Phillipe Schmitter and Gerhard Lembruch (1979) for a valuable collection of essays that define and provide case studies of corporatism.

6. At this level, Durkheim's corporatist methodology runs counter to sociological analysis rooted in naturalism and everyday understandings (Bittner, 1973; Cicourel, 1964; Tiryakian, 1962).

# CHAPTER 6

## *Suicide*, the Corporate Individual, and Gender

Durkheim's methodology and typology of social order exemplify much that is objectionable in social science for theorists who seek to establish the public sphere as a political realm for constituting society through the free participation of individuals.[1] Durkheim's vision of society as a morally regulated metabolism, the incorporation of the private individual into hierarchical public order, defining history through long epochs that are most adequately known through statistical facts and impersonalized codes, and a scientific standpoint based on professionally disinterested norms of truth constitutes a totalizing program. It formulates knowledge through commitments to hierarchy, encapsulating individuals as social actors incapable of constituting their world through a mutually constructed public realm.

*Suicide*, more than any of Durkheim's works, fulfills this methodological approach and defines the individual in strictly social terms (Pope, 1976). *Suicide* attempts to classify and analyze what, at first appearance, is a strictly individualized and private act through sociological concepts and statistical methods. It exudes a profound distrust not only of the self-reports, in the forms of letters and suicide notes, of persons who committed suicide but also of the practical knowledge of suicide developed by investigators and other legal authorities. Durkheim's approach, moreover, is clinical: He starts with categories of corporate holism and establishes the consequences of structural and cultural departures from corporate order. He seeks to analyze suicide as resulting from factors internal to society or by outside social factors that disrupt social integration and destabilize social hierarchy. He proposes social reforms that would locate the individual more fully in corporate structures, securing the private sphere through its relations to occupational associations.

Durkheim's corporatist approach toward suicide, moreover, reveals the centrality of gender to the hierarchical relation between public and private spheres.[2] Indeed, the articulation of the private sphere as essentially feminine and the public realm as masculine is basic not only to the analysis of suicide but also to the problematic role of the family in corporate social order. It is especially striking that Durkheim's hierarchical identification of men with the public sphere and women with the private sphere emerges most fully in his analysis of facts rather than from analytical categories. In this analysis, Durkheim goes beyond his own conceptual limits and recognizes differences between men and women as fundamentally conflictual in part because gender coincides with differential location in public and private arenas.

Durkheim maintains that suicidal tendencies are social phenomena that can best be explained by social causes rather than by either biological or psychological characteristics of individuals or by the features of the physical environment. He classifies suicides by the patterns of collective life that cause them rather than by their "preliminary described characteristics" (1966: 146–47). Through a comparative study of suicide rates, the social conditions that give rise to differential rates are classified so that suicide can be analyzed as an effect that is deduced from causes. This means that data on suicide are formulated through concepts derived from Durkheim's view of corporate holism rather than directly from the context in which they are produced.

Rather than approaching suicide through a study of the "motives reflected in individual consciousness," which are as unreliable as they are unrevealing about the social causes that generate differences in suicide rates, Durkheim locates suicide as a problem of public order. He focuses on suicide rates rather than the private motives of individuals who have manifested suicidal actions (1966: 148). The privatization that leads to the individual's suicidal tendencies are explained by the patterns of association that shape the individual's action. Suicide is not formulated as an issue that reflects problems at the level of the individuals, but an issue at the level of social structure that is manifested as a pathology of public order. At best, the individual is a type constructed in terms of social causation.

In this light, egoistic suicide is caused by a breakdown of social ties that bind the individual to groups in a way that reduces his or her dependence on others. As a result, the individual "depends solely on himself and recognizes no other rules of conduct than what are founded on his private interests" (1966: 209). The egoist is outside of any "pattern of communication that is greater than the individual" (1966: 210). As a social being that cannot be reduced to purely biological needs of survival, the "social man necessarily presupposes a society that he expresses and serves" (1966: 213). Without attachments and associations to objects that go beyond him and survive him, there is no grounding for the individual other than purely self-referential desires and goals. He is isolated in his own private world with, at best, attachments to himself that prove too weak to sustain him since they are overly subjective and fleeting. "All that remains is an artful combination of illusory images, a phantasmagoria vanishing at the least reflection; that is, nothing can be a goal for action" (1966: 213).

In contrast to the disintegration of social bonds that underlies egoistic suicide, anomic suicide is caused by a breakdown in public order that regulates society and its individual members through stable expectations rooted in a justifiable "hierarchy of functions and rewards" (1966: 249–50). The breakdown in public ordering is associated with economic disasters and booms, political catastrophies that disrupt symbolic and territorial stability, and disorienting events such as world exhibitions. In addition, there are more particular catastrophies located in the domestic sphere, such as the death of a spouse, that generate severe disruptions for the individual. The individual is faced by "abrupt transitions" in which passions are unleashed that preclude their satisfaction and harmony; individuals become "declassified" and lose the "standards according to which needs are regulated" (1966: 253).

The absence of regulation requires time "for the public conscience to reclassify men and things" (1966: 253). The anomic phase is characterized by disruption among parts of society, heightened competition at the levels of the individual and group, an unleashing of appetites and jealousies, and a public life charged with intense irritability and "unproductive effort" (1966: 253). The individual, as a result, feels less limited at just the time that any limitation feels increasingly intolerable. The collapse of public order causes the individual to replace a sense of reality with subjective imagination: "A thirst arises for novelties, unfamiliar pleasures, nameless sensations, all of which lose their savor once known. Henceforth, no one has the strength to endure the least reverse" (1966: 256). Society, losing its own coherence and public ordering, becomes less present in the individual, thereby making the individual subject to private passions.[3]

More concretely, Durkheim found through comparative analyses that the disintegration of collective bonds and beliefs in religious, marital, and political associations fostered egoistic suicide. Overall, Protestants had higher rates of suicide than Catholics and Jews because of "higher religious individualism" (1966: 158). The Protestant, who is "much more the author of his own faith" than either the Catholic or the Jew, has a higher degree of autonomy, is critical of tradition, engages in freer inquiry, holds fewer common beliefs and practices, and is a member of a "less strongly integrated church" (1966: 160). The decline of the power of the clergy and his or her religious function along with the breakdown of religious grounds for law and the splintering of the religious community free the individual from practical religious constraints and heighten privatized, self-referential orientations.

Closely associated with religious factors is free inquiry and "the craving for knowledge" as sources of egoistic suicide. The high rate of suicide among the liberal professions is a result of the self-referencing of knowledge that is not bounded by religious organization. The quest for knowledge in the context of a disintegrating religious community makes knowledge an end in itself for the individual rather than knowledge being integrated into established patterns of association under the authority of religious dogma. As a result, "individual intelligence replaces collective patterns of life as society is fragmented. Moreover, it is not the religious precept against suicide that prevents its occurrence but, rather, the degree to which religion is a coherent and cohesive pattern of social organization" (1966: 169–70).

Beyond these associational and structural sources of suicide, Durkheim's analysis of egoistic and anomic suicide raises important issues regarding gender. The differences between men and women and their differential location in private and public arenas culminate in differential patterns of suicide. For example, Durkheim found that the suicide rate for married childless women was higher than the rate for unmarried childless women (1966: 196–99). By contrast, married childless men had a lower suicide rate than unmarried childless men. While wives with children had a lower suicide rate than both childless wives and unmarried women, men seemed to benefit the most from both marriage and family associations. Indeed, based on these findings, Durkheim made a rather radical claim: "Conjugal society [marriage] is harmful to the woman and aggravates her tendency toward suicide" (1966: 189).

There is a clear disparity between the effects of marriage on men and women. Marriage is associated with lower suicide rates for men and higher rates for women. To analyze how this dimension of his thought is related to his formulation of the public/private distinction, we must reconstruct core aspects of his views on the evolution of gender, its expression in domestic law, and through this, how the public sphere has been rendered masculine and the private sphere feminine. Durkheim's theory provides concepts for integrating potentially explosive findings on a core gender issue into a corporatist analysis.

At the beginning is biology. Durkheim initially locates the origins of the functional differentiation of society in physiological differences between men and women: Men and women are physically different, have different roles in sexual activity based on these physical differences and, most fundamentally, play different roles in childbearing and child rearing (1964b: 56–57). He views these differences not only as originating in nature but also as complimentary sources of social cohesion and the moral order. The sexual division of labor requires association.

Based on this initial distinction, Durkheim formulates the development of the relationship between men and women from its simplest to its more complex forms. In simple "segmentary" societies, the sexes shared many commonalities and the only significant distinctions between men and women pertained to their complimentary roles in reproduction (1964b: 58–59). Conjugal ties were weak, there was a sharing of many socially necessary tasks, and the relationships among the sexes were largely unregulated. Indeed, in segmental societies conjugal solidarity is relatively weak in large part because they are formless, that is, "female functions are not clearly distinguished from male functions. Rather the two sexes lead almost the same existence" (1964b: 58).

As the complex division of labor emerges, this patterning of relations between the sexes undergoes changes that are parallel to broader changes in social organization and morality. As social functions become more specialized and as social solidarity becomes grounded in functional interdependence, changes emerge in relations between the sexes, in the structure and function of the family, and in the relationship of the family to society as a whole. As a crucial aspect of this, Durkheim maintains that the role of women changed drastically:

> Long ago, woman retired from warfare and public affairs, and consecrated her entire life to her family. Since then, her role has become even more specialized. Today, among cultivated people, the woman leads a completely different existence from that of the man. One might say that the two great functions of the psychic life are thus dissociated, that one of the sexes takes care of the affective functions and the other of the intellectual functions. (1964b: 60)

This social transformation of the natural sexual division of labor takes a number of directions. Most importantly for our purposes, the public sphere becomes a masculine realm and the private sphere becomes a feminine realm through hierarchical, functional integration. Three aspects of Durkheim's formulation are especially important for establishing a corporatist social order on the grounds of complementary, hierarchical relations of a male public sphere and a female private sphere: (1) Tendencies toward biological distinctions between men and women are heightened as the social division of labor develops. Women are increasingly incapacitated for participation in public life as complex relations evolve. (2) The law and the state are the premier public institutions for establishing marriage and the domestic sphere as functional underpinnings for societal cohesion. Law provides definitions of men and women that support their differential allocation to public and private locations. (3) The more socialized and public character of men compared to the more domestic and privatized character of women accounts, in part, for the differential effects of marriage on the suicide rates of men and women. Moreover, the importance of men for maintaining the social metabolism through their public roles requires policies that favor securing marriage despite the clear disadvantages for women.[4]

Durkheim maintains, utilizing evidence provided in the writings of Gustave LeBon, that the morphological differences between men and women increase with the development of societal complexity. Disparities between height, weight, cranial capacities and the "general form" among men and women are enhanced with the development of the division of labor (1964b: 60). Societal differentiation, in effect, leads to morphological differences. Moreover, since social morality must rest to some degree on a principle of justice and since justice for Durkheim requires that the allocation of social functions correspond to natural capacities, it follows that men and women should be differentially distributed to social positions on the basis of biological differences which emerge with social development (1964b: 375–76). Differences between the sexes justify the very hierarchy that produces these differences on functional grounds.

The development of marital law exemplifies the transition from simple to complex patterns of social organization and the allocation of men to the public arena and women to the private sphere. In segmentary society, marriage was largely a private affair that required no intervention on the part of public authorities. As societies developed in complexity, marriage took on increasing public significance through patterns of religious control. For example, the Christian church took on monopoly control over the granting of marriage contracts. Finally, state intervention and legality increasingly regulate marital relations because of a broadened interest in the domestic sphere as the domestic sphere becomes integrated in complex societal relations. A pattern of law emerges that makes marriage and family life subject to greater state regulation as opposed to defining them as simple contractual relations. While a family regime based on contract law would indicate that family is in the private sphere and results from acts of individual wills, greater state intervention demonstrates the functional importance of marriage and domestic obligations for social metabolism and public order:

> At the same time that domestic obligations become more numerous, they take on, as is said, a public character. Not only in early times do they not have a contractual origin, but the role which contract plays becomes even smaller. On the contrary, social control over the manner in which they form, break down, and are modified, becomes greater. . . . The regulative organs of society are forced to intervene in order to exercise a moderating influence over the functioning of the family, or even, in certain cases, a positively arousing influence. (1964b: 210)

In effect, Durkheim articulates a corporatist, gendered approach to social control: Laws constructed in the masculine public sphere determine relations in the feminine domestic sphere to regulate the moral force of the family to support social integration. The legal regulation of marriage, familial property, domestic violence, family membership, sexual behavior, and divorce develop along lines that secure the mobilization of private sources of morality in the domestic sphere for patterns of social stability, enhancing the very same masculine public sphere where these legal regulations are constructed.

This conceptual framework is pivotal for Durkheim's analysis of anomic suicide, divorce, and family policies. As we pointed out, he maintains in *Suicide* that suicide rates among divorced men are at a much higher order of magnitude than suicide rates among divorced women. Based on these facts, he argues that the moral restraint of marriage is much more important for men than it is for women because marriage serves to reduce egoistic and anomic tendencies that affect men more severely than women. In part, these differences are rooted in nature. Thus, Durkheim points out that marriage tends to fix sexual objects of desire for men and enables them to overcome anomic and egoistic tendencies rooted in "polygamous instincts" (1966: 270–75). Marriage serves to privatize and moralize male sexual passions that are stronger than the sexual passions of women.

More important is the gendered hierarchical relation between private and public spheres for corporatist order. Men require the restraints of family life because they are subject to anomic and egoistic social forces through their involvement and participation in the public sphere. The very fact that men are public actors and are, therefore, directly affected by social, economic, and moral forces that generate anomic and egoistical individualism and suicidal tendencies requires that they be morally restrained through domestic obligations. On the other hand, the very absence of any participation in the public sphere not only reduces these suicidal tendencies for women but also makes family life less necessary for women. Indeed, "from the standpoint of suicide, marriage is more favorable to the wife the more widely practiced divorce is" (1966: 269). A key characterization of women underscores this:

> As she lives outside community existence more than man, she is less penetrated by it; society is less necessary to her because she is less impregnated with sociability. She has few needs in this direction and satisfies them easily. With a few devotional practices and some animals to care for, the old unmarried woman's life is full. (1966: 215)

Because men are more prone to conditions of egoism and anomie that result from their participation in the public sphere, they benefit from a high degree of marital restraint. Women, on the other hand, benefit from a loosening of marital restraint since their relative lack of participation in the public sphere renders them more subject to the pressures of the private household. Thus, where divorce is common and loosens the definition and bonds of marriage, men tend to have higher suicide rates while women have lower suicide rates. Lenient laws regulating divorce and high divorce rates serve to weaken marriage and, thereby, increase suicide among men and reduce it among women (1966: 270).

Yet, because Durkheim associates divorce and a weakening of marriage not only with differential suicide rates for men and women but also, more importantly, with tendencies toward anomie for the public order generally, he does not view the "weakening of marital regulation" favorably (1966: 271). The status of men as public actors gives their needs a higher priority than the needs of women. Nonetheless, he is skeptical about efforts to reinforce the authority of marriage in modern society since the weakening of marriage is a feature of social differentiation and societal complexity that is inherent in social development. As such, efforts to restore the solidarity of marriage are largely futile and utopian.

Durkheim's analysis of egoistic and anomic suicide elaborate his overall corporatist approach by differentiating the public sphere as masculine and the private sphere as feminine because they are associated with gendered patterns of social pathology. The interpenetration of this corporatist formulation and gender are developed further through the contrasting types of suicide.

Altruistic suicide, which is opposite of egoistic suicide, results from "insufficient individuation," especially when the forces of social integration overwhelm the person's capacities to resist collective forces that compel suicide in himself (1966: 217). Although egoistic suicide is characteristic of modern society, altruistic suicide is characteristic of "lower society" where collective life fully penetrated the individual (1966: 217). Suicide was an obligation, a result of duty that maintained collective honor. While altruistic suicides can be distinguished by the degree to which they are obligatory and follow the dictates of "public opinion" (1966: 222), Durkheim focuses on its modern forms in the arena of the military, a paradigmatic masculine location. Officers are more prone to suicide than "private soldiers" because of the greater integration and identification that they have with the military. This is supported by the fact that men who reenlist have higher suicide rates than those who do not (1966: 223). The high levels of training, intense discipline, close associations, the ethic of sacrifice and the "moral constitution" of self-abnegation have historically yielded higher suicide rates in the masculine sphere of the military (1966: 223). While Durkheim points out that the pattern of suicide among men in the military was tending to decline to accommodate modern society's individualistic ethic, it stands as the key example of willful sacrifice of life on the basis of strong, valued association among men outside of the domestic sphere.

Durkheim presents the opposite of anomic suicide in a footnote. Fatalistic suicide "derive[s] from excessive regulation, that of persons with futures pitilessly blocked and passions choked by oppressive discipline" (1966: 276). Durkheim states that this is a type of suicide that characterizes the history of slaves, men who married at very young ages and married women who are childless. Yet he maintains that it "seems useless to dwell upon it" because of the cases that it covers. Thus a major source of suicide among women that results from their lack of liberty in domestic sphere where they face inflexible rules that they are powerless to change does not merit analysis while its opposite, the breakdown of stable matrimonial rules that generate suicides among men, is a key social pathology. Pathologies associated with the participation of men in the public sphere are granted a higher degree of importance than pathologies associated with women in the private sphere. Men and women have different degrees of social importance because of their differential locations in the public and private spheres.

The institutional arrangements that Durkheim advocated for overcoming the social conditions that generate egoism and anomie further demonstrate his commitment to corporatism. On the one hand, he advocated that the occupational association should be reconstructed in a form that would regulate the everyday activities of individuals. The occupational association is ideally suited to this purpose; it "consists of individuals devoted to the same tasks, with solidary or even combined interests, no soil is better calculated to bear social ideas and sentiments" (1966: 378). With the virtual breakdown of religion and the family as institutions for establishing collective sentiments in the individual under modern conditions, the occupational association emerges as a field of relations that replaces private interests with "corporative interest" because it is "omnipresent, ubiquitous and that its control extends to the greatest part of life" (1966: 379). Because "occupational life is virtually the whole of life," occupational associations provide the relational grounds for integrating the details of daily activity and practical sentiments into corporatist beliefs and identities (1966: 379).

Moreover, Durkheim held that the occupational association should be rendered into a "definite and recognized part of our public life, instead of remaining a private group legally permitted but politically ignored" (1966: 379). The occupational association, he maintained, should be given a legal status that places it outside of direct state control, but which provide for collective sentiments and organizational locations that mediate state policies. The legally sanctioned corporation would create a zone of commonality. It would overcome tendencies both toward egoism on the part of private individuals and toward arbitrary, socially rootless policies on the part of the state.

While the occupational association creates a corporatist zone of commonality between the private individual and the state, the individual must be prepared for this pattern of regulation. Here the school is vital. For Durkheim, requisites of discipline and impersonal adherence to rules cannot be inculcated through the family which, in modern society, has "a personal and quite volitional character" (1961: 147). The school, on the other hand, provides for a circulation of teachers, impersonal patterns of authority, and regular control of daily activities. Indeed, "the class is a small society" (1961: 148). As such, it is an initiation in the first organized corporate group that is connected hierarchically to the state through educational policies, curricula, and teachers who have specific functions to fulfill. The school represents an intermediary institution between the personal world of the family, founded on private sentiments, and society as a whole, organized through state regulation of specific functions. The school inculcates the most collective of sentiments into the child to prepare the child for incorporation into more particular locations later in life: "It is by respecting the school rules that the child learns to respect rules in general, that he develops the habit of self-control and restraint simply because he should control and restrain himself. It is a first initiation into the austerity of duty. Serious life has now begun" (1961: 149).

## NOTES

1. Hannah Arendt stated that "statistical uniformity is by no means a harmless scientific ideal; it is the no longer secret political ideal of a society which, entirely submerged in the routine of everyday living, is at peace with the scientific outlook inherent in its very existence" (1959: 40). The parallel with Michel Foucault is strong (1977). The extension of power is accomplished through clinical sciences that accumulate knowledge by generating norms based on averages of observed behaviors within institutional settings (1973). See J. Palmer and F. Pearce (1983) and Turkel (1990) for a fuller discussion of Foucault on law, normalization, and state power. Alan Wolfe, in criticizing the normalizing discourse of states and markets, calls for a sociology that recognizes the norm-making capacity of people in their everyday lives by, in part, "giving voice to ordinary people" (1989: 234).

2. See Mike Gane (1983) for a discussion of Durkheim's changing views on the division of the sexes. Jennifer M. Lehmann has argued that Durkheim's approach to feminism is very much like his analysis of socialism (1990). Carole Pateman provides a clear analysis of alternative approaches to the public/private division in feminist theory by linking it to liberal political theory (1987). Also see Jean Bethke Elstain's discussion of the public/private split (1974).

Randall Collins states that "feminist issues are essentially issues within stratification theory, although they add a new dimension or application to that theory" (1988: 164). Yet, as our discussion shows, gender underlies the core concepts on which knowledge of stratification is constructed. Gender is not so much a feature of stratification as a relation on which stratification is grounded. In part, Collins's construction follows from his disavowal of approaching theory through schools or individual authors but, rather, analytic areas. This approach moves concerns about the nature of inquiry and problem definition from focal to peripheral concerns. By contrast, viewing social theory through authors and schools opens up alternative perspectives. See, for example, Patricia Madoo Lengemann and Jill Niebrugge-Brantley in George Ritzer (1988).

3. Stjepan Mestrovic argues that Durkheim's concepts of egoism and anomie are rooted in Arthur Schopenhauer's notion of will rather than an action framework (1988: 54–55). This not only heightens the objective, natural character of social forces in shaping the private sphere, but also serves to sharply distinguish between individualism, which is socially emergent, and egoism, which is strictly an individual phenomenon. It also sharpens anomie as a socially constructed condition. "In fact, according to Durkheim, the business and economic sector of society has enshrined this state of undisciplined desires as one of the cornerstones of economic theory" (Mestrovic, 1988: 64). Also see M. J. Hawkins

(1977) for a discussion of how Durkheim's views on the society/individual relationship shifted over the course of his work.

4. This underscores Carol Smart's argument against the notion that forms of law, independent of their content, are gender neutral (1986).

# CHAPTER 7

## Dividing Public and Private: Corporatist Law and Politics

For Durkheim, as society becomes more complex, morality is transformed from a core of common beliefs to differentiated moralities that are formed in particular social locations. With heightened moral differentiation, law and state organization become more pervasive sources of social integration.[1] The public/private division, elaborated through corporatist legality and state organization, is fundamental for integrating the proliferating institutional and discursive locations that emerge with social complexity. Corporatist legality and state institutions provide frameworks for ordering the boundaries of the private sphere, intermediate corporate locations like professional associations, market relations, and the state itself.

The public and private spheres are articulated in state organization and law through categories rooted in corporatism: hierarchical knowledge, functional integration, collaborative patterns of interest representation, and marginalizing privatized motives to personal spheres of consciousness (Unger, 1976: 200–202; Winkler, 1976; Gottlieb, 1983). More particularly, in the public arenas of political interest representation and law formation, Durkheim's analysis exemplifies societal corporatism (Schmitter, 1979): It stresses the role of political elites in establishing national consensus on the basis of expert knowledge that filters down to constituencies for more generalized consensus. As such, the public sphere is virtually monopolized by government officials and representatives of corporate groups that are sanctioned by the state.[2]

Legal institutions and discourses maintain formal procedures, define relations among functional interests, establish intermediate groups and recognize their rules of internal governance, and establish rights of the private individual within a functionalist logic of corporatist holism. The democratic character of politics and the legitimacy of law rest on the scientific rationalization of the solidarity, morality, and, ultimately, the underlying pattern of associations that comprise the social whole. The political public sphere manifests the cohesiveness of society which it expresses, communicates, and regulates through expert discourses that are expressed at varying levels of social hierarchy.

Durkheim grounds law and politics in developmental typologies infused with corporatist methodological and policy commitments. Law and politics are indices of social development that manifest underlying patterns of corporatist association and morality. At the same time, law and politics gain autonomy as arenas of public action with increased social complexity. They both manifest social transformations toward corporatism and shape social processes that differentiate private and public spheres through codes and institutional practices. Moreover, law is the most pervasive representation of the corporatist differentiation of public and private spheres. Law articulates the formation of private and public spheres as well as the hierarchical relations among them. Law categorizes private and public spheres within an overall framework of corporatist integration.

Legal categories are grounded in differentiating patterns of association that are the sources of social morality. Despite the differentiation of society and the emergence of private spheres, a core common consciousness continues to form the basis of the public spheres of law and the state. This common consciousness forms the moral grounds for penal law which has as its object crimes directed against rules of conduct and representations of society as a whole. In addition, a moral basis for law emerges that results from the more differentiated sectors of society. Because of the organic quality of social development and the consequent interdependence of sectors within the division of labor, there is a harmony among elements that needs normative definition for both recognition and adjustments when they arise. This type of law, "restitutive law," restores social order to its essential harmony when particular sectors or individuals violate its rules.

For Durkheim, then, social and legal complexity emerge with differentiation from a common morality that is shared by social members. While this common morality is weakened by differentiation, it continues to constitute a feature of individual consciousness. For example, when Durkheim classifies rules that forbid acts "contrary to collective sentiments," he develops a set of classes and subclasses of common sentiments that include the following seven: (1) religious sentiment, (2) national sentiments, (3) domestic sentiments, (4) sentiments relative to sexual relations, (5) sentiments relative to work, (6) traditional diverse sentiments relative to burial, food, dress, and so on, and (7) sentiments relative to the organ of common conscience, for example, encroachments of private individuals on public functions (1964b: 119–32). While the number and force of these common sentiments tend to decline under processes of differentiation and individuation, some of these sentiments continue to be present in complex societies. These sentiments, in turn, are the grounds for penal law and collectively felt urges toward morally charged punishment. Although there is an evolutionary tendency away from repressive law characteristic of a fully shared and consensually binding common morality, elements of such a common moral basis among individuals persist and, indeed, may be enhanced under conditions when they are aroused.

While collective sentiments and, therefore, bases for penal law continue under the evolution of the division of labor, the emergence of the private individual is articulated through the development of legal forms that Durkheim conceptualizes as restitutive. These developments take two major forms: (1) the development of laws that specify the rights of the individual, and (2) laws that express, and serve to maintain, social harmony.

Laws that articulate individual rights segregate individuals from one another and define spheres of private action. These laws express and codify the separation of individuals from one another. They demarcate arenas of action that are not determined through commonly held morals and ethics:

> The rules relative to real rights and to personal relations which are established in their turn form a definite system which has its function, not to attach different parts of society to one another, but, on the contrary, to put them outside one another, to mark cleanly the barriers which separate them. (1964b: 119)

Laws relating to "real rights and to personal relations" are rooted in a process of differentiation that weakens collectively held morality. They are an index of an essentially negative type of solidarity that is constituted through social forces that generate dissociation. Indeed, the very process of privatization and individuation manifested in law is the result of social development. The emergence of a private and individualized realm for Durkheim is part of social progress and results from developments internal to society. Private life and individualism do not exist prior to social complexity but are a result of that very complexity. In this way, Durkheim supports the emergence of private life on the basis of an imminent evolution within social formations. Private life is legitimized by law on the basis of social differentiation and associational complexity. The private sphere of the individual is an emergent structure that is most fully established through legal categories.

While one major development of law in differentiating society is private, personal, and negative from the perspective of social cohesion, another major development serves to regulate the social relations among the differentiated sectors of the social whole. This other direction of restitutive law is along the lines of "domestic law, contract law, commercial law, procedural law, administrative law, and constitutional law" (1964b: 122). Although the actual content of rights that fall under laws defining the private and personal realm are related to property and interpersonal relations, the content of the second direction in restitutive law defines both social functions and obligations associated with those functions. Domestic law, for example, specifies rules regarding marriage, divorce, adoption, and the responsibilities of guardianship. Contract law, as a second example, regulates the cooperation among mutually interacting parties. Procedural law, finally, provides rules for judicial action.

By constructing restitutive law through functional differentiation, Durkheim emphasizes sources of social cohesiveness in legal categories. Laws that are generally considered to be distinguished along private and public dimensions are infused with an integrative social content. Thus, domestic law and contract law are often considered to be included in private law and administrative and procedural law are often included in public law. Durkheim argues emphatically against absolutizing this distinction into a dichotomy on the basis of the autonomy of legal categories and legal reasoning. Rather, he maintains that all of these laws are most adequately formulated as representations that emerge from integrative social processes:

> In order to completely separate the two sorts of law, it would be necessary to admit that there is really a private law, whereas we believe that all law is public, because all law is social. All the functions of society are social, as all the functions of the organism are organic. (1964b: 127)

This is a telling statement. Both public and private law are derived from social processes. Since society, as an object of knowledge and as a realm of representation, predominates over individual manifestations, it has a public character. All law, moreover, is public from the standpoints of social organization and knowledge. This is even the case with laws that define the private individual and exclusive locations and relationships. As in the case of suicide and marriage, public law predominates over the private sphere, legitimating the regulation and control of the private sphere by public authorities. Public regulation fulfills the requisites of social holism rather than the enhancement of private benefits. The integration of society is conditioned, in part, on the incorporation of private spheres into public law and state action.

Durkheim's analysis of property and contract demonstrate the transition from law derived from common morality to private spheres regulated by public law. He initiates his analysis of private property by criticizing both the labor theory of property, associated with liberalism and Marxism, and the theory of first possession. These theories are faulty because they root property in individualism, neglecting its social dimensions and its sources in public morality. While an object that is owned by an individual may be "the product of his own hands," this expenditure of effort is only part of the "raw material" that constitutes property (1958: 126). Beyond this, property has significance that results from "social taste and needs" that give it a fluctuating public value that "depends on public opinion" (1958: 126). Valuation is a collective relation rather than an individual judgment or a material quality. With regard to the theory of first possession, the "tying of individual will to property cannot generate an obligation on the part of others" (1958: 129). First possession is an inadequate ground of an individual's right to property because it is not founded on patterns of association that moralize it. First possession may only be secured through superior force: "The lawfulness of appropriation is dependent on the range of a gun" (1958: 134).

Rather than privatized grounds for property rights, property has its moral grounds in collective possession. With increasing social complexity, collective possession becomes enmeshed in ever more particular relations. Ultimately, property is articulated through individual rights. The moral basis of property develops from collective possession that increasingly takes an individual, private form:

> In order than men may be justified in wishing to appropriate individual things, these things must have been originally possessed by a collectivity. And since the sole natural collectivity is made up of the whole human race (since it is the only one that is complete, all others being partial), the right of the intended appropriation implies an original community of things and derives from this fact. (1958: 129)

Even though property evolves from sacred-communal to patriarchal and, ultimately, to personal and movable forms, the right to the inviolability of property is continually drawn from its original collective source. Forms of property, moreover, manifest patterns of association. The variability of what may be individually appropriated is not settled either by nature or by individual fiat, but by "the public opinion in every society" (1958: 138). In addition, the very notion of individual rights to property has a collective definition that derives from the dissociation of property into its elements. The various ways in which an individual has rights to make use of a thing; has rights to the yield of a thing; and has rights to destroy, consume, or transform it are subject to public determination through law (1958: 138–39). While private property means that there is a private individual who has the legal right to withdraw something from "common usage" for private use, there may be restrictions on private use that are collectively determined and publicly articulated. In effect, the privatization of property is a collective process that defines public and private morality.

At an even deeper level of collective morality, the right to private property has its origins in property that is withdrawn by a society from the "common area" of life and is "insulated" and held to be sacred (1958: 152). Things that are used in a society's religious rituals are held apart from common use and only those people who are recognized to conduct these rituals may have access to them at appropriate times. In this light, the inviolability of private property is derived from sacred property. Indeed, "man's right to property is only a substitute for the right of property of the gods" (1958: 157). Thus, Durkheim views the individual's right to private property, especially the right to exclusive use, as deriving from sacred/collective relations. While other rights to private property, such as the right to transfer property, are subject to high degrees of regulation, private property as a ground for an exclusive location is virtually inviolable.

Similarly, as the contract develops from sacred practices to solemn agreement, consent, the just contract, and ultimately, the equitable contract, there is a process of increased individuation that becomes less ritualized but nonetheless rests on collective norms and public forms of communication. Most fundamentally, changes in the form of contract are associated with changes in spheres of action. As society becomes more differentiated and as individuals engage one another in particularized obligations, the collective ritual of contract that signified collective participation in forming obligations becomes more specific to the individuals directly engaged with one another. The character of contract becomes less a ritualized enactment of collective identity and more a publicly communicated pronouncement of private individuals "declaring themselves exteriorly, of projecting themselves outwardly. They have to become known so that society may attach a moral significance to them" (1958: 184). In this context of differentiated spheres of action, the solemnity of law may substitute for religious ritual, but even if this is missing, the "declaration of will" takes on a character of obligation and power that is rooted in the irrevocable power of society as a whole.

Durkheim emphasizes that the two legal pillars of the private individual, property and contract, have their origins in and continue to draw their moral authority from collective sources. Durkheim's reasoning is worthy of elaboration because it is so fundamental to his formulation of the emergence of private and public spheres. Although these collective sources are lessened as society becomes more differentiated, social integration requires the maintenance of a core of collective norms. With differentiation, there is an expansion of categories of private law and public law; moreover, the quantity of law increasingly expands.

As we have pointed out, one direction of law that follows social development is the elaboration of individual and personal rights. These laws codify the separation of individuals from one another. The other direction has to do with the integration of social functions that are increasingly differentiated as society becomes more complex. Whether these functions are located in the arena of the family, business interactions, or judicial and state apparatuses, they have significance for the maintenance of the entire social organism and are, therefore, public. The elaboration of the social division of labor in the family as well as in political and legal institutions is a central feature of social development. The significance of particular institutions for individuals is not decisive for defining the public sphere. Rather, the function that diverse institutions play in contributing to social integration is decisive. The purely individual and the personal, then, are private locations according to Durkheim while all that falls under the social division of labor and has significance for the social whole is public. Social function determines whether law regulates a private or public sphere; the significance or meaning of that function for the social whole largely determines the legal statuses of institutions.

A distinctly social morality is expressed in the law that is based on the rationality of functional interdependence and reciprocal understanding. As we mentioned, there is no doubt a common, emotion-laden and affective morality is part of organic solidarity. It formed the basis for all subsequent differentiation. There is also a purely private or personal sphere that grows under the division of labor and is elaborated in rights. But what is most pervasive and characteristic of organic solidarity is a public-legal domain that is based on functional necessity of corporate integration rather than an affectively charged common conscience or the aggregation of private interests.

The public domain, grounded in functional necessity and emerging with social complexity, serves hierarchical harmony. It is formed through a social morality and a legal discourse that is even tempered and rational. The main characteristic of organic society that is expressed through the law is to maintain harmony and order and to adjust whatever disturbances may arise within the relations of a differentiating social whole. Rather than expressing a common morality through vengeance, law restores society to an equilibrium state. Specialized institutions articulate and enforce legal norms, regulating individuals and sectors of the social order to maximize their contribution to the solidarity of the whole:

> What distinguishes this sanction is that it is not expiratory, but consists of a simple return in state. Sufferance proportional to the misdeed is not inflicted on the one who has violated the law or who disregards it; he is simply sentenced to comply with it. If certain things were done, the judge reinstates them as they would have been. He speaks of law; he says nothing of punishment. Damage interests have no penal character; they are only a means of reviewing the past in order to reinstate it, as far as possible, to its normal form. (1964b: 111)

This benign character of restitutive law is, in part, a manifestation of the diverse social locations and private orientations of individuals. The conditions for moral consensus in differentiating societies are based on a social division of labor and a pattern of mobility that generates a plurality of meanings and individuated patterns of action. Individuals are engaged by an array of practical activities that they must personally accomplish. For the private individual, social structure is partially internalized as a set of particularized obligations, constraints, and means for fulfilling them.

People tend to have little or no direct contact in public except through exchange, formal roles, and instrumental and strategic interactions. For these reasons, criminal offenses that grow in complexity tend to lose their collectively experienced, affective, and moral force. Rather, crime is increasingly a disruption to the individual's personally significant activities. The private individual is compelled by practical circumstances to have his or her situation restored to what it was prior to the criminal offense rather than to seek vengeance on an unknown, and probably anonymous, perpetrator. What is required above all else is compensation for private loss to continue personally organized rounds of practical activity. It would further disrupt the victim's private life and the conduct of everyday business to be involved in a process of legal vengeance. Thus, the situations of private individuals reinforces restitutive law: to formalize and to maintain conditions of private life and everyday activity rather than to serve as a source of moral gratification.

Just as the dissociation of the individual from collective life yields a sphere of private law and personal autonomy, the differentiation of institutions generates conditions for particular institutional codes and relative institutional autonomy. All the "special functions" of society are institutionalized into distinct "systems of representations actions" that are "outside the common conscience" (1964b: 80). The division of labor transforms social consciousness to go beyond collective consciousness to include more specialized patterns of representation and action.

This pattern of association and consciousness is located in such relatively autonomous institutions as the judiciary, science, the professions, and industry. These institutions, developing out of and contributing to society as a whole, have capacities for independent action that go beyond the limited relations of the private sphere of the individual; yet they are more limited in their scope than the representations that regulate society as a whole.

The rules and moralities that regulate particular institutions engaged in specialized functions constitute professional ethics among each of the specialized groups. Because these groups are largely outside of public consciousness and are constituted through internal practices, shared professional activities and specialized knowledge and education, they lead to a "decentralization of the moral life" (1958: 5–7). To a high degree, professional groups are self-regulating. They constitute particular spheres of morality and action for the individuals included in them. The private scope of the individual's orientations and actions are bounded by their ethical rules and norms of conduct. These norms are closer to the individual's everyday activities than are the laws that support negative and positive solidarity that are directly backed by the state.

The constraining power of professional ethics over private individualism varies widely. Their power to constrain privatism is largely determined by their functional location and by the cohesiveness of their internal organization. The "greater the stability and the better the organization of the professional groups," the greater their authority and their capacity to exercise control over the individuals contained within them (1958: 7–9). Professional groups that have a "strong public character," in the sense that they carry out functions necessary for society as a whole, tend to have great authority, public visibility, and coherent rules. These features provide powerful constraints over individuals. Examples of these strong professional groups are the army, the law, education, and the state itself.

The weakest patterns of professional ethics are found in the institutions of industry and trade through which economic functions are conducted. Since these institutions revolve around market forces that heighten competitiveness, egoism, and self-interest, they tend to foster an "amoral" character in economic life: Indeed, "in this whole sphere of social life, no professional ethics exist" (1958: 9). Establishing patterns of professional ethics and cooperative constraint in the social economy would moderate private individualism: Their absence serves to weaken not only the integrity of the individual but also public order as a whole. Economic functions are in the greatest need of corporate institutionalization and state regulation.

Durkheim's formulation of social complexity, differentiation and corporatist legality are closely tied to his approach to the state. Consistent with his general analytic approach, Durkheim begins his analysis of the state by criticizing other approaches that do not adequately comprehend the social grounding of state organization. He then provides an alternative, sociological approach to the state based on corporatist integration. His corporatist framework stresses the structural conditions of the corporate state and state capacities for maintaining hierarchical order through differential patterns of communication.

Durkheim's corporatist construction of the state is founded on criticisms of socialism, utilitarian economics, and communism. Each of these approaches to the state raise materialism and economic values as the primary social concern, neglecting the role that the state plays as the premier public institution that promotes moral and regulative integration for society. For Durkheim, despite polemical differences, socialism and utilitarianism share a similar economic approach to the state. They undermine the state's political and integrative functions by reducing it to an agency that supports economic expansion to secure the private material well-being of individuals. Communism, in contrast, is an essentially moral doctrine: It is a utopian attack on private property and the accumulation of private wealth that seeks to simplify the social division of labor. Ultimately, communism supports a privatization of production where people are separated through the organization of labor doing the same work. Thus, communism, along with utilitarianism and socialism, heightens tendencies toward privatism at the expense of publicly constructed morality.

According to Durkheim, socialism must be understood on the order of a social fact. Socialist doctrines emerged with the development of a complex division of labor and have been elaborated through manifold repetitions by numerous authors and groups. As such, socialism must be understood as a collective representation that, in part, expresses changes associated with the growing complexity of the division of labor; it seeks to regulate and channel directions of social change. While socialism is a program for social change, it also has the pretensions of a science since it claims to ground itself empirical facts. Yet, socialism is an expression of crisis rather than a scientific analysis of it. It is "a cry of grief, sometimes of anger, uttered by men who feel most keenly our collective malaise" (1962: 60).

Despite its calls for regulation, socialism is essentially reductionist in its approach to the state. Overwhelmingly, socialists see the role of the state as supporting the centralized control of the economy to overcome the chaos of the market and to support economic expansion for utilitarian ends. As such, socialism is bound up with an ethic of liberalizing values at the level of the individual. It supports boundless appetites and enhanced possibilities for pleasure and consumption that are not subjected to moral regulation. By supporting unlimited production and consumption, socialism strengthens privatized propensities for egoistic strivings. This egoistic tendency leads socialism to reject any project of the state beyond administration of the economy. Moreover, socialism lends support to notions of class struggle. This feature of socialism results from the erroneous inclusion of communism in much socialist doctrine, bolstered by egoistic resentment. Ultimately, socialism reduces the state and public order to supports for expansionary economic policy in support of egoistic materialism.

Durkheim is equally critical of the approach to the state put forth by utilitarian political economy. The implausibility of individualism as an ahistorical assumption of utilitarian thought, the reduction of social functions and organization to explanations based on maximizing the happiness of private individuals, the absence of any analysis of the sources of property and contract in social morality and public regulation, and the affirmation of egoistic rationality were all found to be unacceptable to Durkheim in light of sociological analysis.

Similarly, the theory that the state should be reduced to the role of supporting individual rights and enforcing contracts is viewed by Durkheim as an abandonment of public order and social order to the instability of market forces that generate anomie and heighten egoism. While socialists erred in projecting a state that would concern itself only with the control of the economy, utilitarians and political economists sought to limit the state "to the administration of a wholly negative justice" (1952: 52). The heightening of negative solidarity and the consequent dissociation of individuals from one another could only serve to heighten tendencies toward social pathology by reducing public order to the sum of radically privatized individual strivings.

While both socialism and economic utilitarianism are social facts, communism is a utopian ideal that is periodically expressed by individual authors and is lacking in any developed social sources. To be sure, communism is a moral doctrine that expresses both a revulsion to private wealth and an affirmation of collective sources of action based on equality of condition. Yet, it calls for creating a simplified pattern of social organization that flies in the face of tendencies toward organizational complexity and moral differentiation that are characteristic of modernity.

In rejecting socialism and utilitarian political economy, Durkheim calls into question both the egoism that infuses their conceptions of the state and their vision that the realization of economic imperatives should define public order. Communism, on the other hand, not only demands a utopian simplicity but also neglects the way in which social development has generated a public order based on a cooperative division of labor and the negative solidarity that are the grounds for the individual's private sphere. In contrast to these, Durkheim has an affirmative, corporatist theory of the state that supports public morality beyond economism and of the private individual.

For Durkheim, the state emerges as a central agency of control and administration as the social division of labor reaches a degree of complexity that precludes the coordination of social functions by the groups that make up society. The state, as the core agency of specialized control, overviews and regulates society's divisions. The coordination provided by the state is essentially benign and restitutive, provided that the social division of labor is itself harmonious. Although the complexity of society may require a specialized agency of control and organization, the unifying function of the state is not independent of society but conditioned by its internal coherence and stability: "Such is the internal solidarity which not only is as indispensable as the regulative action of higher centers, but which also is their necessary condition, for they do no more than translate it into another language and, so to speak, consecrate it" (1964b: 360).

In addition to coordinating and expressing the underlying harmony of society, the state is also the guarantor of private rights. The rights of the individual as a unique, private, and autonomous agent are elaborated in laws supported by the force of the state. In this dual capacity, the state serves to integrate the divergent parts of society into a unity that maintains society as a whole while legitimating social order to the individual because its integrative rationality supports individual rights.

Optimally, the corporatist state, like corporatist law, is not an independent organization of force that dominates society. The independence of legal institutions and discourses, the internal integrity of institutions intermediate between the state and the individual, and the underlying harmony of an integrated society yield solidarity, moral consensus, and social power. These are sources of resistance to state domination. While the state has a measure of support from individual social members because it recognizes the individual's private rights apart from the individual's associations, its legitimacy rests on the underlying social order that it supports and reflects.

Yet, in the absence of moral cohesiveness and consensus, the state has the potential to rule over society with repressive sanctions. These repressive rules originate in organized state control over instruments of coercion rather than from the functional integrity of society's elements. As the division of labor becomes industrialized, overly complex, and as situations of extreme disassociation among social sectors and among individuals emerge, law and the state no longer manifest internal regulative principles for social order. In this situation, the state assumes the form of an outside agency that maintains public order and control through repressive law and force.

Under these conditions, both the state and law constitute a public realm that has no rational grounding in social institutions or individual private life. In ways parallel to Marx's analysis in *The Eighteenth Brumaire of Louis Bonaparte* and Hannah Arendt's analysis of mass politics in *The Origins of Totalitarianism*, Durkheim sees the state filling a void of social power by politically and administratively organizing instruments of coercion that may respond to the interests of particular groups, but not to a general vision of societal unity. To the extent to which the state reflects private life in a public manner, it does so on the basis of privatized fear, anxiety, and insecurity. Repressive law and state autonomy rest on privatized individualism: The Hobbesian condition of mutual antagonism and aggression among social members is recreated and, with it, the need for a repressive state institution that lords over society's divisions.

Under normal social conditions, the state does more than secure social integration and private rights; the democratic state is a form of public discourse. While all state forms involve government by a minority, democracies are distinguished by the relative fluidity of the governing minority and, most significantly, by a greater openness of governmental power to society and a greater "number of things submitted to collective debate" (1958: 88). In this light, democracy signifies a circulation of power and ideas through government and society, allowing for wider spheres of articulation and criticism than is the case in other forms of government. As a result of this wider scope of discourse that penetrates into deeper levels of society, democracy entails a relatively close form of communication between the public consciousness and the private consciousness of the individual.

Despite these seemingly populist features of Durkheim's theory, there is also a strong element of functional rationality and corporatism in his theory of the democratic state (1958: 95). First, Durkheim distinguished between the democratic state in terms of legislative authority and public administration. His democratic tendencies were more focused on the formation of consciousness and consensus at the level of legislation rather than on popular participation in public administration. Second, Durkheim called for a distance between "the mass of the people" or "the nation" and the state (1958: 92–95). In supporting policies of distance, such as indirect voting for legislators, he maintained that the government could serve as the consciousness of society as a whole only if it were removed from the immediate pressures and interests of particular social groups. Indeed, he maintained that some distance between government and the people was a precondition for public rationality and the formation of a critical consciousness for society as a whole. Thus, while Durkheim was not adverse to popular sources of government and supported a syndicalist form of professional organization, he nevertheless argued for a great deal of autonomy of governmental functions as a condition for the articulation of rational representations of the social whole in the public sphere of politics. Furthermore, he maintained that this gulf between democratic government and particular interests was necessary for upholding the individual. By releasing "the individual from the state and the state from the individual," boundaries between these two spheres could be maintained while communication could occur between them (1958: 108–9).

Durkheim's corporatist construction of law and the state elaborates and supports his sociological approach to the public/private division. He conceptualized the public and private dimensions of society as related features of a complex, unified process of social development. The split between public and private spheres emerges with social differentiation. The split is harmonized through a hierarchical ordering of subordinate spheres of semiautonomous individualism and superordinate public institutions and discourses. To be sure, Durkheim maintained that his science of ethics must be distinguished from efforts to base ethics strictly on scientific inquiry. Yet he provided epistemological, methodological, and empirical grounds for legitimating the split between public and private spheres of society by subordinating the private sphere to public order through mutually related corporatist discourses and institutions: sociological science, law, and state organization. His affirmation of state officials and sociologists as privileged knowers because of their institutional locations in the public sphere in contrast to the partial knowledge of private individuals, especially those in the domestic sphere, manifests this corporatist standpoint.

## NOTES

1. For studies of Durkheim's sociological approach to politics and the state, see Steven Seidman (1983: 145–200), Jeffrey Prager (1981), Steven Fenton (1984: 81–115), and Irving Horowitz (1982).

2. Viewed from Phillipe Schmitter's typology (1979), Durkheim's formulation of state and law is more societal corporatist than syndicalist. This is the case because, in keeping with societal corporatism, he concedes autonomy and a measure of self-determination to entities that are subordinated to the state. His approach is not syndicalist because it is hierarchical.

# Part III

# MAX WEBER

# CHAPTER 8

## Public and Private as Dichotomy: Methodological Condition and Political Dilemma

Critical theorists, beginning with Georg Lukacs (1971: 123–36) through Max Horkheimer (1974), Herbert Marcuse (1968: 201–26), and Jürgen Habermas (1970), have maintained that Max Weber's construction of the public/private division supports capitalist forms of economic domination, and, more generally, patterns of domination founded on instrumentalism. These critics have argued that Weber's theory denies objective truth claims to morality and ethics by privatizing them as values. From the critical theory perspective, rationalizing the public sphere along scientific and instrumental lines lessens capacities to question the necessity of social constraints and enhances tendencies toward the narrowing of action orientations to highly self-interested and personalized values in modern industrial societies. By limiting public rationality to forms constricted by instrumentalism and science, moral issues about social organization and justice are marginalized, often to realms of private discourse.

At the same time, critical theorists have sought to appropriate Weber's analysis of rationalization and power. By historicizing his approach and stressing how rationality is tied to domination, the ideological character of the public sphere is apprehended. This approach, grounded largely in reflections on analytic categories and scientific methods, leads us to consider Weber's theory of the public/private division more fully.

Indeed, the public/private division is at the center of concept formation and the sociological analysis of politics and law for Weber. Yet compared to Marx's scientific socialism and to Durkheim's scientific corporatism, Max Weber's approach to the public/private division is less systematic. It is characterized by pervasive conflict, antagonism, contingency, and an openness to alternative outcomes. The approaches of Marx and Durkheim, despite major differences, agree that the public/private division must be fully integrated in concept formation, social theorizing and practice: The form of the division and its content must be thoroughly socialized for analytic and political purposes. Weber thought otherwise.

Weber maintained that the social must be partially resisted in forming concepts. Weber, like Hannah Arendt, emphasizes the indeterminacy of action that results from nonsociological factors. For Weber, these are sources of action and historical change that are in principle not capable of being analyzed scientifically. Most importantly, they form the public/private division that underlies the role of ethics and the individual politics.

For Weber, public and private elements of social life are inherently separate.[1] They are more than dialectical or functional distinctions within an overarching social process; instead, they are discrete components of action that have incommensurable sources. Weber's science of social action, focusing on the ethical commitments of the individual actor in conflict situations, strives to formulate grounds for a "responsible" actor who recognizes and struggles with the often irreconcilable public and private elements of social life.

For Weber, the division between public and private features of social life is a historically emergent dichotomy that raises dilemmas for the individual and for society.[2] While their combinations yield varying patterns of legitimation and material relations under varying conditions, the main direction of historical change in the West is toward the dominance of public rationality over an increasing range of social relations.[3] Rationalization is a central feature of the social transformation of the public/private division. It facilitates a public sphere of interaction that incorporates more and more localities, traditional cultures and relationships in commodity relations, and modern forms of organization. Rationality is a universal framework for facilitating and coordinating the motives and actions of disparate groups and individuals.

The spread of ever more universal forms of public rationality transforms the private sphere, making it the location of existential value commitments, subjectivity, and personal meaning. The increasing distinctness of the private and public spheres, emerging most fully under modern conditions, combines calculations rooted in institutionalized patterns of public rationality with seemingly irrational values, strivings, and commitments located in the private sphere and, most especially, in the individual's most interior realm of subjectivity. As I show in Chapter 9, while this division provides sources of legitimacy to modern social formations, it also sets the stage for more pervasive and more intense ambiguity, antagonism, and conflict. The public and private dimensions of experience are radically dissociated under modern conditions; the consequences of their interaction is at the core of inquiry.

The consequences of this process are captured and formulated in Weber's methodology and in his analysis of political action. Weber's method aims at combining public and private elements for analytic purposes in ways that recognize both their integrity and incommensurability. His view of politics brings this into a core arena of action.

Weber's methodological focus on the subjective meaning of social action as the grounds for scientific knowledge about society is at the heart of his approach to the public/private distinction. His methodology aims at conceptually organizing the incommensurable public and private elements of social life. Instead of approaching the public/private distinction from its external and objective characteristics or solely as a problem of cultural interpretation, the distinction must be interpreted in terms of antinomies in social action. Conflating the subjective meaning of the public/private division in social action with its material conditions is tantamount to reducing the subjective elements of social action to observable behavior. The public/private dichotomy is embedded in the capacities of human actors to generate a world through meaningful symbols and interactions that yield novel outcomes. These distinctive capacities are conceptually abandoned when subjective meaning is reduced to behavioral observation.

The centrality of the public/private dichotomy for Weber's methodology and concept formation is revealed by analyzing his typology of social action. By ordering the four types of social action through the extent to which they differentiate between public and private, the relationship between the public/private dichotomy and rationality can be demonstrated. Overall, public and private elements become increasingly separated as the types become increasingly rational in an instrumental direction. The most radical separation of public and private is consistent with the most rational type of social action. It is a type of action that is universally understandable on the basis of calculation independent of personal and local knowledges, commitments, and understandings.

Weber specifies four types of social action (1968: 24–26). The first and least rational of these is affectual social action in which the actor is oriented by internal, privately experienced "feeling states" (1968: 25). Here social action is instantaneous and based on feelings that may be known through expression rather than cognitive or intellectually rooted understanding. The second type is traditionally oriented social action which is "determined by ingrained habituation" (1968: 25). Here means and ends, values and instrumental orientations, are locked into a single bundle. The elements of public knowledge and discourse are directly tied to personal identity and form a unity with it. The third type is value-rational social action where commitments to particular values are invariable but means are variable. While value commitments are based on deeply felt emotions and/or traditional identities that have local and private sources, there is variability in the selection of means based on publicly demonstrable evidence and instrumental logic. This type separates the private sphere of value commitments, which have privatized sources, from the rational, public discourse on means. Finally, instrumentally rational social action is rooted in orientations that allow for variability of values that enable a calculation of successfully realizing combinations of means and ends. Here values are more deeply privatized and distantly related to ends that are selected in large part because of the likelihood of realizing them instrumentally. This is the most rational type of social action because it most radically separates the values and feelings underlying social action from universally applicable discourses of calculation that join goals and means.

For Weber, social meanings are established in relation to public discourses, institutions, and practical activities rather than in relations of private, self-referential significance. Methodological concerns with subjective meaning do not focus on personalized, intentional frameworks of interpretation. Rather, subjective meanings are rational to the extent that they are tied to the demonstrable efficacy and logical consistency of symbols and beliefs. They are the cultural aspects of social action and have public consequences.

Consistent with this approach, Weber formulated the individual as the locus of the public/private dichotomy. This is the case because, in general, the individual is the fundamental social element: Social action can only have meaning for individuals. While the public/private dichotomy has cultural and historical importance independent from purely personal relations, it is realized among individuals within social relationships and is maintained through the interaction of individuals. As such, the individual is a primary site for locating the meaning and consequences of the public/private dichotomy. An adequate sociological explanation must, therefore, provide an interpretation of the meaning of the public/private dichtomy at the level of the socially acting individual.

These methodological departures make the private/public dichotomy central for Weber's sociology, shaping the general direction of his inquiries as well as his analysis of specific issues. Most importantly, the public/private dichotomy is at the core of the difference between facts and values.

On the one hand, facts are products of calculating, logical, and scientific forms of public rationality. On the other hand, values, reflection on values, and will are centered in the private sphere. The fact/value dichotomy, as a methodological dimension of the public/private dichotomy, is a critical explanatory framework that is an outcome of historical development. The radical separation of, on the one side, public rationality and facts, and, on the other side, the privatization of values and will, is a methodological standpoint that is self-consciously historically contingent for Weber. By demarcating and formulating modernity as an epoch constituted through a radical separation of the public/private dichotomy, Weber also affirms the distinction between facts and values as a radical separation in private and public discourses. Under conditions of modernity, scientific inquiry and facts are core features of the rational public order, while values are ultimate, irreducible existential commitments that cannot be scientifically determined or adequately understood through scientific categories.

Weber's analysis of religion demonstrates the linkage of an extreme separation of public and private spheres with the development of rationality (1968: 611–34). Those religions foster the greatest rational orientation toward the world in technical and economic rationality that renders spiritualism, faith, and salvation into the inner, subjective realm. Religious rationalizations of the world that link worldly, public activity to salvation—an inner sense of spiritual fulfillment or grace—pose limits to the most rigorous world rationalization. Rather, those religions, such as ascetic Protestantism, that generate inner anxiety about salvation that cannot be overcome by work in the world, shape the most radical separation between private spiritual life and public activity conducive to a fully instrumental, scientific world rationality.

In a very basic sense, then, Weber stresses nondeterministic elements in his logic of explaining social action. By placing the explanatory emphasis for rationality on the privatization of values, which are in principle irreducible to material causation, the primacy of nondeterministic elements is affirmed. This primacy, which is consistent with Weber's paramount attention to contingency and the irreducibility of action, provides a direction for inquiry. Social science, rooted in cultural inquiry, must attend to the meaning and significance of phenomena for historically located subjects of action. Relationships of meaning and significance that are grounded in ultimate values are, thus, central to the analysis of action. This analytic primacy, moreover, is deepened by social inquiry. The disciplined knowledge of social action raises to greater awareness the singular importance of values for the actor in making the social world. In Weber's words,

> the fruit of the tree of knowledge, which is distasteful to the complacent but which is, nonetheless, inescapable, consists in the insight that every single important activity and ultimately life as a whole, if it is not permitted to run on as an event in nature but is instead to be consciously guided, is a series of ultimate decisions through which the soul—as in Plato—chooses its own fate, i.e., the meaning of its activity and existence. (1949: 18)

But how, more specifically, is the public rationality of knowledge and science related to the sphere of values, which is increasingly privatized? And how are the private, existentially based values and the public rationality of science related in action and in theory?

The methodological and, indeed, the political consequences of this dichotomy are articulated in Weber's views on value neutrality in science (Bruun, 1972). Weber formulates relations among science and values to enlighten actors about the consequences of acting on existentially based value commitments. The issue is to analyze how value commitments are related to one another, how they can be realized under alternative conditions, and to assess their actual consequences.

Given this program for knowledge, Weber's argument for value freedom in scientific inquiry does not seek to totally separate the value sphere from scientific inquiry. Rather than arguing either that scientific inquiry and values must be kept separate from one another or that scientific inquiry must be kept separate from values, he argues that the value sphere must be kept separate from scientific elements. He does not argue for a purely value-free science but, instead, for the freedom of values from scientific determination. The value neutrality of science results from the scientifically undemonstrable, private nature of values rather than the character of science.

The key division between the incommensurable discourses of science and values is the objectivity of science and the subjectivity of values. For Weber, claims to scientific truth are constituted through procedures that objectify reality and make it public in causally analyzable forms. The scientific approach, while it involves a value commitment to theoretical truth divorced from immediate practical activity, is primarily committed to delimiting objects of inquiry to develop testable publicly demonstrable and testable empirical knowledge. Ideal types, concepts, and comparative methods are not valued in themselves but, rather, instrumentally, as means for empirical inquiry. All sciences, moreover, share a claim to objective truth that is independent of the personal validity they hold for individuals. Science has a universality because of its public character in comparison to the more personal and particularistic character of value commitments.

While Weber views science from the vantage points of universality and objectivity, he approaches values from the vantage point of subjectivity, practice, and action. Most importantly, values are the subjectively meaningful goals that persons strive for in action. In the course of social action, "the individual, whether consciously or unconsciously, with logical necessity commits his personality, his subjectivity, and stakes it on some ideal" (Bruun, 1972: 31). Values are subjective elements that make the world a realm of activity by shaping the commitments of private individuals. This constitutive, world-making dimension of values is elaborated and deepened through relations among practical values and the fundamental axioms or beliefs that ground them. The dynamism of values that are located in the realm of action may be based on a discursive and, to some extent, logically organized pattern of evaluations. Yet values remain distinguished from scientific facts, whether at the point of action or at the level of fundamental axioms, because they are nonempirical, nonverifiable, and, therefore, nonrefutable commitments. They define the actor as a willful, self-formative agent.

Value neutrality, based on the separation of values from scientific determination, shapes an array of discourses that dominate social action and the public sphere. Value neutrality, while based on the fact/value dichotomy, is an emergent principle of public discourse. It has less to do with strict empirical verification than with the objectivity of discursive relations. As a type of social action and as a discourse, science is an extreme because it is characterized by value commitments to empirical truth. As such, value neutrality in science is not the absence of values but, rather, a commitment to empirical knowledge. Between science based on empirical truth and the nonempirical character of values, there are discourses that are both logical and nonempirical. Disciplines like logic, mathematics, ethics, aesthetics, and jurisprudence usually begin with undemonstrable axioms. These axioms are logically elaborated, providing grounds for objectively binding claims: They have a claim to truth somewhat independent of their initial sources. These forms of public discourse are value free despite the absence of empirical falsifiability.

Beyond generating discourses that are intermediate between science and values, science and values combine directly in the conduct of scientific inquiry. Weber formulates the relationships among science and values in the conduct of inquiry to maintain the nonfalsifiability of values while, at the same time, articulating the multiple roles that values play in scientific inquiry. In the most universal of scientific discourses there are value commitments that go beyond concerns with empirical procedures.

Values are a precondition for scientific discourse and inquiry. While science generates publicly available knowledge that can be reviewed through testing, replication, logical analysis, and other procedures, the impetus for substantive knowledge claims has its origins in the practical value orientations of persons. Because of the pluralistic nature of social reality constituted through the multiplicity of individual value commitments, social science cannot generate adequate knowledge through abstract methods of generalization and quantification alone. Instead, concepts and laws originate in the practical value judgments of acting individuals.

The role of value judgments in scientific discourse undergoes a change as their relationships to inquiry move from practical concerns with the realization of goals toward theoretical knowledge. In this shift, value judgments engage and delimit objects of inquiry by interpreting their significance to the value in question. Connections are made among objects of inquiry through the interpretation of their significance to the values that, in effect, initiate inquiry. In establishing these connections, the objects of inquiry are selected and placed in an ideal typical relation to one another. While the values that initiate inquiry may have generality because they are widely held through society and have broad cultural significance, the personal values of the individual scholar may come into play in determining these values. Indeed, the value origins of inquiry ultimately rest on the willful choice of the individual scholar and may conform to or oppose more generally held values.

Beyond constituting a precondition for scientific inquiry and establishing grounds for different knowledges, values may themselves be posited as objects of inquiry. Indeed, the scientific study of values is a core concern of Weber's theories as well as the focus of much of his substantive research.

The scientific analysis of values can take several distinct directions. One direction is to treat values as "systems of complex ideas" that are detached from immediate practical activity (Bruun, 1972: 149). By analyzing ideas in their connection to one another and by formulating the axioms from which they may be deduced, conflicts, inconsistencies, and conformities can be demonstrated. This direction of inquiry is important for two reasons. First, ideas under certain historical conditions may have shaped action and events through their motivating force. An interpretive analysis, in this light, is preparatory for the causal analysis of the role of ideas in history. Second, an interpretive analysis may perform a critical function for the self-formation of individual actors by demonstrating how the action-oriented values that they hold are theoretically related. This critical function itself rests on the acceptance of an ethic of consistency by the persons whose values are subject to analysis as well as to other interested parties. While inconsistencies in holding opposing values may not always lead to problems at the level of action, the demonstration of relationships among values—whether they are complimentary or antagonistic—is, in principle, clarifying for self-determination. It is a constituent feature of the reflexivity characteristic of individuals engaged in self-formative activities. Consistency is basic to ethical individualism in the private sphere.

A second direction for treating values as a topic of inquiry is to analyze the conditions under which values are realized in action. Here, values are treated as goals, or more precisely, "as an empirical situation which the individual seeks to bring about, not the psychological act of setting the goal" (Bruun, 1972: 162–63). The focus of such an inquiry is to determine empirically both the necessary and sufficient conditions for bringing about the sought after empirical situation as well as to determine the side effects or unanticipated consequences of action.

As a technical analysis of the empirical conditions and consequences of value realization, this type of inquiry has a critical dimension. By assessing the likelihood of goal attainment through empirical inquiry, knowledge is provided to the subject of action for rationally judging which strategy to pursue for the attainment of a goal. In addition, the complexity of outcomes can be used to reflexively determine an avenue of action, including the selection of means. This type of analysis serves to demonstrate the pragmatic difficulties and conflicts that emerge in action beyond the purely ideational conflicts. Hence, privatized value commitments become features of strategic public discourses.

A third direction for value analysis results from combining the analysis of value consistency with the analysis of conditions for implementing values. Here, values, ideals, and goals are analyzed not only in their own consistency with one another, but also in the effects that they bring about under actual empirical conditions (Bruun, 1972: 170–71). The acting person may collapse the realization of self-formation through willful choice into either an objectivism that identifies values with empirical conditions or an intuitionism that reduces empirical conditions to a value element. However, the self-determining, responsible person recognizes the dichotomy of public/private elements in action through a reasoned approach to the division between values and the actual world, truths about the inconsistencies among values, and the gulf between values and their realization:

> Weber sees responsibility as the precondition upon which the function of combined value analysis, the conclusive sifting of means and ends, is based. The aid

which objective knowlege is able to render the subjective goals and actions depends on the assumption that the individual concerned is willing to act in a responsible manner. (Bruun, 1972: 170–71)

Responsibility is a rational approach to action that cannot fully resolve conflicts; rather, it makes dilemmas posed by private value commitments, public discourses and social action more intelligible. On the one hand, divergent practical values are open to interpretation from alternative value commitments. This poses a source of stress at the level of value consistency that cannot be overcome through either an ethic of consistency or through science because science can neither demonstrate the objective truth of one value as a way of ordering others nor can it demonstrate the objective truth of all values by relativizing them. Thus, values remain in the realm of radical subjective choice. Subjectivity and objectivity cannot be combined in an overarching synthesis, despite the dominance of compromises in the leading positions that incorporate majority views. That a view is self-evident does not render it truthful since it merely conforms to dominant values and facts consistent with those values. The actuality of beliefs does not demonstrate their truthfulness.

The coming together of values and science in Weber's methodology, the confrontation of existentially based commitments and objective scientific procedures, is not a condition for the synthesis of private values and public rationality. Rather, it is a foundation for recurrent sources of conflict. This is the case not only in discursive arenas such as science where the orientation is toward theoretical knowledge that is detached from the immediacy of practical concerns with life's necessities, but also in other arenas where the consequences of value conflicts and the incommensurability of facts and values are more direct and widespread.

Nowhere is this more the case than in the arena of modern politics. In politics, public knowledges and power, in the form of the most rational rules for the application of a whole panoply of organized violence, combine with personal commitments and existentially based values. Here is an arena filled with danger for masses of people precisely because it hinges publicly organized, impersonal, and overwhelming forms of violence with personally rooted goals. For Weber, the problem of personal ethics in politics, of the principled control of public and private elements of political action at the locus of the individual, is a paramount issue of modernity.[4]

In *Politics as a Vocation*, Weber defines the state as emerging toward a "human community that (successfully) claims the *monopoly of the legitimate use of force* within a given territory" (1946: 78). The preponderant tendency is for the state to develop along formal, bureaucratic lines. With bureaucracy, the split between the public organization of the means of coercion and the private significance of organized power become increasingly dissociated. The capacity for the exercise of power and violence grows, becoming more concentrated, centralized, and organized just as the means and rationales of administrative state action are differentiated from the private lives and personal significance of individuals who occupy state positions. As a bureaucratic organization, the overwhelming number of positions in the state are directed toward technically and normatively defined tasks that are elaborated through a body of written rules. The officials who hold these positions are expected to fulfill their obligations without undue regard either to their private interests and values or to values, interests, or conflicts outside of their technical competencies and obligations to hierarchical authorities.

In addition to its technical and authoritative bureaucratic order, the state has leaders in the legislative and executive arenas. These leaders provide grounds for emotional commitments to the state through mass appeals based on their personalities. They give direction to state action by mobilizing interests, articulating and exemplifying the values that shape the goals of political action. They assume personal responsibility for the actions of the state through their personal accountability, typically to an electorate.

Normally, the state has a routine, predictable character for those engaged in politics. For bureaucratic state officials, the paramount reality of the state is an occupation that has all the characteristics of a career including a stable income, opportunity for advancement, and retirement with a pension. These orientations may be bolstered through a sense of obligation to perform duties of the office by beliefs in the legitimacy of the state, whether grounded in tradition, the charisma of political leaders and offices, or legality. For political leaders, the state is primarily an opportunity structure made up of offices to be filled by their followers and party members. Whether through elections, political upheavals, or conflicts, a core feature of political struggle is the fight for political offices and the status and opportunities for income that they bring.

To be sure, even at the level of mundane politics, there is a distinction between "living for" politics and "living off" politics (1946: 84). Living for politics is characterized by a preponderance of orientations either toward power as such or toward a course that is to be realized through state power. Living off politics is characterized by a preponderance of orientations toward political action and the state primarily as a source of income and prestige. While mundane politics are generally a mixture of both orientations, the preponderance of either one may serve to render political action with either a lack of objectivity or a lack of responsibility. Thus, living off politics may heighten orientations toward the maintenance of the state as an institution and to purely technical questions that make value questions appear insignificant. In this light, the moral or ethical grounds for formulating political goals and making political judgments may be lost. On the other hand, living for politics may lessen an orientation toward the consequences of action in the affirmation of a value or, in a pure orientation toward power, confuse actual consequences with their appearances and impressionistic effects. An example of this is the demagogue who

> is compelled to count upon "effect." He therefore is constantly in danger of becoming an actor as well as taking lightly the responsibility for the outcome of his actions and of being concerned merely with the "impression" he makes. His lack of objectivity tempts him to strive for the glamorous semblance of power rather than for actual power. His irresponsibility, however, suggests that he enjoys power merely for power's sake without a substantive purpose. . . . It is a product of a shoddy and superficially blasè attitude toward the meaning of human conduct; and it has no relation whatsoever to the knowledge of tragedy with which all action, but especially political action, is truly interwoven. (1946: 116–17)

Beyond these situational features and possible orientations toward political action, Weber presents alternative types of political ethics. For example, vulgarity in political ethics is characterized by "exploiting ethics as a means of being right" (1946: 118). When ethics are used to generate guilt in weak, defeated, or abandoned individuals or nations, the effect is to generate bitterness, anger, and a desire for revenge. Instead of forgoing moral posturing toward the past and looking positively toward the future, this negative use of ethics in politics abandons "objectivity, dignity, and chivalry" in the false glow of self-righteousness, creating the roots of future animosities and conflicts (1946: 118). By exploiting ethics as a moralistic source of identity and justification for the exercise of power, the capacity to fuse ethics with a realistic construction of future relations is diminished and, along with it, any hopes for authentic moral grounds for politics.

A clear vision of ethics in politics can only be realized when it is recognized that the specificity of political action is determined through the special means of politics, "namely power backed by violence" (1946: 127). Given this starting point, the means of politics overwhelmingly determine the actual consequences of political action rather than the content of the goals that are sought. Regardless of the subjective sincerity of individual political actors and movements, to gauge personal conduct on the basis of private ethics without concern for the actions of others or the consequences of outcomes is to abandon oneself to the vagaries of the means of action which, in politics, is violence. The preponderance of means over ends, of the rational organization of the means of violence in the form of the state over commitments to particular values, constitute the real relations that determine the actual consequences of political action. Realism dictates that these relations should underlie ethics in the sphere of politics.

To establish a critical comprehension of these directions, Weber develops two ideal types of political action differentiated by their approaches to subjective values and objective consequences: the ethics of ultimate ends and the ethics of responsibility. The ethic of ultimate ends places trust in the outcomes of action on the validity/purity of the personal value commitments that secure identity and motivate action. By focusing on political action as an expression of values and an arena for demonstrating ethical commitments that define personal identity, political action is valued because it is exemplary for others and heightens awareness in the values being affirmed. Political action is understood solely in the intentions that animate it. There is a tendency to rationalize political action through narratives that transform the consequences of action into exemplars consistent with the value commitments. The world and political action are understood solely through references to existentially held values. In the face of unanticipated results, blame is placed on other people, nonbelievers and their deficiences, or some other set of circumstances. Most pointedly, the indifference toward actual consequences is revealed through an "ethical rationalism that squares every outcome with the conviction of ethics" (1946: 122). Consequences, no matter how they impact on others, are interpreted through values that give them an internal, subjective consistency and coherence.

In contrast, the ethic of responsibility proceeds by taking into account the forseeable results of action. Attuned to the actual consequences of action, the ethic of responsibility does not proscribe that bad results be attributed to the failures of other people or to uncommodious circumstances but, rather, points to the need to anticipate likely outcomes by taking account of the average deficiencies of people. Also, by asserting that the real world is characterized by ethical irrationality and that "anyone who fails to see this is, indeed, a political infant," attention is drawn to the need for objective analysis of the conditions of action and compromise over the goals, if not the ultimate values, that direct action. The ethic of responsibility requires knowledge rooted in value-neutral inquiry so that the calculation of likely outcomes of political action can be understood independently of the value commitments that inspire the action.

At their extremes, the ethics of ultimate values and the ethics of responsibility can yield alternative flights from reality. An extreme ethics of conviction totally divorces the actor from the actual consequences of action, yielding an irresponsibility toward the world that is mitigated solely by the privately held belief in the consistency of values with virtually any set of events and the internally felt sense of doing exemplary acts. Irresponsibility toward the world based on the privatization of the meaning of action is paralleled by the pure opportunism that follows from an extreme ethic of responsibility. Here, there is such attention paid to circumstances and the calculation of likely outcomes that the only criteria for political action is its likely success. The sole orientation is toward outcomes that maintain and enhance the political positions from which action is taken and the augmentation of power. Politics becomes divorced from any purpose. The identity of private interests and personal meaning with the perfection of the public rationalities that organize instrumental means of violent action renders value judgments independent from the exercise of rationally organized power meaningless. With this, the insensitivity to the realization of ethical goals that are not embedded in the routines of exercising power is enhanced.

Grounding action in either of these extremes is damaging to the very foundations of political action in the long run. The abandonment of concern for the actual consequences that result from value commitments may generate cynicism toward values in general. The basis for belief in values may be undermined by the destruction of the world that follows from an ethic of pure conviction. On the other hand, abandoning value commitments for an orientation toward success may lead to a spiritual deadening, confusion over goals, and denial of felt needs that may lead to a mistrust of leadership and cynicism toward technical rationality. In both cases, the fragmentation of collective action frameworks are likely results.

In rejecting both of these extremes, Weber advocates the need to bring the irreconcilable public and private elements of political action together. The confrontation of decision making based on existential value commitments and the rational calculation of outcomes cannot be avoided in politics without creating disasterous conditions. For Weber, the mature person recognizes that the incommensurability between the ethics of conviction grounded in existential value commitments and the ethics of responsibility, grounded in the socialization of the means of action, requires a commitment to compromise. While for such a person, the ethics of responsibility is paramount because he "is aware of a responsibility for the consequences of his conduct and really feels such a responsibility with heart and soul," ultimate values and principles cannot be compromised beyond some point. The drama, and, often the tragedy of life is shaped by this conflict and the will to act on it. In this light, "an ethic of ultimate ends and an ethic of responsibility are not absolute contrasts but rather supplements, which only in unison constitute a genuine man—a man who *can* have the 'calling for politics'" (1946: 127).

The issues raised in our discussion of Weber's methodology and politics have broad significance for the public/private dichotomy. The priority afforded to the actor as an agent of self-determined, nonempirically based, and reflexive values is more than a methodological starting point and a focus for poignantly depicting the dilemma of political action. Rather, it serves as the main framework for analytic concepts that cut across a wide range of issues. For it becomes a focal issue of Weber's studies, no matter how disparate they may appear, to analyze how the private and public dimensions of society have become separated in a manner that yields the radical privatization of values and an objective and publicly meaningful context within which personal will can be exercised and developed.

The conceptual commitment to the distinctive human capacity for willful choice of values and the distinction between values and facts has major consequences for Weber's core analytic concepts (Kronman, 1983). Most importantly, it accounts for the "privileged position" (1983: 51) given to legal rationality that legitimately bounds political action by ordering state actions and provides the legitimate boundaries for economic action. Compared to other types of public rationality, legal rationality has a primacy because it is the foundation for the legitimate application of state violence whether on the grounds of political action or as the guarantor of economic relations.

Through this basic relation to the state and the economy, legality secures the full scope to the willful positing of values: "Legal rational authority rests on the assumption that norms are made, not discovered, and on the belief that it is this attribute which confers on them their normative status as standards for the evaluative assessment of human conduct" (1983: 52). While tradition grounds values and norms in the world itself and views them as features of an unalterable reality that human beings are bound to adhere to with little possibility for deliberate change, legal rationality locates values and norms in the very "purposeful acts of human legislation that bring them into being" (1983: 52–53). Norms are not part of an unalterable fate, but have their basis in the human capacity for self-direction and self-formation. They gain their justification from purposes and goals that are distinct from the facticity of the world.

Legal rationality, then, has conceptual priority because it focuses analytic attention on human will and self-determination and also allows for the analysis of other forms of belief and action that limit these capacities. The vantage point of legal rationality serves to frame issues in conditions for and limits to human self-creation. The realization of the private individual through the exercise of a self-grounded will is conditioned by the formation of a public order that is rationally organized. The public order, indifferent to the private ends of action, is instrumental to those ends. For this reason, legal rationality serves as the premier critical concept. It enables the causal analysis and interpretive understanding of a fully humanized world that maximizes the exercise of willful choice and self-generating identity.

## NOTES

1. Anthony Giddens states, from his standpoint of structuration, that there is "*duality of structure*, which relates to the *fundamentally recursive character of social life, and expresses the mutual dependence of structure and agency*. . . . Structural properties of social systems are both the medium and the outcome of the practices that constitute those systems" (1979: 69). The public/private division in Weberian theory lacks this systemic relation between structure and agency. Their underlying sources, while having overlapping elements, have some elements that are completely distinct. Ann Swidler (1973) has analyzed the various ways in which "rationality" is used by Weber.

2. In this analysis, I focus on Weber's programmatic writings closest to his formulation of social action. This is in no way intended to discount the structural, historical, and material dimensions of his work that are valuable for empirical research (Turkel, 1981). Bryan Turner's comparison of the parallel between the scholarly treatment of the young and the mature Marx and Weber is very instructive here (1981) as is the underlying Weberian approach in Immanuel Wallerstein (1974). Just as there are disputes about the relationship between continuity or discontinuity in Marx's early philosophical work and the more concrete analyses that he wrote in his maturity, so there are debates about the relationship between the views Weber expressed in programmatic and methodological writings and in his historical studies. Guenther Roth (1979) stresses the importance of generalizing from experience, both at the level of ideal types and historical studies, that characterizes Weber's approach.

3. As Wolfgang Mommsen points out, these "predictions are part of a pluralistic model of societal change that considered history as open-ended in principle and regarded development as not unidirectional" (1987: 50). Again, the stress on nondeterministic features of social action is critical, even in Weber's approach to historical development.

4. Jeffrey Alexander argues that there is a distinct difference between pre-secular and contemporary vocational situations, including the vocational situation of politics: "The Puritan maintained his vocation and his work serving to maintain the fabric of cosmological meaning. In Weber's view, the modern vocation cannot allow this intellectual sacrifice. The fruits of rationalization must be maintained" (1987: 200). In effect, the pattern of autonomy initiated through rationalization, including the privatization of values, is irreversible. There is both liberation from a subordination to cosmological service and a new degree of responsibility for action.

# CHAPTER 9

## Public Rationalities: Discontinuities and Conflicts

The incommensurability between public and private sources of action are most dramatic in the political sphere. Combining private values and will with publicly organized means of violence in the form of the state establishes a classically tragic arena. The political actor is at the center of ethics, of decisive action that defines the human condition in privately held convictions and public consequences.

By comparison, the public/private dichotomy in the spheres of economic action, law, and bureaucratic organization are more mundane. Although these spheres of activity are related to politics because they are arenas of domination, they are focused on the maintenance and extension of mundane need satisfaction, stability of institutional life, and grounds for individual experience. In these spheres, especially under modernizing conditions, the dichotomy between privatized values and rationalized public order is more complimentary than conflictual. Indeed, in these spheres of life, the public and private dimensions of action often facilitate one another, interpenetrating in the subjective orientations of the individual.

In these arenas, the problem that Weber poses is not centered on the confrontation between public and private elements of action. Rather, it is formulated through the mutually supporting but conflicting rationalities of the public sphere and the private orientations associated with them.

Rational economic action, formal rational legality, and bureaucracy are mutually supportive yet conflictual. Their relations, based on divergent imperatives, set the stage for ambiguities and conflicts in public discourse.

While these rationalities come into greater contact with one another and partially blend as social structures become more open and universal, they retain independent principles and institutional practices. They are divergent rationalities that cannot be fully integrated through shared logics, quantification, and instrumentalism.

This is best demonstrated by reconstructing each of these rationalities in light of their underlying principles and then demonstrating the disparities and conflicts among them. Through this reconstruction of the sources and principles of economic rationality, formal legal rationality, and bureaucratic rationality, strains in public discourse that facilitate substantive discourse and conceptual spaces for alternative approaches to social organization and for conflict are presented. In their most ideal forms, public rationalities generate tensions and conflicts that require non-instrumental resolution.[1]

## ECONOMIC RATIONALITY

A rational economic orientation requires deliberate planning in the use of resources that establishes both the desire for utilities and the provision for their satisfaction (1968: 63–68). In addition, rational economic action is distinguished by an absence of both direct appropriation by force and direct coercion. This formal requirement of the peacefulness of economic action differentiates it from the state and law which, as we shall see, often buttress economic action but are not bound by its specific criteria, that is, costs, benefits, and profits. Furthermore, the rationality of economic action is distinguishable from pure technical rationality. It focuses on the costs associated with the use of resources for different ends rather than the most rational means to a particular end. By contrast, technical rationality requires the least effort in realizing a particular goal. It is indifferent to the scarcity of resources and the economic requirement that resources be allocated to maximize their usefulness for the realization of a range of utilities.

Economic action enhances subjective orientations that facilitate public choice and planning. These include such orientations as a distinction between present and future, the allocation of utilities through a systematic ranking based on the "estimated relative urgency," and the systematic procurement of them through the control of the means of production and transportation (1968: 71–72). Also, the control and disposal of economic resources is accomplished through agreement with other actors through some stable organization that rations procurement, use, and consumption or through exchange based on reciprocal compensation based on bargaining or competitive bidding and offering.

Money plays a decisive role for expanding the range of rational economic action. While Weber discusses different types of money, including differences between money that has a value independent of its role as a medium of exchange and the role of the state and law in regulating currency, stress is placed on the expansion of the scope for calculation that money facilitates:

> In substantive as distinguished from formal terms, monetary calculation means that goods are not evaluated merely in terms of their immediate importance as utilities at the given time and place and for the given person only. Rather, goods are more or less systematically compared, whether for consumption or production, with all the potential future opportunities of utilization or of gaining a return, including their possible utility to an indefinite number of persons who can be brought into the comparison insofar as they are potential buyers of the powers of control and disposal of the present owner. Where money calculations have become typical, this defines the "market situation" of the good in question. (1968: 81)

Money expands the range of economic action into a public sphere that includes ever more actors and relations. Moreover, money expands the arena of willful choice for private individuals by rationalizing time in terms consistent with quantifiable exchange. Will may not only be exercised within present social relations but also by tying future activities in calculable ways to present activities. The subjective sense of time is itself transformed. It becomes socialized as a dimension of planning and exchange. Time is a mode for a calculus of utilities not bound by either a private sense of duration or purely physical limits. In this way, the actor has available a fully rational ordering of time that drastically alters the framework of willful choice through calculations that cut across time and render it homogenous.

The subjective rationality enhanced by money is not only extensive over time; it is also intensive, opening ever-new opportunities for exchanging objects for money. The "market situations" for an object are "all the opportunities of exchanging it for money which are known to the participants in exchange relationships and their orientation in the competitive price struggle" (1968: 82). The arena for the exercise of subjective will through the expansion of the opportunities for exchange, while it may be restricted by legal, traditional, conventional, or monopolistic factors, expands with the number of actors engaging in exchange and the diversity of differentially priced objects that are brought to the market. Economic rationality expands the sphere of private will as the market expands, by homogenizing time orientations and by expanding the range of participants and objects on the market.

Rational orientations toward time, the market, and its related activities are expressed in public forms of budgeting and capital accounting. Budgeting is "the continual utilization and procurement of goods, whether through production or exchange, by an economic unit for purposes of its own consumption" or to procure other goods for consumption" (1968: 87). Weber maintains that the maximum degree of budgetary rationality is realized when calculation is conducted through money rather than physical units and when there is a linkage between efficient production and shifts in market conditions. Moreover, and most importantly from the standpoint of the private individual, economic rationality is enhanced through "an expansion and refinement of everyday wants" (1968: 89). Limitations on both traditional and extraordinary expenditures facilitate greater calculation of utilities among rationalized, mundane choices. The budgetary orientation to everyday life through private consumer wants partially constitutes and supports the objective relations of economic rationality. This is the nexus where private calculation of wants converges with the public ordering of preferences through the intertwined calculi of homogenous time and money.

Profit making is an activity oriented to opportunities for seeking "new powers of control over goods on a single occasion, repeatedly, or continuously" (1968: 90). Indeed, the highest form of rationality is characterized by an economic enterprise engaged in profit making that relies on market calculations and production calculations. The calculation of risks and profits, both before and after economic actions have taken place, based on the changes in the valuation of assets is central to capital accounting.

Capital accounting, resting on a multitude of factors including the availability of an extensive market for both the sale of products and the acquisition of resources and labor, a stable monetary system, and adequate legal and technical means for realizing production and sale, is the hallmark of rationality in the Western world. The presuppositions of society as an aggregate of mobile individuals, double-entry bookkeeping, the intensive growth of calculation within enterprises and, indeed, across all social relations are the foundations for the total rationalization of profitable production and exchange. Moreover, because needs are met solely through effective demand that depends on the money income of consumers and because the satisfaction of everyday wants requires stability and growth of production by profit-making enterprises, the most mundane everyday life activities of private individuals are tied to the formal processes of rational economic calculation. Everyday life takes on the character of a quantitative ordering of interdependent private desires and the fulfillment and shaping of them through rational accounting practices. The very creation and destruction of wants are accomplished by enterprises oriented toward profit making (1968: 99).

Beyond the formal requirements and the pervasiveness of the calculating orientation through which economic rationality conditions the will of the private individual, there are also deeper and more tangible motivational sources toward economic rationality. These motivational sources are differentiated by the degree to which social members are owners of property. For those with little or no property, economic activity is motivated by "the risk of going entirely without provision" for themselves and for their personal dependents. In addition, there may be a personal value placed on an ethic of work. For those who hold property, motivation in the economic sphere follows from the opportunities for income, ambition, valuing work as a source of prestige and acquisition, as well as calculations of risk (1968: 110). In particular, both material and ethical sources that motivate labor and that provide incentives to labor support profitable production and want satisfaction.

The restlessness accompanying the expansion of wants, the motivation to labor along profitable lines, not only set the formality of economic rationality in motion but also characterizes the rational division of labor. Weber constructs the rational division of labor along three intersecting lines (1968: 114). First, the technical division of labor refers to the combination of differential skills and procedures of production that are cooperatively linked through technical criteria along with the technical characteristics of nonhuman means of production. Second, the social division of labor refers to the social characteristics of the economic units within which labor is combined. Among the most prominent social criteria is the degree of autonomy of a unit and its jurisdiction regarding appropriation along with its relation to occupational differentiation and the market. Third, the strictly economic division of labor refers to whether the economic unit and the combination of units falls under budgetary administration or capital accounting, that is, profit making.

Cutting across these different categories is the distinction between managerial action and labor subject to managerial control.[2] While managerial action is labor in the sense that it involves expenditures of effort and time, the term *labor* is most strictly reserved for activity that follows managerial instructions.

Weber considers a range of historical possibilities for determining the most rational division of labor. These range from slavery, which is the extreme of unfree labor since the slave's labor is appropriated by the owner of the slave, to cases where managerial functions are appropriated directly by workers. For Weber, each of these extreme possibilities is lacking in either the realization of individual self-determination or in the maximization of profit-oriented calculation. The greatest penetration of rationality in the sphere of production is facilitated by the expropriation of workers from the means of production. For the individual worker, the sources of expropriation are located in the development of the technical division of labor through the differentiation of technical procedures and their complex combination in coordinated production processes. These technical developments underlie the differential training and subordination to discipline. The mechanization and technologizing of work both controls the speed of work and standardizes the effort required to perform it.

The exproporiation of workers in general follows from the economic requirements for the control, selection, and use of workers along criteria of profit making. The freeing of labor, both from the private domination of personal ownership and from the public exercise of managerial power, is thus in keeping with the combined technical and economic rationality in its most ideal public form. In keeping with the segregation of private individual will from the rational demands of technological and economic rationality, Weber also views the separation of business ownership from management as consistent with a heightened public rationality. While owners are oriented to the returns of profitability, managers have a more focused concern with the technical and market sources of capital accounting directed at the realization of profit.

## FORMAL LEGAL RATIONALITY

Weber maintained that the segregation of indeterminate values and will formation in the private individual combined with technical and economic rationality publicly institutionalized in budgeting, capital accounting, markets, free labor, and the managerially controlled firm maximize both public rationality and the exercise of private will. In keeping with his outlook on the essentially conflictual nature of social life, however, Weber also points to conflicts among public rationalities. This antagonism is manifested in relations among private will formation through economic rationality and legal rationality. To be sure, there is considerable overlap and consistency between the economy and law (Trubek, 1972). Yet, there are also departures and inconsistencies between them. In discussing these issues, I first delineate the interplay among private values, will, and rationality in law. Then I discuss some of the major potentials for divergence, inconsistencies, and conflicts between economy and law.

Weber's analysis of law is rooted in the fact/value dichotomy that is fundamental to socially established public/private dimensions of action. The sociological study of law neither affirms particular values that underlie private commitments nor demonstrates through scientific methods the rectitude of particular value commitments. As such, Weber views law as an institutionally elaborated, normative ordering of social relations that has observable consequences for social action. Rather than viewing law from the evaluative framework of extralegal ethics or as jurisprudential efforts to rationalize the norms internal to legal decision making, Weber is primarily concerned with the factual analysis of law. He seeks to determine the ways in which law modifies conduct as a result of the relationships of actors to legal standards and institutions. In addition to the empirical variability of law, there is a rich empirical variability of the consequences of legal norms under different historical conditions.

To facilitate this empirical approach, Weber develops an ideal type of legal rationality. This is central to his analysis for several reasons: First, the emergence of legal rationality and its relationship to rational economic action and the state is the core theme of Weber's comparative analysis of law. Parallels, convergences, and inconsistencies between the public/private elements in economic action and the public/private elements in the realm of legal action are analyzable through ideal types. Second, the ideal type of rational law is part of a larger typology of legal decision making. The typology enables the analysis of the causes and consequences of types of law that depart from a fully rational model. The elaboration of the typology of law extends the analytic concepts available for comparative studies. Third, and most significantly for our purposes, the ideal type of rational law and its empirical variants are formative for analyzing the exercise of private interests and choice and the public rationality that facilitates them in the legal sphere.

Just as economic rationality forms a public framework for the exercise of private capacities for free will and self-determination in the economic sphere, so legal rationality provides a public framework for the exercise of private capacities in the public sphere of legal relations. Law, like the economy, becomes a means for realizing an increasingly privatized pattern of value commitments and will formation in the individual. The rationality of law, as a source of predictability in action, is a condition for individualizing and subjectivizing goals, value commitments, and will.

In its most rational form, law is an internally consistent and logically coherent public discourse that has the universal scope of formal logic and the deductive depth of detailed fact. As extensive as it is impersonal, the law expands to cover all social action in a systematic construction that derives decisions from abstract propositions through logical procedures.[3] Moreover, grounding law in rational logic and procedure is so great that anything that cannot be viewed from its perspective is, at least provisionally, not legally relevant.

The importance of law for individualizing and privatizing will hinges on its rational extension through stable, logically derived, and ethically neutral contexts of normative meanings. Rational law elaborates its internal coherence along impersonal lines of deductive logic as well as by abstracting facts from personal and local meanings and defining them through rules of evidence consistent with legal procedures. To be sure, there is a place in legal rationality for tangible facts such as the "utterances of certain words, the execution of a signature, or the performance of certain symbolic acts with a fixed meaning" (1954: 63). Yet, for full legal rationality, the meaning of such facts must be logically reconstructed and systematically derived from universal legal propositions. Thus, the basis of facts in local and private contexts of meaning has legal relevance only to the extent that these meanings can be logically reconstructed, analyzed, and interpreted through systematic legal discourse. The legal reworking of social action into formally constituted facts is a requisite for rational law as a distinct public discourse. Legal rationality develops without requiring that spheres of personal meaning and legal meaning coincide.[4]

The capacities of private choice and will formation in production and consumption that are realized through patterns of public rationality in the economic sphere result from a multitude of factors as indicated earlier. This is also true for the realization of private will and choice in the legal sphere. These capacities rest on rational law that is itself part of a wider process of rationalization. Among the most prominent factors in facilitating rational law are the development of a political public sphere dominated by the modern bureaucratic state and legal specialists.

Modern state apparatuses increase tendencies toward rational law by increasing the scope and density of bureaucratic organization. The proliferation of institutions embodying legal norms tends to eliminate areas of personal and traditional authority in public life and to codify the norms of public life into legal rules. The expanding scope of the state, combined with the intensive definition of the legal limits and obligations of political authority and state action, fosters impersonal and rule-oriented social relations. In addition, as the legitimacy of the modern state increasingly rests on rational legal principles determined through legal institutions, the very bases of political action, including private values and interests, are expressed through legal discourse and discourses influenced by law.

The development of legal specialists is fundamental for the formation of legal rationality. This development stems, in part, from the spread of bureaucratic state apparatuses. The increasing complexity and pervasiveness of bureaucratic rules, and the impersonal relations that they foster, not only require a greater number of legally trained officials but also generate the need for a "further category [of] private counselors and attorneys" who heighten the density of legal orientations and interaction in social life by transforming social issues into legal matters (1954: 96). As bureaucratic differentiation and the influence of lawyers increase, law grows as a professional status group that has an interest in its own power and distinctiveness. Moreover, through specialized legal training and legal scholarship, the law is increasingly formulated as a distinct, abstract, and logically consistent specialty. In this sense, the efforts of the legal profession itself are at the center of enhancing the formal rationality of law. The intellectualization of law along formally logical lines is facilitated by the professionalism and scholarship through which law develops institutionally.

Beyond expanding the scope of rational action for the private individual through the spread of legal rationality in state bureaucracies and through the rationalization of law by legal specialists, the legalization of contracts further rationalizes the most mundane spheres of everyday life: market relations and the economic orientations of private individuals. Beyond the durability that legal guarantees give to an individual who exercises the power of control over objects or persons in specific ways, the recognition of freedom of contract by the legal order grants the "individual *autonomy* to *regulate* his *relations with others* by his own transactions" (1954: 100). Contract law "consists in the grant to everyone the power to create law by means of engaging in private legal transactions of certain kinds" (1954: 146). Backed by the normative and coercive power of the state, lawmaking and public power are, in effect, decentralized to the willful purposes of private individuals. The growth of contractualism, by facilitating market orientations and the expansion of economic relations facilitated by money, enhances the legal rationalization of the norms of everyday life for individuals engaged in private pursuits.

The expansion of contractualism increases the differentiation of the private core of the individual as values, will, and interests from publicly defined roles that constitute the societal means for realizing privatized commitments. Contractualism enhances the public definitions of roles that are related to specific goals, capacities, and performances through the juridico-economic discourse of legal action. Contractualism is at the center of the increasing privatization of values and will expressed through private meanings and the explosion of publicly defined means for their realization through legal discourses that are ultimately tied to the exercise of state power.

The private individual is partially defined through inheritance based on "a legally recognized family relationship"; this is largely a "survival of modes of acquisition derived from the familial household economy" (1954: 101). As such, inheritance is merely the starting point for the individual's self-initiated activities that require public rationalization through law. Most important, the rationalization of life is accomplished through the expansion of purposive contracts that are specific, quantitatively delimited, abstract, and economically conditioned compared to the greatly declining role of status contracts. Status contracts involve the entire personality of the individual; indeed, the very identity of person in law. Even though individuals have an identity and an independence from specific purposive contracts, they are totally immersed in and defined by status contracts. As Anthony Kronman has pointed out, the expansion of purposive contracts constitutes a basic condition for the individual's autonomous and willful identity:

> To conceive of an individual as a legal person whose identity transcends the sum of his *expressed* purposes, we must think of him as having—or, more accurately, as being—a capacity for purposive action which his concrete aim regarding interactions (and, in particular, his contractual relations) with other individuals actualize but never exhaust. The person who stands behind every purposive contract and whose basic identity is unchanged by the contractual relationship he enters must therefore be thought of as a bare power or capacity, the capacity for purposive action itself. It is this capacity, viewed abstractly, which constitutes the core of his legal personality. (1983: 104)

Because contract law is predicated on individualized will, it must have limits that prevent the violation of individual attributes and capacities that constitute the conditions for the exercise of will and value commitments. Contracts are overwhelmingly concerned with the extension of actions involving goods and services; yet transactions that violate the moral agency of the actor and/or the rights or interests of third parties are not supported by contract law. Thus, it is generally the case that sexual relations are not open to legal contract with the exception of monogamous marriage. Even in cases that are not in keeping with the legal formalities of marriage, such as prolonged cohabitation, the rights asserted are based on the expectations that follow from marriage. Contract law also precludes slavery. The sale of one person to another and the rights of ownership of persons, whether transacted between the two parties or by a third party, are illegal. While no doubt conditioned by changes in economic and political forces, there is a tendency for unfettered sexual exploitation and unrestrained exploitation of labor services to lose their support in contract law. Indeed, they are increasingly subjected to criminal law. Whatever the sources and specific tendencies of these limits, they further the contract law distinction between the agent of contracts as a purposive individual and the specificity of obligations that are affirmed in contracts. Limits to the range of what is contractually permissable heighten the conditions for the exercise of private individual capacities through choice in purposive contracts.

While private persons exercise their will by entering into contracts to realize specific purposes, individuals may also exercise their wills by combining their resources and interests organizationally. Partial commitments by individuals acting through legally created persons can expand the range of willful activity. The formation of legal combinations, such as corporations, extends the sphere of action and power of the individual by creating a sphere of law that regulates organizations independent of the legal regulation of the individual. Under the coercive and rational capacities of the state, "associational contracts" are "the most rational actualization of the idea that the legal personality of organizations consists in the complete separation of the legal sphere of the members from the separately constituted legal sphere of the organization" (1954: 156–57). While the forms of this association may vary depending on membership and specific rights, they center on the limited liability of associated members along with the designation of persons who assume obligations and enter into contracts for the organization. The individual can legally distinguish private resources and personal obligations from the organizations with which he or she is affiliated.[5] These forms of association increase the scope of the individual's effective action and choice by differentiating the individual's private sphere from the realm of limited association.

## BUREAUCRATIC RATIONALITY

Although economic rationality and legal rationality provide frameworks for a calculating intellectualization of activity through which private will and values are realized, the epitome of rational public order for Weber is bureaucracy. Whether in the state, in the capitalist enterprise, or in military organization, bureaucracy "goes hand in hand with the concentration of the material means of management" and the growth of power through the extension of markets, political power, and military professionalism (1968: 980–81). Its development is spurred on by the spread of rational law, market orientations and capital accounting, modern communication, and the intensification of technically defined tasks in all spheres of activity. Bureaucratic organization pacifies social order and enhances support for an everyday world constituted through mundane economic calculation and consumer orientations. Indeed, consumer orientations and bureaucracy are mutually supportive. Consumer goods define "the standard of living and makes for an increasing subjective indispensability of public, interlocal, and thus bureaucratic, provision for the most varied wants which previously were either unknown or were satisfied locally or by the private economy" (1968: 972). Bureaucracy is the legally constituted organizational form through which routine political and economic action are conducted.

The success and legitimacy of bureaucracy are consequences of its rational, impersonal features. Bureaucracy organizes and mobilizes highly specialized scientific and technical knowledges for the realization of technically defined goals. As an organization of knowledge, bureaucracy is elaborated through specialized "administrative functions according to purely objective considerations" (1968: 975). By allocating individuals to specific offices based on their documented performances and specialized training, bureaucracy enhances the utilization of experts and technical discourses. In addition, by proceeding through documentation and calculation grounded in rationally organized rules, bureaucratic rule formation and implementation constitute public order through logically coherent and quantifiable standards that depersonalize both means and goals. Consistent with the equalizing and universalizing imperatives of the market and formal legality, "bureaucracy develops the more perfectly, the more it is 'dehumanized,' the more completely it succeeds in eliminating from official business love, hatred, and all purely personal, irrational, and emotional elements which escape calculation" (1968: 975).

Bureaucracy has its counterparts and concomitant orientations in the private sphere. Weber points to the strict separation between the private and public relations of social action in modern organizations. Whether state or private enterprise, the private property of officials is divorced from the organization's resources. The separation of the office from the household and the predominance of codified rules in coordinating the interaction of officials depersonalizes bureaucratic action and, importantly, generates a means-ends relation between the private sphere and the bureaucratic public realm. Entering into a bureaucratic order commits the individual to accept an allegiance to "impersonal and functional purposes" for a "secure existence" (1968: 959).

Bureaucracy does more than provide a sense of security and a stable location for the individual: The private life of the individual is defined and directed through the coupling of educational certification and official performance with incremental progress in salaried careers. For the private individual, the range of possibilities for commodity consumption and, therefore, material life, is largely projected over time through the stages of a bureaucratic career. Fixed career lines and ranks are tied to both the individual's status and income not only during working life but through pensions to retirement as well. Career is a privatized appropriation of public functions at the level of meaningful personal action. Bureaucratic rationality orients the private individual to the future along calculable lines of income and status tied to official actions of public institutions and economic enterprises.

Politically, bureaucracy coincides with democratic elitism. The technical superiority of bureaucracy and the order provided for the individual through career support mass democracy. On the one hand, this is the case because both technical capacities and individual rights within bureaucracy are legitimated through principles of "equality before the law" and, especially, equality of educational opportunity. As a feature of democratic elitism, bureaucracy fosters an affirmation of hierarchy based on knowledge and rational rules and equality of opportunity, largely through educational certification, to the widest possible range of official positions. On the other hand, the affirmation of equality

> heightens orientations toward the prevention of a closed power group based on official position and to limit the power of political elites through shortening terms of office of elected officials and other efforts to make political officials subject to mass public opinion. Thus, bureaucracy mitigates against direct rule by a community by separating individuals from one another and by *leveling of the governed* in face of the governing and bureaucratically articulated group, which in its turn may occupy a quite autocratic position, both in fact and in form. (1968: 985)

## DISCONTINUITIES AND CONFLICTS

For Weber, the private/public dichotomy does not serve to fully incorporate the private sphere of values and will into the sphere of public rationality through either a harmonious functionalism or through a dialectical opposition. Rather, the division between the will of private individuals and the rationality of public order is mutually dependent and antagonistic. While the privatization of values and willful action develop along with the rationalization of the public sphere, their interdependence is as conflictual as it is pervasive. The realization of the private individual's value-oriented will depends on a rational, interdependent, and extensive social order. The partial incorporation in the individual of rational calculation along with the instrumentalizing of the public sphere as the location for the fulfillment of private projects are highly problematic contingencies of action. They generate discontinuities and conflicts within the rationalized spheres of society and within modern culture.

In the economic sphere, the rationalization of wants through money and the maximization of economic efficiency through managerial control of the labor process have the negative consequences of reducing the sphere of willful determination of workers in the design and control of their work. The absence of cooperation, substantive communication, and the heightening of dehumanized production generate income inequalities, class antagonisms, and sources of conflict both within the economy and politics. Moreover, the expropriation of workers from the means of production, while it may further technical and economic calculation, does not necessarily further legal rationality. Rational law is neutral toward the ownership of the means of production and the substantive patterns of association at the workplace as well as in private spheres of production. Indeed, the associated ownership of the means of production by workers may expand individual rights, combinations and contractual opportunities for private individuals. In contrast and partial opposition to economic rationality, workers' ownership of the means of production is minimally consistent with rational legality and, indeed, may lead to its expansion.

Just as there are internal contradictions in economic rationality and potential contradictions between economic and legal rationality, so there are internal contradictions within rational law. Weber points out, for example, that formal legality has the greatest affinity with high income groups that have the capacity to purchase legal talent and use the legal system for their own benefits. While legal rationality is logically autonomous from economic resources, in actuality it is much more likely to serve the substantive interests and private values of those who are financially well-off.[6] Moreover, lower-income classes are more likely to push for the democratization of law so that their own interests and values can be realized. Thus, the inequality that is generated by economic rationality undermines the formal equality of law, setting the stage for demands for democratic forms of justice. To the extent to which formal legality serves the private interests and values of economically dominant classes and suppresses the substantive demands for justice of low-income classes, it becomes enmeshed in conflicts that erode its autonomy from politics and from class-based social movements.

The effects of concentrated ownership of the means of production and market power on the universality of rational law are another source of conflict.[7] As ownership and market power become more concentrated, tendencies toward legal particularism are enhanced. Not only does the financial power of dominant enterprises serve to create opportunities for a vastly unequal distribution of legal expertise but the functional relations of dominant enterprises in the economy also set the stage for demands for particularistic laws on their behalf. Since it can be maintained, often with justification, that the maintenance and growth of dominant enterprises is necessary for the stability of the economy as a whole, these enterprises are in the position to make political and legal demands that smaller enterprises can neither plausibly argue for nor marshal the financial and political resources to sustain. Whether in the arenas of legislative, judicial, or administrative lawmaking, enterprises that have a measure of monopolistic power are able to secure benefits that enterprises in competitive relations cannot. Thus, economic concentration and market power provide an additional source for the erosion of rational law beyond the demands for democratic legality that is fostered by income and class inequality.

Compounding the discontinuities between private and public dimensions of social action in the economic and legal spheres are antagonistic relations between these spheres and bureaucratic organization. First, there are tensions generated between economic rationality and bureaucracy that result from their divergent principles (Bell, 1976: 291). Although both forms of rationality share instrumental orientations that are indifferent to ultimate values grounded in the experiences of individuals, they are based on alternative principles. Economic rationality is oriented toward the maximization of production and utilities in the face of scarce resources and unlimited wants. Bureaucratic rationality is oriented toward the control of outcomes through the expansion and rational organization of knowledge. To be sure, these divergent principles and patterns of action can and often do converge in the planning and implementation of technologies and in defining issues and problems to be solved both economically and with a maximum of knowledge and predictability of outcomes. Nonetheless, economizing the use of scarce resources may pose limits to the expenditures on expanding knowledge which, on strictly bureaucratic criteria, are not justifiable. Conversely, because the focus of bureaucratic attention can be determined by a multitude of values—whether related to religion, ecology, national security, health, education, race, gender, or justice—the bureaucratic organization of knowledge may be put to uses that oppose the economizing mode. While these conflicts are not basic contradictions, since bureaucracy rests on a money economy and expanded production just as economic rationality rests on the expansion of knowledge in the form of bureaucracy, there is nonetheless considerable latitude in conflicts that can follow from their divergent principles.

Bureaucracy and economic rationality are fundamentally different. Bureaucratic knowledge and organization are not bounded by principles of maximization of resource utilization in the face of scarcity while economic rationality limits the expansion of knowledge and constrains the scope of rational decision making to criteria of profitability. Similarity, legal rationality, based on strictures of legally relevant language and legally conceptualized facts, conflicts with the more pervasive spread of knowledge and more diverse construction of facts characteristic of bureaucracy.[8] Bureaucracy and law, lacking in internal principles of efficiency of resource allocation, may conflict with economic rationality. Yet legal expertise can be challenged by more substantive bureaucratic expertise, especially when the scope of law comes to include the realization of public policies beyond conflict resolution, contracts, and administrative law fostered by democratic pressure and corporate capitalism.

Without attempting to articulate the multiplicity of potential discontinuities and conflicts that flow from the triad of economic rationality, rational law, and bureaucracy, I have suggested their pervasiveness. Beyond these conflicts at the level of public rationality, there are deep tensions between the personal dimensions of the private sphere and rational public order that follow from Weber's theory.

Rationality is a type of legitimacy that links the activation of the private individual's will and the projection of a stable social order through the impersonality and anonymity of social relations. The individual is able to project the fulfillment of wants through money, security of social relations through contracts, and the mapping of a career precisely because social relations take on a logical, quantitative, and objective quality that is abstracted from personal and emotional realities. The individual's personal plans, material fulfillments and private initiatives rest on an abstract order: The world is filtered through instrumental, technical, and depersonalized norms that limit the recognition of self and others to partial constructs derived from the publicly institutionalized rationalities of economics, law, and bureaucratic organization. These rationalities provide discursive and institutional contexts for action and personal life. The formation and presentation of the public world of power and activity through rational categories generates a highly depersonalized context in which the willful capacities of the private individual are maximized.

In constructing a rationalized public world, people tend to become operationalized as resources, means, and population aggregates for the instrumental projects of political and economic bureaucracies. The definitions of these operational categories take the forms of employee, consumer, and citizen. There is, however, a disjuncture between the public purposes and organization of social action and their cognitive appropriation as individual means to realize personal, willfully chosen ends. The organizational power and direction of rationalized social order is but partially known to the private individual as consumer possibilities, career opportunities, and political preferences. The active relationship of the individual to the public order is manifested as a detached functional position that contributes in more or less unknown ways to a more total process. Yet these positions are privately significant because they partially constitute the individual's resources for personal self-determination. A technically necessary public sphere becomes the condition for individual freedom and subjectivity; The condition for active private freedom is a public sphere that the individual can neither personally nor collectively control.

Antagonisms and conflicts among diverse sectors of rationalized society are central to Weber's analytic framework. Beyond these antagonisms among public rationalities, however, Weber formulates a deeper opposition between public and private aspects of action: The concentration and expansion of rationalized power and the isolation and entrapment of the private individual in an increasingly self-referential subjectivity. Indeed, this dilemma is the source of Weber's sense of irony and fatalism about modernity. The image of modernity as a "cage" that takes on the character of unreflected constraint, so central to Weber's pessimism, is based on the realization that rationalization channels the will and activity of the private individual in ways that undermine the scope and force of private values (1958: 182).

In the rationalized public sphere, the orientations and activities of the individual are channeled by the functional demands of position along lines of certified competence, codified procedure, and anonymity (Berger, et al., 1974: 41–62). In the public sphere of work, the range of activity is limited overwhelmingly by the authority of the rational order rather than by the individual's value commitments. Departures from rational and organized boundaries that are directed toward personalizing relations are evidence of public corruption and impermissible uses of official positions.

Beyond channeling action orientations, the very cognitive structure of the individual is shaped along rational lines that increasingly depersonalize the world and restrict the sphere of private values to the farther reaches of subjectivity. The taken-for-granted cognitive features of orderliness, based on the rational organization of the world, are patterned along lines of predictability of outcomes rather than judgments about personally held values. These rational cognitive constraints are accompanied by the control of emotional states, in itself a feature of rational authority relations. Expectations regarding the passivity of clients, patients, students, workers, and other categories of actors subject to bureaucratic action conform to the discourses of organizational hierarchies that process them.

Yet, because of the conflictual nature of the social world and the disjuncture between action and consequences, the stability of the private/public dichotomy is always precarious. Private life rests on the maintenance of public rationalities that promise to secure arenas where expectations can be calculated and personal identity depends on the maintenance of abstract, impersonal frameworks buttressed by economic expansion and progressive technical control. When these relations that support private life and personal identity are disrupted, questions are raised about their economic, legal, and political sources. Every crisis puts the rational grounds of social life into question and, with this, the maintenance of the public/private dichotomy. The power of a rationalized public world that makes the private individual autonomous and self-referential also serves to call its own fundamental principles into question. The very strengths of a self-positing private individualism and a self-positing rational public order turn into weaknesses in the face of crises.

Charismatic authority and traditionalism, which are the main alternatives to legal rationality, serve to overcome these strains and crisis tendencies by transforming the private/public dichotomy and by reducing the range of self-positing orientations. Charisma radicalizes the private/public dichotomy by emphasizing the person of the charismatic leader (Sica, 1988). Charisma marshals the private sentiments of followers in collective efforts to forge a new ethical community based on conversion and personal renewal. At the same time, the affirmation of the charismatic leader displaces private will and rational principles of public organization, thereby undercutting the sources of a self-positing private individualism and legal rational social order. Traditionalism, which Weber viewed as the most stable form of social action and social order, reintegrates the individual in household and kinship relations. It fuses public authority with the person of the incumbent, usually through principles of heredity and through narrative justifications. The force of the past, in narratives and religious legitimations, provide external sources of social legitimacy that displace self-positing rationality. Whatever their differences, charisma and tradition reorient the private/public dichotomy, undermining the rational grounds of social order and individualized privatism.

Even though Weber viewed the formation of the private/public dichotomy as central to the rational transformation of society, he recognized that it had more to do with the elaboration of power than with truth. Its historical contingency rested, in part, on its inherent discontinuities. Because of his analytic openness and disavowal of progress, his writings raise dimensions of the public/private dichotomy that are profoundly problematic for social action, individual integrity, and historical development. The private/public dichotomy, as a core Weberian concept, has its greatest analytic force when its internal conflicts are most fully exposed and its contingent character most fully affirmed.

## NOTES

1. This approach is quite independent from the problem of rationality in everyday life posed by Harold Garfinkle (1967) or critiques of ideology rooted in practice (Smith, 1974). It is also independent of analyses of law as ideology in Weber's writings (Albrow, 1975; Beirne, 1979). Rather, it is rooted in the limits to rationality posed by Weber's method of analysis and concept formation.

2. This is similar to Harry Braverman's analysis of the separation of management from labor and the homogenization of labor through instrumental rationality is striking (1974). Yet Braverman opposed his analysis of "power, of class antagonism" to the "Weberian system of bureaucratic rationality" (1974: 145). Weber was, of course, analyzing power because he understood rationality as a form of legitimate domination, itself a form of power. Weber's categories of rationality are not descriptive; rather, their analytic direction is shaped by the problem of power.

3. In developing the ideal type of rational law, Weber proceeded from the following five postulates:

> First, that every concrete legal decision be the "application" of an abstract legal proposition to a concrete "fact situation"; second, that it must be possible in every concrete case to derive the decision from an abstract legal proposition by means of legal logic; third, that the law must actually or virtually constitute a "gapless" system of legal propositions, or must, at least, be treated as if it were such a gapless system; fourth, that whatever cannot be "construed" legally in rational terms is also legally irrelevant; and fifth, that every social action of human beings must always be visualized as either an "application" or "execution" of legal propositions, or as an "infringement" thereof. (1954: 64)

4. By contrast, common law accumulates cases that are associated through comparative meanings that are largely external to the rational principles of law. While comparability based on precedence allows for continuity and stable

outcomes as features of common law, there is a relative absence of articulated general principles along with a heightened authority of the judge. Decisions, while they may be backed or supported by reasons grounded in precedent, take the form of pronouncements made by judges. Both the character of facts and the form of decision making do not rely on logical consistency of meaning as is the case in strict formal rationality.

5. In some respects, despite its coercive character, the state is such an association in that individual citizens are partially distanced from state decisions and obligations while the state can enter into contractual obligations based, in part, on the individual's membership as a citizen.

6. Michael Walzer (1983: 100) argues for a "complex" theory of equality that separates income and wealth from public forums of criminal justice. This is supported by Weber's divergent principles of rationality. On the other hand, Jerold Auerbach demonstrates that there is a rich history of elites preferring private forums for dispute settlement to prevent information and secrets from going public (1983).

7. See, for example, Joyce Rothchild-Whitt on economic discontinuities between managers and workers that lead to legal patterns of worker ownership (1984). Also valuable on the confluence of economic rationality and legal rationality in the context of the development of labor law and the labor movement are Robin Stryker (1989) and Michael Wallace, et al. (1989).

8. Another split is between the bureaucratic handling of claims and the need to legitimate those claims on other than organizational criteria. See, for example, Jerry Mashaw's study of the management of social security disability claims (1983).

# PART IV

## TALCOTT PARSONS

# CHAPTER 10

## Socializing the Public/Private Division in Action Theory

Formative critical approaches to Talcott Parsons's writings have viewed them as symptomatic of tendencies toward oversocializing the private individual in directions that erode individual autonomy, absorb the individual into social processes that severely restrict self-determination, and favor the growth of mechanisms of social control rooted in professionalized bureaucratic administration and technical knowledge (Mills, 1956; Lockwood, 1956; Gouldner, 1970). These criticisms are heightened by efforts that demonstrate inconsistencies in Parsons' theory as a whole (Savage, 1981) along with charges of faulty interpretation of the classical social theories on which it is grounded (Pope, 1973; Pope, Cohen, and Hazelrigg, 1975). From these criticisms, it appears that Parsons forced concepts into a preconceived social totality, making the private sphere a resource for fulfilling society's collective requirements and goal attainment. Parsonsian theory represents the total collapse of the public/private distinction into a totalizing sociologism and social metabolism.

To be sure, reconstructing Parsonsian theory through the public/private distinction generally supports the view that Parsons conceptualized relations between the public and private sphere in a rigorous sociologism: The preeminence of society over the individual is accomplished in large part through the expansion of public discourses and institutionalized action that remake the individual and the private sphere in conformity with societal imperatives. Yet locating Parsonsian theory in the public/private framework also provides grounds for a renewed appreciation of it.

Talcott Parsons reconceptualizes a wide variety of theoretical approaches to the public/private distinction in an overarching synthesis that maximizes their social and relational content. In large part, his theory is a culmination of earlier conceptualizations of the sources of the public/private distinction, its transformation through processes of social development, and its importance for the constitution of society.[1] The subtlety and intricate conceptual relations provided by Parsons are grounds for more fully understanding and appropriating the sociological formulation of the public/private distinction for critical inquiry.

My reworking of Parsons's theory argues that the transformation of the public/private distinction is pivotal for theorizing society as an interrelated system of social action that maintains itself and enhances its capacities in the face of internal and environmental contingencies. Formulating social action in terms of society's survival and development weakens the distinction between public and private spheres of action by unifying their contents through ever-denser social relations. The public/private distinction is elaborated through social processes that dissociate and recombine action elements from the hierarchically integrative requirements of societal maintenance and development. Elements of societal action move across public and private categories, including the elements that distinguish between aspects of the private individual and aspects of the individual as a participant in institutional processes. Moreover, the overall direction of the public/private transformation is toward enhancing the formation of societal goals and the growth and mobility of societal resources. A highly elaborated analytic framework is established that partially reconstitutes the private sphere as a source of action and identity. The dynamic underlying the framework revolves around how society's action elements undergo internal change and transformations in their public/private relations under conditions of systemic pressures toward adaptation.

This chapter focuses on *The Structure of Social Action*, centering Parsons's early concerns with social action around the public/private distinction. In *The Structure of Social Action*, Parsons reconstituted general categories and particular concepts of earlier theorists by transforming the public/private distinction of classical liberalism and utilitarianism into a social discourse that emphasizes the social sources of action and indeterminacy. Especially important is his critical appropriation of Emile Durkheim and Max Weber, along with Alfred Marshall and Vilfredo Pareto, into an overarching theory of action. Their concepts are reshaped to heighten the socially emergent nature of values, the dissolution and the incorporation of the individual as an element of action. The individual is an element of action that includes social values and socially organized means of action that go beyond the requisites of economic rationality, technical efficiency, and positivist determinations. The systemic and voluntaristic character of the social order preclude the formulation of the public sphere as a realm of strict causal necessity. Rearranging features of the liberal private sphere across the more socialized public/private division has the consequences of weakening the tensions between public and private spheres while leaving the remnants of private individualism undersocialized.

*The Structure of Social Action* is the beginning point of an ever more elaborated socialization of the public/private division. Here Parsons was concerned with developing a sociological theory that reduced neither the values that people pursue to their social conditions nor to the intentions of private individuals. He maintained that reductionism in either direction undercuts the autonomy of action, characterized by capacities to shape novel alternatives in the face of given conditions. Reductionism would result either in a form of sociological determinism or biological determinism. In addition to constituting an inadequate analytic framework, such reductionism would severely restrict the formation of knowledge and, hence, the scope of the possibilities of collective action.

In rejecting approaches that would result either in sociologism or biologism, Parsons focused on the commonalities of a plurality of actors mutually oriented to each others' action. Since such commonalities could not in any ultimate sense be derived from purely social or biological determinants, Parsons centers on the integrative role played by publicly shared values. Thus, he defines sociology in *The Structure of Social Action* as "the science which attempts to develop an analytical theory of social action systems in so far as these systems can be understood in terms of the property of common-value integration" (1937: II, 768).

In keeping with his concern with the commonalities of social action, Parsons takes neither the private individual nor established public order as primary concepts of sociological theory. Rather, the simplest and fundamental concept for Parsons is the unit act. The unit act provides a focus for relating the means and ends of action that is both analytically abstract yet adequate for explanatory purposes in much the same way that supply and demand encompass economic action (Bierstedt, 1981: 403). By centering on the unit act, analysis is focused through a concept that relates public and private elements to one another at the most basic level of action. Public and private dimensions get their analytic significance from their relations in realizing the common values that shape action rather than any essential differences they may have due to their respective internal relations.

Central to conceptualizing the features of the unit act and the action frame of reference is the distinction between rational action and social action (Sciulli, 1986). While rational action is oriented toward the most efficient means of realizing a given end, social action involves more than technical criteria. The defining feature of social action is the mutual orientations of a plurality of actors to one another's action through common values; hence, the integration of ends and the normative relation among means and ends has the highest analytic primacy. Given the importance of integration for social action, all aspects of the unit act must in one way or another be subsumed under the normative relation of means to ends. This includes such apparently privatized features of social action as individual subjectivity, the individual body, and subjective choices.

The unit act is made up of four components or dimensions: (1) an actor, (2) an end, (3) a situation, and (4) a normative orientation. While under purely rational action, efficiency could serve as the sole criteria for realizing a given end under specified situated conditions involving environmental contingencies and available means, the issue is more complex under conditions of social action. Most importantly, conceptualizing the individual actor as an element of action rearranges privatized aspects of the individual through categories of the unit act. This changes the location of elements of action across the dividing line between the private individual and the public spheres of knowledge, norms, and values.

First, in locating the individual actor in the act, some aspects of the actor are located as internal properties of the individual through which a private sphere is realized while other aspects are located in the external situation of action. For Parsons, "the actor is not an organism but an 'ego' or 'self.' The principle importance of this consideration is that the body of the actor forms, for him, just as much part of the situation of action as does the 'external environment' " (1937: I, 46–47). Within the context of the unit act and, therefore, social action generally, the body is conceptualized through its external aspect as "powers" or means to realize anticipated states of affairs or as conditions that are beyond the actor's capacities of control in much the same way as the physical environment and the biological organism. The self or ego is cognitively dissociated from the individual's body.[2] The body, in effect, is part of the publicly available and rationally knowable reality that has an analytic independence from the ends and values that give direction to social action.

Second, the category of choice takes on greater societal significance and determinacy. A fundamental characteristic of action is that the actor faces choices with regard to means and ends within the context of normative orientations. Choice is located in the public/private duality: It is both an objective, indeed, definitive aspect of social action and a privately determined experience of the acting individual.

Although choice is a feature of the private and subjective experience of action, its objective significance and analytic import are formulated from the standpoint of the scientific observer. This gives the category of choice its scientific/public character, allowing for distinctions between nonrational sources of social action based on shared values and irrational sources of action. Action requires "the *difference* between the anticipated future state of affairs and that which it could have been predicted would ensue from the initial situation *without the agency of the actor having intervened*" (1937: I, 49). This difference may be based on the value element in action through which choice is constituted and/or it may be based on "error," that is, "the failure to attain ends or to make the 'right' choice of means" (1937: I, 46). Whatever the experiential and private significance of choice, it is a central category for Parsons's scientific theory of action that enables the observable and publicly demonstrable distinction between the role of values in social action and error. Choice is not merely a matter of private preference but, rather, from the viewpoint of social theory, a basic aspect of social action that signifies the capacity of the actor to have effects on the world that are independent of situational contingencies and errors in the selection of means for realizing ends.

As the use of the category of choice suggests, the concept of the unit act and the reformulation of the individual across the public/private division have both critical and positive analytic dimensions. On the one hand, Parsons uses aspects of the unit act to argue that individualistic, positivistic, and utilitarian theories cannot adequately account for social order or the complexities of social action. As we have seen, part of this critique revolves around the reductionism of positivistic theories that limit action to its conditions and undermine the independent effects of the actor by privatizing ends and normative orientations. Grounded solely in public norms of efficiency based on scientific notions of causality, departures in action from strict logics of efficiency between means and ends are viewed either as personal errors by private, atomized individuals acting on purely subjective motives or as random variations reducible to publicly knowable biological or sociological factors. From these approaches, the very legitimacy of social action as an objective reality is undermined.

More positively, an adequate theory of action must account for the issues that it finds wanting in utilitarianism and positivism. Most importantly, a theoretically adequate explanation of the sources of ends and norms must be articulated that both overcomes the randomness of ends and that locates norms in a framework that goes beyond privatized rationality and the logic of technical efficiency. Without reducing action to either the personalism of the private individual or the public determination of narrow scientific causality, an adequate theory of action must develop a framework for irreducible aspects of action that allow for choice on the part of the actor.

Parsons develops the "voluntarisitic theory of action" as the positive solution to this challenge (Sciulli, 1986). In his reconstruction of sociological theory, Parsons develops the idea that the integration of ends is only possible "if there is some higher form of existence of ends towards which the separate ends of action can be directed" (Savage, 1981: 108). Parsons critically incorporates a range of theoretical approaches in formulating nondeterministic sources of integration. He locates these sources of integration first in economic practices, then in the organization of social activity and then, most definitively, in the sphere of values that constitutes a society's morality and culture. Voluntaristic action is grounded "in aspects of social life that must remain both worldly and qualitative" (Sciulli, 1986: 747). In opposition to notions, on the one hand, of privatized free will and autonomy limited to individuated goal formation and, on the other hand, publicly demonstrable empiricist accounts of values based on observation and quantification, voluntarism accounts for shared and realizable values that define social action in opposition to simple standards of efficiency, coercion, and otherworldly beliefs.

The nondeterministic core of this approach indicates both the importance of the interpretation of the meaning of values at the expense of strict causal explanation as well as the centrality that the critique of positivism has for the substantive direction of Parsons's theory. Yet a major problem in Parsons's formulation is the distance of nondetermination from actual situations of action. By deprivatizing sources of value nondeterminacy at levels higher than the individual, values become overly abstracted from the social contexts of action. While the movement away from positivism enhances the notion of freedom, it does so at the level of culture and emergent values rather than at the practical level of social relations or the private individual. By locating the nondeterministic features of action at the highest levels of symbolism, the public sphere is rendered impersonal. At the same time, the private sphere becomes a realm of motivational resources and directed energies or effort. The constitution of values in arenas of public discourse becomes increasingly distanced from situations of action in which the elements of private individualism are distributed across society/individual boundaries.

In formulating the concept of voluntaristic action, Parsons interprets writings of Marshall, Pareto, Durkheim, and Weber in ways that support this distancing of nondeterminism. He accomplishes this, in part, by reconstructing the elements of each of these theoretical approaches at higher levels of abstraction, moving the principles of nondeterminism in each of the approaches to the level of abstract values and culture. The overall tendency is for nondeterministic features of action to be located at higher levels of complexity in the constitution of the socialized public sphere while individualized privatism is rendered into a motivational aspect of action.

In attacking both the utilitarian notion that ends are random and the positivistic view that ends are reducible to pure natural conditions, Parsons reconstructs Alfred Marshall's writings to show that his economic theory was developing a perspective through which wants are viewed as conditioned by economic activities. Marshall pointed out there are wants that are similar to biological needs. More importantly, he argued there are wants that increase the efficiency and productivity of labor; these wants are socially created through everyday economic activity (1937: I, 167–73). Through the satisfaction of these socially created wants, the productive capacity of labor increases. In addition to these nonbiological but natural wants, there are also wants that "appear to be wholly arbitrary, mere whims with no foundation in life" (1937: I, 140). These wants, while socially conditioned, are not socially determined. Although Parsons views Marshall as lacking a full-blown analysis of the role of values in shaping wants, he nonetheless sees Marshall as contributing to the voluntaristic theory of action because he locates the aims of life in the ends of socially generated economic activities. Because neither biologically induced wants nor the whims of private individuals are decisive for economic development, the public sphere of everyday economic activity is central in shaping the wants that direct and motivate action.

Several additional points regarding Marshall merit comment here. First, because Parsons views Marshall as laying such great stress on the role of wants in fulfilling and expanding economic activities, he considers Marshall as moving away at least partially from hedonistic utilitarianism that focused solely on remuneration as the source of efficient labor. Rather than efficiency being motivated by wages that provide for privatized satisfactions, Marshall emphasizes the adjustment of wants to productive relations within a general process of economic development. The satisfaction of wants maintains and enhances efficiency in specific economic activities. Want satisfaction facilitates the social process of production. For this reason, it is opposed to individualized, privatized enjoyment through wages as a motivation for labor. Second, to the extent that economic activities are the source of ends and wants, efficiency is a type of public rationality that has normative features. Efficiency is itself embedded in social relations of production that generate shared patterns of wants and satisfactions. It has sources that go beyond the individual's hedonistic impulses and is a value that emerges from what actors do collectively. Finally, since Marshall views a private, competitive economy as the framework through which economic activities most fully evolve, the evolution of free enterprise is a condition for the spread of public rationality as opposed to private pleasure seeking and hedonistic ends. This lends a dimension of social organization to the social sources of want creation, satisfaction, and efficiency. By viewing ends and wants as forming through social action, Parsons is able to claim a nondeterministic and nonprivatized element in Marshall's economic theory that contributes to the voluntaristic theory of action.

Parsons is also clear about the limits of Marshall's contribution to the voluntaristic theory of action. For one thing, Marshall's commitment to the rationality of efficiency blocks out the role of other norms and higher values in social action. His vision of linear evolution is tied to the disciplinary constraints of economics that stress empiricism and, consequently, relatively undertheorized conceptual schemes such as supply and demand (1937: I, 171). Indeed, Marshall raises the concept of activities primarily because of the inability of utilitarian theory to explain behaviors involving the price mechanism. Because Marshall was concerned with practical economics, his view of action lacks a place for noneconomic values central to a voluntaristic theory of action.

It is in this light that Parsons considers writings of Vilfredo Pareto. In his assessment of Pareto, Parsons finds much that is congenial to the voluntaristic theory of action. As a critic of enlightenment thinking and of the belief in progress, Pareto eschews ideas of linear evolution and rationality. His vision is one that sees increasing limits to the autonomy of private individualism and rational public order. Instead, the future for Pareto is to be characterized by increasing constraints on the individual, a revival of faith, and greater reliance on force for social cohesion (1937: I, 179). While Pareto valued science and rationality, he was concerned with pointing out its limits for social action and social order. Perhaps most importantly for Parsons's purposes, he laid great stress on the subjective and nonreducible character of nonrational action in shaping social order.

Pareto formulates action in its logical and nonlogical character. This formulation is an advance for the voluntaristic theory of action over Marshall because it provides nonrational grounds for action beyond the rational grounds of economic efficiency. Sources of nondeterminacy, moreover, are introduced at higher levels of abstraction and historical generality.

In conceptualizing logical action, Pareto stressed the way in which means are logically tied to the realization of ends and to the empirical knowledge that supports this cognitive relationship. As in economic action, which is an exemplar of logical action, the relationship between means and ends is both subjectively known by the actor and, even more extensively, by the scientific observer (1937: I, 187). Since the actor's rationality is formulated by combining objective criteria and subjective knowledge, the actor is viewed as an element in action rather than an agent that autonomously determines action. Parsons's reconstruction of logical action supports the diffusion of action elements from the actor to the situation of action. More importantly, it delimits a range of action that roughly corresponds to economic action and, by exclusion, it establishes a residual category of nonrational action that is both the focus of Pareto's analysis and a departure for the voluntaristic theory of action.

At its most inclusive level, Parsons takes action for Pareto "to designate the total complex of concrete phenomena comprising the life of human beings in society in relation to each other, seen from the objective and the subjective points of view combined" (1937: I, 192). Beyond logical action that is the result of a process of reasoning, there is a category of action that is based primarily on sentiment and unconscious elements. This category of action encompasses moral, religious, and other nonempirically based theories. These elements of nonlogical action cannot be known through strictly scientific means but, rather, through their manifestations and the theories associated with them. While these theories are nonscientific, they can be at least partially analyzed by focusing on their major component elements, that is, "residues" that are the "constant element of such theories" and "derivations" that are "the variable elements" (1937: I, 201).

Parsons takes pains to demonstrate that the "nonscientific" theoretical grounds of "nonlogical" action are distinguishable from ignorance and error, the "unscientific" elements of positivism. Indeed, these features of Pareto's analysis support Parsons' distinction between nonrational and irrational action. The sources of nonlogical action are diverse. They may be based on privatized sentiment that can be scientifically reduced to features of heredity or the environment. In addition, collective sources of nonlogical action are neither scientific nor reducible. Rather than being error, ignorance, or irrational sources of action that follow from instinct, they are those justifications of action and the ideas that link means to the realization of action that cannot be verified through strict scientific logic or empirical methods (1937: I, 204–5). Although derivations, as the variable element in nonlogical action, may be characterized by error and ambiguity, residues constitute principles of nonlogical action and have higher degrees of consistency. They organize the ends of action, providing the normative grounds of action on other than a rational, scientific basis.

For Parsons, residues have important implications for establishing a theory of social action that cuts across the utilitarian liberal public/private distinction. They are irreducible subjective elements of action in Pareto's analysis that are both nonrational and nonprivatized. More specifically, residues organize action through procedures that involve the interpenetration of symbols and their meaning rather than through positivist categories of cause and effect. Beyond their normative and interpretive features of nonlogical action, they are nonprivativistic since they are shared features of action and have objective manifestations and consequences for action, as in the case of collective rituals. Moreover, these shared subjective elements of action may combine with logical action so that, in effect, they may become partially rationalized. Thus, these subjective, public, and nonreducible elements of action are pervasive aspects of action in general.

Beyond incorporating Pareto's conception of nonlogical action into an emergent voluntaristic theory of action, Parsons reformulates Pareto's theory along holistic lines by tying the integrative elements of social action to Pareto's concept of collective utilities. He links means-ends relationships and the integration of means and conditions through ultimate ends to Pareto's view that there are collective utilities that supercede individual utilities. Social action becomes the analytic framework for realizing collective utilities that are ordered through common values conditioned by the structure of social action itself. Since "the utility *of* a collectivity cannot be interpreted without conceiving the action system of a society as culminating in a common system of ultimate ends," the predominance of the social over the individual elements of action is axiomatic (1937: I, 267). Moreover, ultimate ends are nonlogical categories since they are both nonempirical and are not subject to falsification. At this level of abstract theory, social action is integrated through publicly expressed ultimate ends. These socially rooted and publicly expressed ultimate ends incorporate individuals in action beyond calculations of private interest or privatized derivative value commitments.

At a more empirical level of analysis, Parsons focuses on force and conflict as decisive in Pareto's views on social change. Elites tend to be divided into "foxes" and "lions" (1937: I, 284). Foxes are speculators whose propensity is toward caution in social affairs, a combination of disparate interests, and skepticism. Lions, on the other hand, tend to be rentiers whose propensities are toward decisive action, single interests, and faith. Foxes typically exercise power through manipulation and fraud; they are loathe to use direct force because of their multiple interests and their sensitivity to sacrifice and costs. Lions try "to make others conform to the standards demanded by faith by whatever means are available. Force is the ultimate means when all others fail" (1937: I, 289). In the cyclical view of history, lions are the initiators of civilization while foxes dominate toward the end of the process.

These features of Pareto's theory provide Parsons with further grounds for the critique of liberal visions of progress and linear evolution. If changes in social order are demonstrably cyclical, the vision of a public order based on linear, incremental, progressive change characteristic of empiricism and positivism is clearly inadequate. Moreover, the tying of force to nonrational action as decisive for establishing public order undercuts attempts to explain public order primarily on rational, deterministic principles. Indeed, the capacity to act on nonrational beliefs—even to the point of using force—is fundamental for establishing public order and social integration. In the face of collective capacities for realizing nonrational commitments, egoism and private interests are as fragmented as they are ineffectual.

The reconstructions of Marshall and Pareto provide grounds for weakening the public/private boundaries in Parsons's voluntaristic theory of action. The approaches of these theorists demonstrate the preponderance of social elements of action over the private individual and the participation of the individual in action frameworks that are integrated by shared nondeterministic and nonrational commitments. As we see, his interpretations of Durkheim and Weber are of even greater significance for socializing the public/private division.

Parsons's discussion of Durkheim focuses on several key themes. First, he focuses on the role of moral constraint in shaping individual action (1937: I, 383). Based on a reconstruction of Durkheim's analysis of the causes of the division of labor, suicide, and methodology, Parsons maintains that Durkheim moved from physicial and biological causation to social causation and, ultimately, to the effects that collective representations have on shaping individuals engaged in social action. From this vantage point, Durkheim's writings support the position that social action rests on moral values that are independent of both the individual and material causation. Second, in considering Durkheim's views on socialism, corporate groups, and religious rituals, Parsons emphasizes the notion that normative constraints emerge from the patterns of association established by a plurality of actors. Moreover, the ordering of ends is viewed as a socially emergent phenomenon that shapes action through shared norms. Finally, Parsons emphasizes Durkheim's critique and paradigmatic alternative to writers such as Herbert Spencer who are associated with individualistic positivism. By emphasizing the collective over the individual and the role of moral norms over private interests, Durkheim is seen as a main contributor to the voluntaristic theory of action.

While Parsons's reconstruction of Durkheim emphasizes the individual's location in social institutions and the compulsion of socially rooted norms, there is also a critical edge to his discussion that is equally significant. On the one hand, Parsons emphasizes the importance of moral obligation in Durkheim's theory. On the other hand, he characterizes Durkheim as a positivist who overly stresses the sociological determination of collective representations such as moral norms and religious symbols. Because Durkheim "never explicitly or in any way consciously abandoned his positivistic position," his theory does not allow for "elements of reality not susceptible of empirical scientific treatment from the points of view of both the observer and the actor" (1937: I, 426). At both a methodological level and at the substantive level of morality, Durkheim severely restricts the autonomy of values and the interpretive accomplishment of social reality. This overly deterministic and, ultimately, reductionist stance denies the role of nonempirical aspects of reality in shaping social action. For example, regarding Durkheim's analysis of religion, Parsons states that

> it is not possible to agree with Durkheim's view that the ultimate "reality" in general symbolized in religious ideas is the reality "society" taken either as a concrete entity or as a factor in the latter. What is true is, rather, that it is in terms of what we call religious ideas that men attempt a cognitive apprehension of the non-empirical aspects of reality to which they are actively related. (1937: I, 425)

To remain consistent with his view that the shared pattern of values through which social action systems are integrated have nonempirical and nonrational elements, Parsons is lead to reject some of Durkheim's central methodological tenets. He rejects Durkheim's view that sociology can play a critical and policy-oriented role in the formation of publicly symbolized morality and the private motives of individuals precisely because of the ultimate reference that public symbols have to social organization. Thus, in his appropriation of Durkheim, Parsons accepts the importance of the force of social morality in public life and at the level of the private individual while rejecting the, at least, potential determinism of social morality.

Yet Parsons sees an important shift in Durkheim's theory of religion toward an approach that stresses the autonomous role of ideas in action. By focusing on the active side of Durkheim's theories, Parsons maintains that religion provides symbolism through which the collective actions of public rituals serve to stimulate "solidarity and energy of action" (1937: I, 467). In effect, by stressing the interpenetrations among the symbolism of religious values and public activities that affirm the normative grounds of social order, values have autonomous effects that Durkheim recognizes but that cannot be accounted for on the basis of his lingering positivist concern with determinism and causal explanation.

Based on these considerations, Parsons affirms Durkheim's contribution to the voluntaristic theory of action. The actor is located in collective actions grounded in ultimate values in a virtually all-encompassing nonrational public sphere. The inner motivations of the actor are tied to communal solidarity rather than privatized dissociation.

The affirmation of a nonrational public sphere and the normative limitations on private individualism led Parsons to give primacy to Durkheim's moral idealism over his positivistic methodology. His reconstruction of Weber follows a different path. Since Parsons locates Weber in the tradition of German idealism, the independence of ideas from purely material factors can be unequivocally affirmed. Parsons can justifiably state that "Weber came quite decisively to the view that an indispensable (though by no means the only) element in the explanation of the system lay in a system of ultimate values and value attitudes, in turn anchored in and in part dependent upon a definite metaphysical system of ideas" (1937: II, 510). This view is buttressed by a discussion of religious ethics and, most prominently, the consequences of the Protestant ethic for the mental attitudes associated with capitalist economic activities. That the religious ideas and attitudes associated with protestantism support a spirit of capitalism that is not directly derivable from material factors demonstrates the independent consequences of values on social and economic development.

In addition to Weber's analysis of the role of religious values for economic development, Parsons views Weber's formulation of social action and, most importantly, the stress laid on the subjective aspect of action as contributing to a version of science that goes beyond the observation of external uniformities. That social science is grounded in the recognition that shared meanings are a condition of action and that these meanings are not reducible to external conditions serves to underscore the interpretive character of social science as well as the implausibility of positivist approaches.

These key features of Weberian theory, especially the interlacing of collective ideals in the formation of the actor, support the voluntaristic theory of action. Yet there are aspects of Weber's approach that are at odds with Parsons' analytic concerns. These differences, which raise problems for incorporating Weberian theory into the voluntaristic theory of action, hinge around the divergent approaches that Weber and Parsons take toward the relationship between facts and values and their sources and locations in the public/private division.

In his effort to incorporate Weber's theory, Parsons shifts the emphasis of Weber's fact/value dichotomy from their differential sources in science and existential commitments to a discourse that stresses a more continuous relationship between facts and values as elements of action integrated in social action. The dichotomous terms of public/private discourse characteristic of Weber shifts to a discourse that stresses the continuity of public and private elements of action. While for Weber, the core of private value commitments rests on extrasocial sources in the private sphere, Parsons seeks to maximize the social and collective character of values. He accomplishes this by, on the one hand, arguing that the divergence that Weber is concerned with is not as strong as Weber maintains, and, on the other hand, by comingling these divergent categories in a way that gives predominance to the more collective, publicly knowable, logically demonstrable, and more universal elements over the more individual, privately affirmed, habitual, and particularistic elements. Most centrally, he elevates the theoretical discourse on social action, which includes nondeterministic and nonrational categories, to a dominant discourse that analytically integrates concepts across the fact/value and public/private division.

Several key examples may serve to demonstrate this: First, Parsons maintains that the distinction between scientific rationality and values for social action is not as sharp as Weber takes them to be. He argues that instrumental and value interests characterize natural science as much as social science and, moreover, instrumental interests derived from scientific rationality may predominate value interests for both social action and the individual. Indeed, certain religious values stress that God can be known through His works and, thereby, focus on a knowledge of the physical world (1937: II, 595–96). Secondly, Parsons maintains that, at least insofar as theory is concerned, there is a tendency for sciences to become logically closed systems that yield an "integration of instrumental and value interests" (1937: II, 597). Ultimately, the comingling of values and instrumental orientations in a logically closed system tends to lead to the predominance of the theoretical system itself for the formation of cognitive interests. Finally, the logical closure of scientific theory incorporating instrumental and value elements is consequential for the analysis of social action since scientific methods and knowledge are themselves comingled with the analysis of action: "Thus the two are elements of the same fundamental complex; a knowledge of action and its elements is indispensable to ground the methodology of science and, vice versa, scientific knowledge is itself indispensable to the analysis of action" (1937: II, 600).

Parsons strives to overcome the categorical conflict that Weber posits between scientific rationality and values by relating them through the voluntaristic theory of action. Since scientific knowledge and a knowledge of action presuppose one another, and since both have nonrational value elements incorporated in them, there is justification for locating nonrational elements, including values, within public spheres such as science over their privatized sources in individual experience. Parsons also seeks to overcome Weber's views on the irrationality of values by an appeal to science. Here, however, the argument is factual rather than theoretical. As we pointed out in our discussion of Weber, the plurality of values is not an empirical issue for Weber but, rather, grounded in his version of radical individualism and existentialist values. In reconstructing this issue, Parsons counterposes Weber's theoretical approach with the fruits of his historical research:

> It is one of Weber's basic theorems that while there is a plurality of possible value systems, their number is, in fact, limited. From this it follows that on Weber's own principles there is a limited number of possible constructions of historical individuals from the same concrete objects of experience, on the one hand, and of systems of theoretical concepts, on the other. From this it follows further that there is in principle a finite totality of humanly possible scientific knowledge. (1937: II, 601)

While there may be an infinite and, therefore, unknowable number of ultimate values rooted in the existential experiences of individuals, there is a limited plurality of value systems through which history, science, and social action can be constituted. Moreover, Parsons's stance is consistent with his view that analytical concepts are real, that is, they are necessary features of social action that go beyond Weber's view that concepts are ideal fictions. Parsons's adherence to the nonrationality of values as an aspect of social action enables him to expand values to the public sphere of scientific discourse, in comparison to Weber's more privatized view of ultimate values that relies on their sources in the individual's subjective experience.[3]

Much of Parsons's consideration of Weber culminates with his interpretation of legitimacy. Parsons emphasizes the notion that legitimacy is, first and foremost, a property of an order (1937: II, 652) rather than a feature of privatized belief. Legitimacy is, analytically, a system of organized norms that structures the relationships between means and ends and that coordinates unit acts. While actors may differ in their attitudes toward legitimate norms from taking them as instrumental conditions to affirming them as moral obligations, there is an independence that legitimacy has from such individual attitudes because legitimacy is characteristic of a structure of action rather than separable individual orientations. To be sure, legitimacy is most fully fulfilled "for one who holds an order to be legitimate, living up to its rules becomes, to this extent, a matter of moral obligation" (1937: II, 661). Indeed, Parsons virtually equates Weber's concept of legitimacy with Durkheim's concept of moral obligation (1937: II, 652). In this light, Parsons incorporates Weber's theory in a way that accentuates the role of public values associated with institutional processes over methodological and private individualism.

## NOTES

1. As François Bourricaud has pointed out, Parsons's theory sought "to establish itself in relation to a catalog of authors and problems—in short, in relation to a tradition" (1981: 2.) See Paul Colomy's analysis of how the functionalist approach associated with Parsons has undergone revisions as a result of criticisms (1986).

2. R. Stephen Warner has argued that Parsons, in *The Structure of Social Action*, overemphasizes the importance of norms and values in social action while minimizing the importance of interests and cognitive elements (1978: 1317–49).

3. At other levels of theory, Parsons reformulates Weber's typology of social action and historical individuals in a more unified and systematic direction. While Weber is concerned with the problem of rationality primarily through comparative studies, Parsons maintains that specific concepts and empirical studies developed by Weber are most coherent in an explicit theory of rationality. By emphasizing the theoretical over the particulars of empirical research, Parsons again strives to totalize Weber's sociology in a universalistic direction. By stressing unity and rationality as theoretical principles, public elements of collective action are given primacy over privatized elements.

# CHAPTER 11

## The Weakening of Tensions

Parsons's formulation of voluntaristic action was a self-conscious effort to provide a theoretical alternative to both the economic determinism characteristic of the private individualism of liberal theory and the statist domination of society of socialism. Voluntarism afforded conceptual space for the formation of noneconomic collective values in arenas between the privatism of individual experience and self-interest and the public authority of the state. Yet the reconstruction of social theory in terms of value integration did not achieve an adequate analytic theory (Parsons, 1968: I, vi–vii). In large part, these limits resulted from not incorporating an analysis of "the internalization of cultural norms and social objects as part of personality" (1968: I, xi).

In writings after *The Structure of Social Action*, Parsons constructs a set of distinctions through which the complexity of social action and its relationship to both values and physical and biological reality are established. In conceptualizing the systemic and evolutionary character of social action, Parsons depicts a socialized public sphere that increases in determinacy and complexity and a private sphere that is increasingly enveloped in functional social relations. Indeed, the private individual merges into the semiautonomous personality system that is integrated through its capacities to mediate organic, cultural, and, most importantly, systemic requirements of society.

In writings that center around *The Social System*, Parsons weakens tensions between the public and private spheres by focusing on the individual/society relationship. There are a range of tensions between the individual and society. These tensions follow from a basic distinction: The integrity of the individual and the integrity of society as a social system are not identical. Because they are defined by different levels of organizational complexity and have different requirements, the individual and society have distinct properties and principles of integration. While they condition one another, are mutually dependent and interpenetrate, they do not collapse into one another.

Yet beyond the analytic distinctness of individual and society, Parsons elaborates their relationships in a dynamic that tends to weaken tensions between them. Their different analytic locations and principles of organization are mediated through symbolic and interactional processes that minimize sources of strain. Although society and the individual are never formulated as fully identical, they tend to interpenetrate along lines that are mutually supportive and complementary.[1] However, the analytic preponderance of society over the individual serves to delimit the individual as a social entity that represents social values, norms, and action orientations internally in the personality system.[2]

Leon Mayhew (1984: 1300) captures this aspect of Parsons's theory by stating that Parsons replaced "reason in the individual" with "intelligent choice." This change occurs as a result of the differentiation of the individual into a pattern of roles that emerges with societal complexity (1984: 1300). Social processes render the individual into an actor suited for highly differentiated activities, incorporating the individual more fully in social processes, including integration and control. Autonomy, considered from the standpoint of "reason in the individual," includes capacities to pattern structures of choice as well as to exercise choice. The individual, relatively separate from institutionally integrative processes, acts on a "reason" that is relatively independent from the pattern of choices that are embedded in social institutions. Autonomy as "intelligent choice," on the other hand, is limited to exercising capacities to choose within preestablished, institutionalized patterns. While the range of action subject to "intelligent choice" expands for individuals, the choices as well as the nature of the individual are more socially constrained. The interpenetration of the individual and society generates increased commonalities between them through socially driven processes: institutionalization, socialization of the individual into roles, and personality formation.

In *The Social System*, analysis continues to focus on interactive patterns of a plurality of individual actors (1951: 24). While this is consistent with his concerns in *The Structure of Social Action*, the features of action, including the actor, are more rigorously elaborated through analytic concepts. The actor, for example, may be either an individual and or a collectivity. Moreover, the actor is seen as a "*bundle* of statuses and roles" (1951: 26). The actor is an author of action as an organized system of statuses and roles that performs social action through reciprocal orientations toward other actors. Perhaps most importantly, the actor that is manifested in social action can only be partially accounted for by social action; rather, the individual as a personality is a prior condition or a functional prerequisite of the social system and social action at the same time that the individual as a personality is formed through social processes.

At first blush, it seems that Parsons is conceptualizing a location for the private individual that is largely autonomous from social relations. To some degree this is the case since the personality is integrated at the level of the individual ego and has its own organizational integrity. Yet, as the concept of the personality is developed, the core concern is with analyzing the individual as a requisite of the social system and the social processes through which the personality is generated. Indeed, the individual as a personality is problematic primarily in relation to fulfilling social statuses and roles. Thus, Parsons views individuals as units for the maintenance of the social system:

> From the point of view of functioning of the social system, it is not the needs of participant actors which must be met, nor all the needs of any one, but only a sufficient proportion for a sufficient fraction of the population. It is indeed a very general phenomenon that social forces are directly responsible for injury or destruction of some individuals and some wants or needs of all individuals, and though this may be reduced it is highly probable that it cannot be eliminated under realistic conditions. To cite a very simple case, a war cannot be won without casualties, and acceptance of war is sometimes a condition of survival of a social system as a distinctive system. (1951: 28–29)

Parsons develops the concept of the personality from this standpoint of social realism. Society does not require either the maximum of individual autonomy nor, for that matter, the full satisfaction of the needs of participant actors or even the survival of individuals beyond an unspecified minimum. To be sure, there is no necessary inconsistency between society and the maximization of individual autonomy, material circumstances, and protection of life. Maximizing satisfactions for individuals may serve to enhance their attachments and contributions to society. Yet the analytic focus is on social processes that shape the individual to meet minimal requirements for participation in a social system that, based on its own integrity and contingencies, may threaten or deprive individuals of their socially unnecessary aspects, up to and including their lives.

In keeping with this paramountcy of society, Parsons delineates those individual requirements that must be minimally met so that the individual may function socially. In addition to minimal biological requirements that include nutrition and physical safety, the stability of the personality requires adequate socialization relating affectional support to security so that the individual can be adequately motivated to engage in social action. Since the absence of stable personality may result in deviance that either positively disrupts social interaction or leads to withdrawal from action, the social system cannot take stable personalities for granted but, rather, must adapt to these minimal needs in a way that integrates stable personalities into systems of social interaction.

Closely tied to the concept of the stable personality as a prerequisite of the social system is the issue of motivation. From the point of view of the social system, there is a "motivational problem of order" in that there is no necessary or instantaneous fit between the action orientations of individuals and the requirements of the social system (Parsons, 1951: 30–31).[3] For this reason, the satisfaction of the minimal needs of individuals is most fruitfully viewed as a societal issue rather than as a problem of private individuals considered in isolation from one another as psychological entities. Rather than formulating the individual in psychological terms that stress disjunctures or contradictions with society, Parsons analyzes the specific mechanisms through which the "motivational systems of personalities" are related to social structure and role behavior. Indeed, Parsons asserts that it is this focus on the individual as an agent socialized into publicly significant activities rather than a primary concern with the character of private individuals that delineates the modern sociological perspective. Most directly, the analysis of integrative institutions and processes emerges as a key conceptual issue.

In *The Structure of Social Action*, Parsons analyzed private individualism as leading to inadequate explanatory frameworks for social action that required a more socialized analytic approach through the emergent theory of voluntarism and value integration. In *The Social System*, however, the very integrity of the private individual and the capacity to act are inseparable from categories of interaction in the socialized public sphere. The private individual is more fully absorbed in the life processes of society that are constituted in public.

*The Social System*, because of its concern with elaborating integrative institutions and processes from the vantage point of a stable system of social interaction, analyzes aspects of the public/private division at levels of societal analysis that go beyond a focus on personality. Two aspects of the public/private division are central to this wider scope.

First, privatism is reconceptualized as an orientation toward social interaction that may be either conducive to social integration or to disruption. Here the stress is on dimensions of privatism as features of role definition requisite for publicly consequential action. Second, privatized orientations may emerge from the ego integrity of the individual and may yield orientations toward action that are differentiated from role orientations. Here the stress is on potential conflicts or, more mildly, tensions between the integration of the personality as an ego and the personality as an element of social interaction. In effect, the ego integrity of the individual may generate privatized orientations that are disruptive to publicly consequential action.

These two aspects of the public/private division come together in Parsons's presentation of the pattern variables (1951: 52–53). Pattern variables have broad significance for the development of Parsons's theory (Münch, 1982: 781–83; Savage, 1981: 160–65). The pattern variables are not themselves aspects of social action. They do not formulate aspects of the personality or the social system that directly comprise elements of action; for example, motivation or conduct. Rather, they are categories for describing types of action that establish observational standards for evaluating direct motivational and situational elements of action (Bershady, 1973: 107–11).

With regard to relations between the individual and society, the pattern variables serve to delineate the duality of action orientations that come from institutionalized roles and orientations that come from the individual actor's ego integrity (Parsons, 1951: 52–53). On the one hand, the pattern variables define acceptable goals by specifying orientations for the individual actor consistent with societal goals. In addition, they describe limits to the choice of means faced by the actor. On the other hand, the orientations described in these patterns may be internalized by individual actors, enabling them to orient themselves toward one another so that interaction can be coordinated. Thus, the pattern variables serve to describe action orientations of individual actors that are in conformity or tension with the overall institutionalized pattern of action orientations of the social system. In this way, the pattern variables enable the description of the boundaries of orientations for congruence or divergence between individual actors and the social system.

The five pattern variables point to alternatives that are possible from the point of view of the social system and the choices that are faced by individuals in their orientations toward roles. Generally, integration is optimized when there is consistency between the systemic alternative and the individual choice. With regard to expressive action through which gratifications are realized, for example, social interaction may require more or less of a suppression of immediate gratification on the part of the individual actor (1951: 60). An orientation of affectivity, which minimizes the suppression of immediate gratification, may characterize a role orientation both from the point of view of the social system and the actor. On the other hand, an orientation of affective neutrality may be characteristic of a role orientation both from the point of view of the social system and the individual actor that requires a maximum of suppressed immediate gratification. Societal integration is enhanced when the orientations of the social system and the actor toward the degree of suppression of gratification through expressive activity converge.

The second pattern variable distinguishes between action orientations on the basis of private and collective interests. From the point of view of the individual actor, there may be "instrumental and ego-integrative orientations" that define interests as private since they do not coincide with any collective interest (1951: 60). A "self-orientation" is characteristic of a role orientation from the point of view of either the social system or the individual actor that defines activity through private interests while a "collectivity orientation" defines a role from the point of view of either the social system or the individual actor through the common interests of the collectivity. As with the case of gratification, the distinction between self and collectivity orientation is one of degree: The higher the convergence between social system and individual actor, the higher the degree of societal integration.

Beyond the issue of role orientations, the distinction between private and collective orientations raises issues of identity for both the individual and the collectivity. For the individual, self-orientation signifies indifference to "the integrity of a valued social system of action" (1951: 97). Here, the social system is taken purely as a framework for orientations toward the realization of private interests. Collectivity orientation, on the other hand, signifies that the actor recognizes responsibilities toward, and has an identity that is shaped by an interest in, the integrity of the social system beyond private interests. This affirmation of commonality, moreover, supports an organization of sanctions rooted in orientations toward the integrity of the system. A collectivity orientation, by engendering responsibility through common identity, generates patterns of solidarity that are both institutionalized in role expectations and emerge as uninstitutionalized values and sentiments. This is generalized in the form of loyalty beyond any specific agreed on obligation. While collectivities may be expressive, instrumental, or based on formalized rules, solidarity is grounded in a preponderance of orientations toward the integrity of the system as a whole over private interests.

The two pattern variables that we have discussed so far relate the individual to social action by describing patterned orientations; the other pattern variables are somewhat more distant from action. The distinction between universalism and particularism, for example, refers to types of value orientations as categories of knowledge rather than as direct orientations toward action. Universalism refers to value orientations that are logically organized and have an empirical component that can be constructed along principles of science (1951: 62). Particularism refers to value standards that are grounded in emotional attachments and relations specific to gratification. Because universalism is primarily a cognitive orientation that can be elaborated through logic and science, it has a more public character than particularism, which is local and appreciative. Moreover, since universalism yields general values, it may serve to expand the orientations of the social system as a whole.

Similarly, the distinction between achievement and ascription refers to how the actor is viewed as an object from the point of view of the social system (1951: 64). In the allocation of personnel through the social system, an achievement orientation serves to detach the individual from specific locations and to maximize the mobility of human resources. Ascription, on the other hand, tends to limit the plasticity of individuals from the point of view of the social system and to block resource mobility.

Taken together, universalism-particularism and achievement-ascription are descriptive of the relations of societal power. The combination of universalism/achievement enhances the formation of societal power while particularism/ascription limits the extent to which societal power can be mobilized. While the "breakdown of particularistic ties is the first condition of the extension of the power system," it leads to "instability" unless it is developed through patterns of universalism/achievement or reverts back to "particularistic restrictions" (1951: 122). Thus, these combinations of pattern variables condition one another along lines that either enhance or restrict societal power.

While achievement and ascription can be differentiated in terms of the usefulness of individuals as personnel for wider arenas of social action and the accumulation and expansion of power, Parsons's final pattern variable distinguishes between the scope of interest that either the social system or the individual has in the object of action (1951: 65). Specificity refers to a restricted interest and diffuseness refers to a relatively general interest. Here the focus is on the evaluation of action in the range of impact on either restricted or relatively open expectations.

As alternative role definitions, the distinctions put forth in the pattern variables delimit alternative orientations for the actor and shape alternatives, goals, and means for the social system. Those alternatives that are relatively public in orientation, such as affective neutrality, collectivity orientation, universalism, and achievement, tend to enhance both the scope of action and the expansion of power by opening up goals and the selection of means that are conducive to greater mobility of resources and to greater inclusiveness of personnel. Just as these alternatives tend to expand the social system, their opposites—affectivity, self-orientation, particularism, and ascription—tend to restrain mobility, restrict power, and limit the scope of action. Tensions between the individual and society are minimized when there is consistency across pattern variables at both the level of the personality system and the social system. It must be stressed that these analytic categories indicate the direction of action. Any concrete society will be characterized by a combination of alternatives that would yield more complex relations than are indicated by the comparisions pointed to here.

A major source of tension for integrating the social system is the extent to which there is either convergence or divergence between orientations described through pattern variables that are institutionalized in roles and the integrity of individual personality. While the convergence between institutionalized orientations in roles and the orientations from the individual personality does not have to be exact, there is a range of overlap that must be fulfilled for integration to be realized. The individual/society distinction is reestablished at a higher level of complexity where processible relations are paramount.

Our discussion of the pattern variables points out that a major source of conflict or tension with regard to the integration of the social system is the extent to which there is either convergence or divergence between orientations that are institutionalized in roles and orientations that follow from the integrity of the individual personality. While the convergence between institutionalized orientations in roles and the orienations from the individual personality does not have to be exact, there is a range of overlap that must be fulfilled for integration to be realized. In effect, this formulation reestablishes the individual/society distinction that is basic to the public/private dichotomy. It is to Parsons's analysis of this issue that we now turn.

Parsons (1951: 205) claims that the stability of the social system as a set of complimentary role expectations "once established is *not problematical*, in other words that the 'tendency' to maintain the interaction process is *the first law of social process*." In large part, this stability results from conceptualizing role sets in their inherent reciprocity and equilibrating tendencies rather than analyzing them as problematic from the standpoint of discrete individuals creating public order through interpretive processes. More central, the problem of social system maintenance revolves around establishing orientations within the actor that enhance orientations toward conformity with role expectations over orientations that lead the actor to deviate from role expectations. Directing the individual's inner drives through conformist social orientations maintains the social system.

In keeping with the analytic primacy of the social system over the individual, Parsons (1951: 207) conceptualizes the allocation of personnel between roles and the socialization of the individual as mechanisms of social control that "are clearly the same processes viewed in different perspectives." Just as allocation of personnel is a requirement of the social system if it is to be maintained over time, so socialization is a mechanism through which the individual actor learns those motivations and orientations that are "of functional significance to the operation of a system of complimentary role expectations" (1951: 208). In effect, the institutionalized orientations required for social action and the motivations of the individual actor are unified through parallel processes of allocation and socialization.

Internalization of value orientations is embedded in socialization processes that have mechanical, personal, and symbolic features. Reinforcement and extinction, inhibition, identification, and imitation are the main mechanisms through which the individual, especially in the infancy stage when the capacities to learn alternative patterns and to form attachments around basic gratifications are high, learns the values requisite for participation in roles. These mechanisms, however, require personalized reciprocal attachments based on needs for security. Learning is realized through psychological mechanisms combined with personal attachments. Moreover, that which is learned is both behavioral and symbolic since meaning is basic to value acquisition. Most importantly, the convergence of need dispositions at the level of personality and institutionalized value orientations is the foundation for specific role expectations. This convergence develops through socialization generally and early socialization especially.

Since internalization is complex and becomes increasingly differentiated, Parsons does not discount the possibility of problems emerging in the fit between socialized individuals and the social system. Indeed, just as conformity emerges so does subjective alienation. Alienation is a negative orientation toward institutionalized role expectations. It "is always a possible product of something going wrong in the process of value-acquisition through identification" (1951: 233). As a general condition, alienation results from a lack of congruence between need dispositions and value orientations. It emerges from the distinct requirements for integration of the personality system and the social system. More locally, alienation is manifested in specific role expectations that combine specific need dispositions and specific value orientations.

Deviance is the major result of a lack of congruence between socialization processes and the social organization of complementary role expectations. From the point of view of the individual actor, deviance is a "motivated tendency to behave in contravention to one or more institutionalized patterns" that, from the point of view of the social system, leads to a disturbance "in the equilibrium of the interactive process" (1951: 250). The consequences of alienation in specific role expectations can be minimalized by "fear of the consequences of sanctions," or a pattern of rewards and punishments, tolerance, or alternative role opportunities (1951: 234). While forces of social control may provide countervailing tendencies toward deviance, this is always a matter of degree. Rather than leading to congruence between individual motivations and role expectations, the general tendency is toward patterns that yield various degrees of strain, frustration, and disturbance in the fit between individual actors and interaction systems.

In this light, Parsons reinvigorates the distinction between the private individual and public order in the effort to analyze the problematic nature of the individual from the standpoint of societal stability: There is always a residual privatized sphere that resists full societal incorporation. Indeed, in ways that go beyond the naturalism of early liberalism (Sennett, 1977) or Durkheim's (1951) formulation that stressed the importance of conjugal solidarity and stability in the private sphere as basic sources of public order, Parsons (1951: 261–62) maintains that deviance is, to a large degree, generated by "alienation from social objects (and) tends to focus on problems of security, on anxiety about being able to count on their receptiveness-responsiveness or their love, approval or esteem." Moreover, the personalism of socialization rooted in the private sphere yields background expectations that may generate the individual's "alienation from normative patterns" that "focus on a problem of adequacy on one or both sides of the interactive relationship, that is, ego's own capacity to fulfill the expectations of conformity, or alter's capacity (including motivation) to do so, or both." Resistant privatism, no matter how residual, is problematic from the standpoint of social control and public order.

To be sure, Parsons's focus on the distinction between the actor as a personality and the social system as a stable order of integrated roles is formative for the analysis of deviance in a form that raises the public/private dichotomy to a degree of complexity not encountered in theories that we have discussed previously. Yet, it is also the case that the psychologizing of the private individual in an interactive process reaffirms the dominance of the social system at the same time that the individual's autonomy is asserted. Thus, without denying problems of faulty socialization and the autonomy of individual motivation, Parsons's overarching framework of the integration of the individual in stable patterns of social interaction resurfaces in his psychological account of the personality. Parsons is concerned with oppositions within a unity that, at most, yield disharmonies and tensions rather than contradictions and conflicts.

The analytic distinction between the actor as a personality and the social system as integrated roles raises crucial issues about the psychological requirements for societal stability, sources of strain between individual and society, and the depth psychology of the individual. If the individual is conceptualized at the psychological level as dependent on society yet in fundamental conflict with it, as Sigmund Freud theorized in *Civilization and Its Discontents*, then the force and pervasiveness of tensions between individual and society grows with social development. Society and forces of psychological repression at the deepest levels of private emotion and desire go hand in hand, generating accumulated sources of aggression. If on the other hand, the individual is conceptualized psychologically in a way that tends toward the full incorporation of the individual as a social actor without any fundamental antagonism, then strains are minimized. To be sure, there may be problems of individual or behavioral maladaptation to society and concrete situations that generate neurotic or even psychotic tendencies. These sources of individual problems and breakdown, however, are not basic to developing patterns of social differentiation and complexity. Rather, processes of social integration and complexity are overwhelmingly conducive for stable personality integration.

Parsons's psychology of the individual is conceptualized in an asymmetrical interactive process that infuses the overarching control of the social system into the processes through which the individual's autonomy are established. The agencies through which mental life is constituted are conceptualized from the standpoint of stable interaction and shared culture. Without denying problems of faulty socialization and independent sources of individual motivation, the integration of the individual in stable patterns of social interaction is reproduced in accounting for the personality psychologically. The individual and society, despite the differences in the mechanisms through which they are each integrated, are infused with the same symbolic and cultural content. Oppositions between the individual and society appear as disharmonies and tensions within a symbolic unity rather than as fundamental contradictions and conflicts.

One of the clearest statements of this is "The Superego and the Theory of Social Systems" (Parsons, 1982). In this essay, Parsons formulates the personality in a way that stresses both the integrity of the individual and the dependence of the individual's integrity on social interaction and the common culture. Because Parsons reformulates the personality as essentially harmonious and integrated through the internalization of a common culture by way of social interaction, the sense of a unified relation among the personality, social interaction, and culture is heightened.

Parsons accomplishes this by first stressing the mutual relations among the id, the ego, and the superego. He builds on Freudian categories by maintaining that the ego is primarily engaged in mental processes of cognition and conceptualization, and that the id is primarily engaged in forming emotional attachments or aversions, and that the superego is engaged in evaluation through a combination of both cognition and emotion. But beyond the integrative view that the superego, as an agency of evaluation, is somehow a combination of cognition and emotion, Parsons (1982: 132) also maintains that these three mental agencies are "modes of orientation" that constitute a "common symbolic culture" through which social interaction is conducted. Indeed, "not only the cathectic attitudes, but also the cognitive images, of persons relative to each other are functions of their interaction in the system of social relations" (1982: 134).

These departures from Freud are based on the argument that "all the components of the common culture" and not only moral standards are "internalized in the individual's personality" (1982: 134). Where Freud saw opposition and conflict among biological drives, reality, and a repressive morality as the sources for the formation of individual personality, Parsons frames the personality at the level of social interaction. Since the personality is formed through a socially constituted reality, the contents of personality are penetrated through an asymmetrical relationship with the social system. In this light, the ego is viewed in terms of interpenetration with a social reality that includes moral standards, the id is viewed in terms of "emotional symbolism" through which affect is communicated rather than as the individual's presocial drives, and the superego is viewed in terms of individual's internalized understanding of "prescriptions and prohibitions" toward social reality (Parsons, 1982: 136–39). Parsons saw the implications of his view, especially with regard to the id, as a singularly novel theoretical departure:

> This may be felt to be a relatively radical conclusion, namely, that emotions, or affect on the normal human adult level, should be regarded as a *symbolically generalized system*, that is never "id impulse" as such. Affect is not a direct expression of drive motivation, but involves it only as it is organized and integrated with both the reality experience of the individual and the cultural patterns which he has learned through the processes of identification. (1982: 143)

This statement is radical in the sense that it provides a critique of instinct theory and theories of repression that are crudely reductionistic. Indeed, there is some similarity between Parsons's insistence on the symbolic mediation of organically rooted impulses and Jürgen Habermas's (1971) reformulation of Freudian theory. There are, however, crucial differences between Parsons and Habermas on this issue. For Parsons, the symbolism infused through psychological mechanisms in the individual is overwhelmingly an internalization of the symbolic culture integrating nonproblematic patterns of social interaction. For Habermas, on the other hand, this symbolism is the object of critical inquiry since it is rooted in authoritarian modes of life and exploitation. The critical analysis of patterns of interaction and social organization as relations that repress and distort communication provides the basis for emancipation. For Habermas, the autonomy of the individual is enhanced by revealing understandings of habitual behaviors and opening up new possibilities for action through critical inquiry and practice.

Our discussion of Parsons's (1951: 295) formulation of deviance and the personality points out that for analytic purposes the individual never meshes with the orientations necessary for stable social interaction perfectly because socially imposed "disciplines are never completely and fully accepted in the sense that they are fully integrated in the personality structure of the actors without alienative elements and hence ambivalence." Nonetheless, the individual is viewed as socially produced along the lines of functional integration with the system of social interaction. Society, through the organization of roles and the expectations that characterize interaction, fully penetrates the individual up to and including the mental agencies through which private desires, reality, and evaluations are made. While the personality has some autonomy, it is an autonomy that emerges out of the integration of the individual as a complex, sensate organism through social interaction.

## NOTES

1. Richard Münch (1982) states that Parsons analyzed relations among subsystems solely as interpenetrations, both at the level of abstraction (772–73) and at the level of concrete action (791). Münch maintains that there are alternative relations that Parsons did not consider: accommodation, reconciliation, mutual isolation, and extinction of one subsystem by another. Parsons's exclusive focus on interpenetration suggests a predisposition for minimizing the potentials for strains among subsystems.

2. While the social system requires the activity of individuals conceptualized as personality systems, the social system integrates individuals as personalities (Parsons and Shils, 1951: 109). Parts of the individual actor's activity are required as inputs for the social system; on the other hand, the social system is the source of integrity for the individual:

> No personality system can exist without *participation* in a social system, by which we mean the integration of part of the actor's system of action as *part* of the social system. Conversely, there is no social system which is not from one point of view a mode of the integration of parts of the systems of action which constitute the personalities of the members.

3. Both Jürgen Habermas (1973) and Daniel Bell (1978) have focused on motivation as a core problem for social integration. In contrast to Parsons's analytic approach, however, these writers develop analyses rooted in contradictory tendencies within the relationship of commodity production to culture. Motivation is a site of disruption and potential crisis that is internal to processes of commodity production.

# CHAPTER 12

## Fusion and Societal Autonomy: The Public/Private Division and Adaptive Culture

Culture is of singular importance for weakening the boundaries of the public/private division for Parsons. From the intimate relations through which identification processes shape the personality system to the public zones of institutionalized interaction that constitute the social system, culture integrates various structural components of social action by providing "patterned or ordered systems of symbols which are the object of orientation of action" (1951: 327). Cultural symbols cut across the personalized spheres through which internalization of values of norms is accomplished to highly impersonal institutionalized relations. In transversing public and private spheres of social action, cultural symbols provide the standards through which the mutual expectations in interaction are communicated and regulated. Culture integrates the meanings through which public and private levels of social action are rendered coherent and cohesive.

Culture facilitates the coordination of the public and private components of social action by establishing a discourse that mediates aspects of social action through symbols that combine rational and nonrational meanings. Culture forms symbolic systems that combine cognition, normative judgments, and expressivity in various combinations in the social system. Reality, or the cognitive dimensions of belief, may be empirical or nonempirical, that is, more or less amenable to the public procedures of scientific verification. Normative judgments, or the evaluative dimensions of belief, are related to the relationship between reality and the interests or significance reality has for actors. These norms result from interactional processes and are subject to public deliberations that include referencing to personal valuations and emotional expressions. Cognitive dimensions of belief are combined in various ways with orientations toward gratification/deprivation orientations that engage expressive symbols. These combinations are subject to evaluation based on some system of collective values.

Since Parsons locates culture primarily in relation to stable social interaction, his analysis is directed both at the public organization of culture and, as we have seen, the internalization of values at the level of individual personality. With regard to cognitive dimensions of culture, Parsons focuses on the development and characteristics of the public sphere of science, especially within the institutionalized setting of the university and associated scientific communities. It is in the university, moreover, that much of the values associated with the humanities along with the sciences are developed and socially transmitted to wider publics.

The focus on science, the university, and the scientific community is indicative of the importance that Parsons places on the institutionalization of culture for the public sphere for creating and disseminating socially cohesive symbolism. This holds not only for cognitive and evaluative dimensions of culture based on empirical knowledge but for religion and expressive symbolism as well.

In addition to the roles that culture plays in providing the values through which the individual is integrated as a personality in patterns of interaction based on shared norms and the ways in which culture is itself institutionalized as patterns of action, Parsons stresses the function that culture plays as a major source of social control. Indeed, Parsons locates culture at the apex of a hierarchically ordered system of control that constrains lower levels of organization and that ties cultural institutions and symbolism to societal imperatives:

> The behavioral organism is the point of articulation of the system of action with the anatomical-physiological features of the physical organism and is its point of contact with the physical environment. The personality system is, in turn, a system of control over the behavioral organism; the social system, over the personalities of its participating members; and the cultural system, a system of control relative to social systems. (1982a: 157)

The hierarchy of control is a cybernetic concept. For Parsons, the upper reaches of the hierarchy of control are composed of "informational elements which define and control lower-level elements of energy and matter" (Mayhew, 1982: 20). Analogous with such biological processes as the control of genetic processes by the informational content in genes and the control of various metabolic processes by the information embedded in the molecular structure of enzymes, patterns of organization and categories of knowledge are low energy/high informational elements that reproduce the social system in the face of environmental contingencies. They direct material and motivational elements along lines that maintain and enhance the social system as a cohesive entity.

Formulating culture at the apex of cybernetic control heightens the interpenetration of culture with societal capacities for environmental adaptation, making a number of features of Parsons's approach to the socialization of the public/private division explicit. First, problems generated by inadequately incorporating the private sphere through socialization and a lack of motivation at the level of the individual are not the only threats to the integration and maintenance of the social system. To be sure, overly privatized and other alienative orientations at the level of the individual are threats to systems maintenance to the extent to which they are generalized. These are problems that focus on constraining and shaping the interface between private and public requirements at the level of the individual. Problems of control at the levels of the social system and culture, however, raise problems at higher levels of the organization. They involve problems of collective constraint not only in aggregating individuals but also, more systemically, in social organization and categories of knowledge.

This shift in the sources of problems for stable social action and the maintenance of the social system from incorporating the private sphere to higher levels of organization changes the focus of analysis from primarily subjective dimensions of social action that we have discussed with regard to *The Structure of Social Action* and *The Social System* to the more objective structural relations that maintain the existence of society. To be sure, Parsons does not depart from his concern with social action since he sees ideal elements as central to the social system and institutionalization as the dominant relation between values, ends, and means. The institutionalization of values, ideology, and legitimacy in directing the motivation of private individuals and creating coherence in public spheres of interaction remain focal for Parsons's theory. Yet, by focusing on the role of culture and social organization as the major defining and controlling elements in the struggle for existence that society faces in the confrontation with environmental contingencies, the relative importance of those dimensions that shape the social system as a material process emerge more forcefully. In a very real sense, ideas, at both the level of cognition and values, and organizational patterns are collective material forces.

Reorienting his theory in objective structural relations leads to a heightened analytic attention to "the functional problems that face a system of action and the structures and subsystems that exist to meet them" (Savage, 1981: 59–60). In this shift from subjective orientations to structural relations, the functional prerequisites of the social system are elaborated as objective elements that maintain and enhance societal unity, resources, and power in the face of environmental contingencies. In effect, the culture of collective purposes and needs is transposed into a public discourse of objectivity and instrumental categories that emphasizes pragmatic necessity over private autonomy and freedom.

Functional requisites have broad implications for the subsequent development of Parsonian theory and its underlying formulation of the public/private dichotomy. By formulating the social system in terms of generalized control over environmental conditions for the realization of societal goals along lines that maintain and enhance the system's integration and overall patterning, public and private dimensions of social action are given a much higher degree of interrelation than in either Weberian conflict theory or even in Durkheim's theory of harmony and functionalism. The character of the interrelation between public and private elements of social action, moreover, stresses the preponderance of societal needs and structures for the maintenance of public order over the autonomy of the private individual. While this approach is central to both *The Structure of Social Action* and *The Social System*, these works focused on individual actors whose private orientations and needs were incorporated in interactional contexts shaped by available instrumental means, social norms, and cultural values. The framework of functional requisites goes beyond this construction. It transposes this approach into a much more hierarchical and formal integration of public order and private orientations by "organizing the relations of complex institutions rather than merely coordinating the expectations of actors in face-to-face situations" (Mayhew, 1982: 31). These departures can be appreciated by reconstructing the functional requisites, differentiation, institutional exchange, and social evolution.

The first functional requisite is adaptation, the "development of generalized means for pursuing a variety of future goals and for meeting a variety of environmental conditions as they change over time" (Mayhew, 1982: 25). Adaptation is essentially an instrumental function that enables the accumulation facilities for controlling the environment. The economy is the subsystem that is specialized in adaptive functions involving the production and command of goods and services that are both physical and generalizable (Parsons and Smelser, 1956: 47).

Goal attainment, the second functional requisite, serves to mobilize societal resources for the attainment of collective goals (1956: 47). The polity is the organized subsystem through which political power is accumulated and directed toward realizing goals in relation to the environment. Through the polity, resources are mobilized for effecting specific goals.

Integration, the third functional requisite, "relates cultural value patterns to the motivational structure of individuals" (1956: 48). Integration relates the elements of a social system to one another to facilitate coordination and mutuality of expectations. Through the institutionalization of value patterns in the societal community subsystem, solidarity is enhanced and, thereby, adaptation and goal attainment are facilitated.

Latent pattern maintenance, the fourth and final functional requisite, provides overall stability and continuity for the system as a whole by securing consistency in the patterned relations of subsystems, their units, and the individuals of which they are composed. This functional requisite can be likened to the tendency in organisms to "maintain a normal state of internal stability through coordinated responses of organ systems that compensate for environmental changes" (Mayhew, 1982: 26). In effect, latent pattern maintenance refers to the general tendency toward equilibrium that continues the overall structure of the social system and gives it its identity as an integrated whole. The stability of normative order and its underlying values along with the mechanisms through which norms and values are institutionalized through the fiduciary system serve to maintain general structural stability.

Implicit in the analytic framework of functional requisites is the material process of differentiation. While any social system, including the simplest, must meet the functional requisites, there is a tendency for social systems to split functions off from one another into ever more specialized structures and institutions. Increasingly, specific subsystems become differentiated within the social system as a whole to meet the functional needs of adaptation, goal attainment, integration, and latent pattern maintenance. Moreover, each subsystem has an internal tendency toward differentiation as specialized structures develop to meet each of the four functional requisites of each subsystem.

The process of differentiation is neither random with regard to functional requisites nor are its possibilities for extension boundless. Rationalization is viewed "as the tendency of social systems to develop progressively higher levels of structural differentiation under pressure of adaptive exigencies" (Parsons and Smelser, 1956: 292). To be sure, it would be too gross to reduce structural differentiation to a reflection of either purely material or economic conditions. Adaptive contingencies result from relations among material circumstances and the internal relations of the social system as a whole that include goals, norms, and values. They are relative rather than absolute. Yet, the compelling conditions for directing and limiting structural differentiation are located in necessary adaptations of the social system and its environmental contingencies. The maintenance of all of the aspects of social action, from the incorporated private sphere to the highest symbolic spheres of cultural discourse, face these environmental constraints through processes that socialize adaptation.

The significance of this for the character of the public sphere in Parsonian theory is twofold: First, the nodal point at which the process of the overall differentiation of the social system is shaped is that of societal necessities which condition the scope and limits of differentiation if not its specific direction. Second, the public ordering of differentiating subsystems takes on the character of a pragmatic relationship with the environment because of the instrumental nature of adaptive structures and institutions. Pressures toward the instrumental control of the environment in the direction of enhanced production and the generalized accumulation of mobile resources socialize the public sphere as a realm of necessity. Both the public discourses of the social system that facilitate its expansion and the pattern of structural differentiation are shaped by instrumental necessity.

The force of adaptive exigencies and instrumental processes also have major consequences for the integration of the social system. As structural differentiation proceeds through enhanced control of the environment and economic growth, subsystems emerge that require more elaborate forms of integration. As Parsons points out in his discussion of institutional interchanges, these forms of integration have both structural and symbolic dimensions. In effect, the specialization and growth of adaptive capacities has qualitative as well as quantitative consequences for structural differentiation.

The consequences of relationships among functional differentiation, system integration, and institutional interchanges for the public/private distinction can be fully appreciated by analyzing several examples. A central instance of differentiation is between the private household and the social economy. While under relatively simple conditions, the household is the undifferentiated location of production, consumption, and social integration, the splitting off of generalized production from household consumption along with the household as the center of pattern maintenance is basic to functional differentiation. As the process of differentiation occurs, the "boundary relationships" between the economy and the household become "symmetrically reciprocal; each exchanges 'primary goal outputs' with the other" (1956: 55). A reciprocity of private and public spheres is established through an overall socialization of needs. The economy generates income for the satisfaction of consumer wants while the household provides labor services for the economy. This interchange, in turn, maintains and enhances the adaptive capacities and the pattern maintenance capacities of the social system as a whole.

Parsons's analytic approach to the interchanges between the social economy and the private household stresses their mutuality and their combined effects for the social system. Their institutional capacities are formulated in functional differentiation and societal requisites. As such, the analysis cuts across private/public distinctions between them, conceptually reducing their tensions by highlighting their functional affinities. Because the overall process of systems maintenance and differentiation is rendered public through hierarchical control and overall systems integrity, specific elements that are located in the private sphere of the household take on public significance. Despite their boundary differences, the economy and the household overlap in important ways. Consumer durables, which may appear as private consumer goods, are actually important elements of society's "working capital" insofar as they contribute to the household's ability to provide labor services to the economy. The interchanges among the economy and the household, moreover, require the development of such public institutions as contract law, an occupational order, and money that facilitate their relations institutionally and symbolically. While the private household and the social economy have core functional differences, they are systematically related through public symbolism and institutions that enhance their combined contributions to societal adaptation.

The category of capital also intermeshes public and private elements in an overall social process. Capital is a facility that maintains and enhances generalized production (1956: 56). As differentiation increases, the provision of capital by households tends to decrease relative to the provision of capital by the polity's capacity "to create or restrict facilities for the pursuit of economic goals" through credit (1956: 56). By regulating generalized purchasing power through the provision of credit, the polity provides for the general adaptive needs of a highly differentiated society. By enhancing generalized purchasing power through credit creation, the polity generates capital funds which, in turn, yield productivity growth in the economy. This relationship is reciprocal in the sense that the polity's creation of credit leads to a growth in the adaptive capacity of the economy and, on the other hand, the growth in the economy's adaptive capacity provides for an increase in general facilities available for the realization of political goals. The polity dominates the economy, moreover, during periods of societal emergency such as mobilization for war. The overall direction here is to socialize capital as a category of political economy beyond its private, entrepreneurial boundaries.

Parsons's functional focus reconstructs public/private distinctions by bringing together apparently diverse elements into the polity. In this light, "government, central banks which are semi-independent, private agencies with a public purpose such as insurance companies" are deemed political because they all are engaged in the creation and regulation of credit and capital formation (1956: 60). As in the case of the household, elements of the internal relations of the polity are viewed from the vantage point of their consequences for the social system as a whole rather than merely in terms of their location. Viewed in functional terms, the political sphere—the epitome of the public sphere—includes private as well as public institutions.

Parsons's analysis of property further demonstrates the extent to which the formulating issues through functional requisites reduces the tensions between the public and private dimensions of action. The public/private dimensions of property are ordered through their combined contributions for maintaining their underlying social conditions. The core relations of property are established through interchanges that fulfill society's systemic requirements under conditions of institutional differentiation. Hence property is defined as "the institutionalization of rights in objects of possession or non-social objects which function as facilities in the process of production and as a reward to the factors of production" (1956: 123). Property is not viewed primarily as a right that adheres in private individuals over which they can exercise exclusive use or, as in classical liberalism, a location that secures the right to participate in the public sphere of politics. Rather, property is conceptualized as institutionalized rights that link capital to the economy through differentiated patterns of allocation in a way similar to the allocation of labor through occupational institutions. From the perspectives of functional requisites, the features of property that are most important for the maintenance of the social system have the greatest analytic significance.

By thoroughly socializing the concept of property, the stage is set for transforming the sociological definition of ownership. Ownership is transposed from privatized to more public forms rooted in rationalities of functional integration. Parsons conceptualizes ownership as contractual and interactionist rather than as exclusionary and proprietary. Ownership is a "contractual relation" through which property holders provide their property to a specific organization's productive capacity (1956: 123). Central to this approach is the view that property is primarily a contract through which property holders invest their property in an organization. The analytic and normative focus is shifted from property as private entitlement, possession, use, and exchange to property as socially productive investment. In much the same way as the creation of credit is a public and political activity regardless of whether the institutions that engage in credit creation are in the private or public domain, so ownership is public and political regardless of the private or public character of property owners:

> The receipt, manipulation and application of capital funds by the borrower places him—whether he recognizes it or not—in a role of public responsibility. By the same token the contract of investment, which is the commitment of capital funds to particular firms, is a political decision; the relevant environment which imposes exigencies on the investor is not in a differentiated society the household but the polity or some organizational subsystem with political functions. (1956: 125)

Tendencies toward structural differentiation under pressures to meet functional requisites of the social system weaken the public/private distinction. Both sides of the division are increasingly rooted in common social conditions that institutionally and symbolically combine them by heightening their functional interdependence. While private domains of action appear to remain a feature of differentiating social systems, especially at levels of personal interaction through which identifications with cultural values and norms are formed, they are increasingly incorporated in organizational and institutional relations rather than as exclusionary preserves of the individual. Moreover, the compelling requirements of the social system for both external control over environments and goal attainment as well as for internal integration reorder key dimensions of the private sphere. Categories such as capital, property, and ownership are increasingly transformed from personal powers that adhere in individuals and that ground the private sphere as distinct from social processes. Rather, these categories are rendered into aspects of society. They are increasingly conceptualized in terms consistent with their societal consequences, as resources and as capacities for social production through their organizational and contractual relations. The polity, moreover, is the institutionalized public sphere through which societal goals are formulated and mobilized. The problem of maintaining and enhancing generalized adaptive capacities, furthermore, infuses the political public sphere with a discourse of instrumental necessity that reverberates through societal subsystems, institutions, and role relations.

Parsons's approach to social evolution provides a dynamic framework for analyzing the socialization and weakening of the public/private division. Functional requisites, structural differentiation, and institutional interchanges are grounds for capturing the dynamic transformation of the public/private distinction when they are located in evolutionary processes. Most pointedly, the central importance that Parsons places on universals in social evolution that heighten adaptive capacities lead to an analysis that further reformulates public and private dimensions of social action as resources that can be organizationally mobilized for societal survival and goal attainment.

Parsons's perspective on social evolution, like Durkheim's, is both an analogy with and an extension of Charles Darwin's theory of biological evolution. Despite their similar foundations, however, they take different directions that have important consequences for the public/private division. For Durkheim, evolutionary developments are largely caused by population increases and other physical causes; their main social consequences are at levels of the social organization of morality. Evolutionary pressures lead to moral differentiation in a way that compartmentalizes both normative control and competition among members of society. Durkheim utilizes Darwin's theory of the diversity of species and specialization in environmental niches to account for the moral differentiation of occupational organization and the development of private locations for individual actors and their identities.

Although these themes are not totally lost in Parsons's approach, his departures on these issues are quite different. He focuses on generalized mechanisms that emerge in evolutionary processes that facilitate an active adaptation of "living systems" to their environments. Rather than focusing on the "passive adjustment to environmental conditions," Parsons is concerned with conceptualizing universal mechanisms that enhance capacities for mastering the environment to secure survival and further development. For these reasons, Parsons views social evolution, not in terms of symbiosis, specialization for environmental niches, and the proliferation of life forms, but, rather, in terms of attaining "higher levels of general adaptive capacities" (Parsons, 1982b: 298–99).

Parsons's theory of social evolution extends theories of cybernetic hierarchy and functional differentiation by centering social change on survival problems of enhanced adaptation, societal cohesiveness, and control over environments. In processes of social evolution, "cultural innovations replace Darwinian variations in genetic constitution" as adaptive mechanisms are enhanced and normative relations to the environment are developed (1982b: 300). This conceptual change focuses culture on the relationships among instrumental rationality formulated through the public discourse of science, norms formulated through nonrational public discourse, and the relatively private spheres of interpersonal relations and motivation.

As we have seen at other problematic conjunctures that require a blending of public and private elements of social action, Parsons secures conceptual integration by grounding apparently divergent elements in more universal symbolic and social relations. This approach is maintained in his theory of evolution by locating public and private features of social action in shared prerequisites that conflate their origins. Evolutionary changes shaped by cultural innovation and structural differentiation have linguistic and social organizational prerequisites (1982b: 300–301). Language is the prequisite that enables culture to be transmitted and shared through processes of communication. The simplest, least evolved form of culture is religion. Kinship, which "is an extension of the mammalian system of bisexual reproduction," is both the carrier of culture through socialization and the location of norms involving incest, residence, and descent. All higher forms of evolved societies develop through the differentiation of religion and kinship. Because of adaptive requirements that characterize all life forms, Parsons includes technology, the "synthesis of empirical knowledge and practical techniques," as a constituent element of culture.

These groundings are originally closely bound through the overlapping of culture and kinship. A core evolutionary problem is how the bonds that unify these requisites for survival and enhanced control over the environment can be overcome while maintaining the integrity of society. This is partially accomplished through a pattern of differentiation that distinguishes public and private spheres of action while maintaining their cultural identity.

An integrated pattern of differentiation is shaped through combined developments of social stratification and cultural legitimation. Social stratification has its initial sources in the distribution of resources, most importantly, residences and land through kinship relations. The more prestigious or senior lineage groups tend to get the more advantageous resources while the less prestigious "cadet" groups tend to get the "less advantageous bases of subsistence" (1982b: 302). This process is driven by the interaction between population growth and the natural environment. As cadet groups move to inferior residences with poorer economic resources, advantages emerge with the concentration of responsibility for certain functions by more advantaged groups. In effect, growing complexity, conflict, and defense requirements from the outside generate needs for maintaining internal order, power, and solidarity. Under these strains, political and religious centralization occurs through the differentiation of groups along prestige lines. Processes of centralization and differentiation allow for innovation on the part of prestigious social members and also provides for the accumulation of resources that can be used in innovative ways. This process, facilitated by written language, tends to become institutionalized through endogamy and ascription so that a two-class system of a ruling class and mass develops. These tendencies toward statification become more complex as urban centers, political-administrative functions, and economic specialization increase. Finally, the very growth in functional complexity and diversity leads to a weakening of ascription and the growth of mobility within a stratified structure.

Cultural legitimacy provides a symbolic framework, initially in religious form, that distinguishes the society as "meritorious" in relation to other societies (1982b: 306). By providing a positive understanding of "we-ness" in religious and political terms, cultural legitimacy enhances the society's capacity for coordinated action in relation to other societies and the natural environment. In addition, cultural legitimacy provides the grounds for "justifying advantages and prerogatives *over against* burdens and deprivations" that serve society as a whole (1982b: 307). Cultural legitimation tends to become differentiated along with the complexity of the public order as a whole.

Beyond the primitive stage of social evolution, other universals become functionally differentiated in ways that secure enhanced adaptation and publicly articulated relations of institutional interaction. Among these are bureaucratic administration, money and markets, generalized universalistic norms, and the democratic association based on leaders elected by enfranchised members. Bureaucratic administration allows for the exercise of power through hierarchically organized authority and specified spheres of competence. It facilitates the mobilization and use of resources for the realization of decisions outside of private and kinship-based obligations because it locates authority in offices or official positions differentiated from each incumbent's other roles. Through money and markets, resources are generalized and their mobility is enhanced for the realization of collective goals. The extension of money and markets frees resources, including human services, from kinship relations and renders them open to alternative uses. Universalistic norms, of which law is a leading example, define the rights and obligations through generalized principles and standards that underlie bureaucratic authority and markets.

They tend to become differentiated from religion as well as from the government. The democratic association, which is a tendency characteristic of modern nation-states, provides for a pattern of consensus in the political sphere that allows for increased participation by members through the extension of the franchise while, at the same time, removing "the consequences of the act from the particular actor" (1982b: 322).

Each of these universals provides specific functions for society as a whole through their capacities to coordinate social relations around specialized goals. Yet, they add more to societal cohesion and adaptability than would be indicated by the sum of their parts, especially in tension management and legitimation. Tensions and legitimation problems within the arena of money and markets can be displaced to the arena of universalistic norms. Tensions and legitimation problems in the arena of universalistic norms may be displaced to the arena of the democratic association. In addition, bureaucratic organization generates a pattern of role differentiation and, indeed, role segregation, that buttresses the diffusion of tension and legitimation through the social system. Because they are rooted in a common societal process and articulated through meanings grounded in a common culture, they are mutually supportive and, to a high degree, legitimate one another.

Parsons's approach, with its emphasis on cultural cohesion and mechanisms that interpenetrate hierarchical levels of action systems, undermines distinctions between public and private elements of action. It does not conceptualize social evolution as a process through which public ordering generates divergent spheres of private individualism as in both Durkheim's views on social evolution and Weber's theory of rationalization. With Parsons, the public and private dimensions of society tend increasingly to merge analytically as unified structural consequences of adaptive change and cultural cohesiveness. Because differentiation is directly tied to patterns of integration generated by instrumental adaptation, the fusion of private and public elements is accomplished through functional relations that are absent in other theorists that we have considered. This fusion is buttressed by tying social stratification to cultural legitimations that stress functionalism, internal unity, and the appropriateness of inequality. While voluntarism is a feature of this pattern of evolution, it is increasingly located at the levels of culture and the polity that orient social members to patterns of action that are institutionalized through specific roles and integrated through universalistic norms. The public sphere, in its political and scientific arenas, becomes increasingly bounded by problems of adaptation and environmental controls.

In his later writings on social evolution, Parsons reaffirms these conceptual departures in a way that strengthens adaptive and hierarchical aspects of collective holism over the private sphere. Thus, the inequalities of stratification serve to increase the "mobility of human and nonhuman resources" while cultural legitimation serves to "justify asymmetries of authority and prestige" (Toby, 1977: 12–13). Law, far from grounding the private individual in rights backed by the state, serves to develop a normative order that increases "independence . . . from the exigencies of political and economic interests and from the personal, organic, and physical-environmental factors operating through them" (1977: 13). The universalism, formal rationality, and procedural aspects of law heighten the society's capacity for adaptation, the flexible use of power, and the mobility of resources. The democratic polity links "collective and coercive features of power" through "an approximation of voluntary participation" in a way that generates consensus for "greater adaptive capacity" (1977: 16–17). The societal community, the integrated subsystem of statuses and roles, defines obligations in loyalty, "a readiness to respond to properly justified appeals in the name of the public interest," the hallmark of which is "the willingness to perform military service is a test of loyalty for men but not for women" (Parsons, 1977: 135). The central problem of modern societies, moreover, are integration, the maintenance of institutionalized values, and appropriate individual motivation (1977: 186–93).

To be sure, the success of social evolution and the fusion of public/private elements is not without countertendencies and tensions. For example, the inclusion of diverse groups in hierarchically organized subsystems heightens requirements of public ordering through social mobility and value generalization that may be resisted on the privatized grounds of kinship and particularism. Thus, Parsons discusses fundamentalism "as a resistance to value generalization" that emerges with tendencies toward inclusion (1977: 94). In addition, Parsons focuses on stresses in the nuclear family (1977: 195–196). On the one hand, the nuclear family, by tying occupational earnings to residential mobility, is functionally related to the mobility of human resources that facilitate society's adaptive capacities. On the other hand, this fosters a high degree of experiential privatism in the family as intimacy with neighbors declines and as the family takes on the function of providing the emotional support for participation in the public sphere. In particular, this puts a great deal of stress on the housewife whose privatized role in providing emotional support increases along with her responsibilities in the polity and the public economy. As another example, Parsons points out that the growth in collective responsibility concentrates power in the polity in a way that both heightens the role of elected leadership and generates greater demands for private rights on the part of citizens. These stresses are felt in the polity and in the electoral process in particular. A similar pattern of strains are located in bureaucracies, especially with regard to their responsibilities and accountability. In this light, the hierarchical and technocratic character of bureaucracy has tended to become at least partially transfigured by the spread of professionalism and collegial decision making.

But beyond considering the strains and stresses generated by social evolution that cut across public and private dimensions of social organization, Parsons also associates social evolution with liberal values most directly related to the formation of individuals as agents of action: individual choice, private rights, and individual initiative. He is quite explicit about the freedoms brought forth by modern societies at the apex of social evolution:

> Such freedoms begin with freedom from some of the exigencies of physical life: ill health, short life, and geographical circumscription. They include reduced exposure to violence for most of the population most of the time. Higher incomes and extensive markets enhance freedom of choice in consumption. There is also general access to services like education and public accommodations. There is freedom of marital choice, of occupation, of religious adherence, of political allegiance, of thought, speech and expression. From a comparative and evolutionary perspective, the more privileged societies of the later twentieth century have successfully institutionalized the liberal values of a century ago. (1977: 208)

This roster of both negative and positive freedoms does, indeed, appear to fulfill liberal notions of progress. They suggest that the growth of autonomous individualism associated with liberal democratic notions of private rights, reason, and public participation. Yet, as we have shown, Parsons's notion of individual freedom takes on a distinctive antiutilitarian character when considered in light of his overall theory. Given the general processes of adaptation and integration, Parsonian theory constructs agency from the vantage point of freedom within structurally integrated and institutionalized roles rather than from a standpoint that emphasizes equality, self-determination, and full participation in a public sphere collective debate and action. The focus is on actors in socially consequential roles rather than on the active freedoms through which public life is constituted. The liberal notion of individual reason is replaced by an institutionalized individualism characterized by a highly structured and institutionalized form of "intelligent choice" that is shaped by normative order and patterns of gratification (Mayhew, 1984: 1300).

The notion of freedom, then, is derivative of societal processes that are not fully redeemable at the level of individual reason but are rather formulated through culturally bounded choices. That actors are dispersed in differentiated roles characterized by patterned choices has less to do with private freedom and autonomy in creating a public sphere than it does with systemic needs for mobility of human resources in the collective process of enhanced adaptation that Parsons affirmed as the general trend in evolution (1966: 110).

Even when the boundaries between public and private aspects are weakened and made permiable by a thoroughgoing adaptive functionalism, the public/private division remains crucial for defining distinctive features of social action, especially at the level of agency.[1] At the very least, it has roots in personal spheres of interaction that are basic to processes of identification and personality formation. It also has continued importance for processes of cultural legitimation by providing a conceptual space for displacing societal tensions and conflicts. The division may be marginalized and incorporated as fragmented elements in dominant processes of social evolution and the formation of systemic requisites, yet it resists conceptual disintegration. While the private sphere is socialized through institutional relations and public discourses about the necessities of system's maintenance, cohesion, and growth, its persistence is indicative of its significance for social action.

## NOTES

1. See David Sciulli (1988), especially regarding the difference between voluntaristic action and normative action. Paul Colomy (1986) presents some of the flexibility that has developed in functional theory regarding issues of conflict and politics.

# PART V

# CONCLUSION

# CHAPTER 13

## A Social Affirmation of the Public/Private Division

The transformation of the public/private distinction is part of a broader process of social change. As separate spheres of human activity merge into an all embracing social life process, they become increasingly less independent and less distinct compared to the mutual effects that they have on one another and on society as a whole. Connections affect the possibilities of maintaining and recreating life itself. Culture, politics, law, technology and science, family life, friendship, economic relations of production and consumption, personality formation, and the interior of intimate experience are increasingly shaped through social linkages that define their most important features.

The transformation of distinct spheres of activity into coordinated elements of social action creates a common realm of significance that cuts across personal and collective boundaries. Links among strangers who are unknown to one another except through their products, relations of consumption and effects on such global arenas as the environment, ecology, society, the economy, and the state become as important to sustaining stable social life and individuality as the most intimate personal relations and the relations of local community. The separation of public and private spheres of life in an age when world events are televised into the bedroom through technologies and equipment that are themselves globally produced seems barely justifiable even on the basis of personal experience let alone through theoretical reflection on society and social action.

Processes that cut across the public/private division and interconnect ever more spheres of action into a social metabolism raise deeply troubling prospects. They redefine the public/private distinction in terms consistent with a world driven by necessity and survival: a world of material dependency, hierarchical knowledge and social organization, and a kind of equality based on maximizing social control and minimizing political autonomy. The emancipatory value of moving aspects of social life from private to public relations has become increasingly questionable. As postmodernist thinkers such as Michel Foucault have maintained (Foucault, 1977; Lemert and Gillan, 1982; Turkel, 1990; Goldstein, 1990), modern society's initially progressive categories of the individual, private rights, politics, law, and economy are increasingly transformed through social processes into a generalized system of surveillance and therapeutic intervention. These instrumental processes create social institutions and individuals through techniques that facilitate imperatives of organizational control. They are supported by moral claims rooted in societal commitments to labor, productivity, secure life, and privatized freedom.

As it becomes a dimension of an interconnected social life process, the public/private division is recreated through legalized forms of power that render it into a mode of societal domination. Legality increasingly combines with scientific discourses that transpose the private sphere, especially the interior of the individual psyche, into a zone that cannot be directly seen but is made knowable through technological interventions because it is the location of primal threats to ordered social life.[1] From Jeremy Bentham's Panopticon to Big Brother of Orwell's *1984* to the routine analysis of blood and urine, the revealing of the interior, of the private body indicative of the private mind, for purposes of social order is rationally justifiable and, indeed, consensually legitimated on grounds of social necessity, public safety, and life.[2] Perversely, even resistance supports the formation of a private sphere as an arena of public control. Resistance, local and ephemeral, serves the expansion of social power. It occasions the extension of social power through law, science, and the state into zones that have either escaped surveillance or have not been found to be controllable. The public and private dimensions of power are absorbed into a social process founded on control and necessity.

Since the public/private distinction in law is continually reconstituted as part of the transformation of societal power, one direction of criticism is to foster the distinction's demise as a legal category. Tendencies toward the diminution and virtual collapse of the public/private distinction have been encouraged by legal critics who view the breakdown of the distinction as part of an opening to realism, emancipation, and a more spontaneous, authentic form of social life and self-identity formation. The public/private distinction in law, since it supports hierarchical power and manipulation, is criticized as fostering domination and ideological mystification.

Among critical legal scholars, for example, Duncan Kennedy (1982) has argued that the public/private distinction has lost its capacity to plausibly capture features of reality and specify differences that are consistent and relevant for legal decision making. In common with deconstructionist efforts to demonstrate that oppositional concepts are interdependent and have shared meanings (Johnson, 1980; Culler, 1982), the public/private distinction is viewed as resulting from particular legal activities and is neither natural nor logically sustainable. The decline of public/private distinction is largely internal to legal discourse and consciousness associated with legal practices. Although the public/private division begins as a dichotomy, it is eroded through case law that turns it into a relative category that locates issues along a continuum of public and private dimensions.[3]

The public/private distinction stereotypes issues for routine decision making: Does a proposed shopping center fulfill a public purpose or does it merely serve the interests of developers? Will the proposed extension of a roadway serve a public interest or will it needlessly reduce private property values? In the absence of any outside standard for its application, an extreme relativism infuses public/private discourse (1982: 1354). Ultimately, the public/private distinction becomes "loopified": The ends of the continuum become less distinct so that everything is both thoroughly private and public. For example, the family fulfills a public purpose at the same time that it is the most private of human relationships. The exercise of individual consumer preferences is intensely subjective and private just as it is open to government regulation (1982: 1354). For purposes of legal decision making, it is difficult to take the public/private distinction seriously as a description, as an explanation, or as a justification for anything (1982: 1357). The public/private distinction raises problems for the rationality of law and, more importantly, for acting juridical subjects. Abolishing the distinction, it is argued, would further rational discourse.

Beyond the public/private distinction's potentials for incoherence and mystification raised by legal critics, there are more substantive charges leveled against how it operates in dividing markets and social policy. To the extent to which law supports and defines the public/private distinction in terms consistent with private competitive uses for public and common property, the very sustainability of biological resources are imperiled. As Arthur McEvoy has shown in his analysis of California fisheries (1983), private property in the means of catching, processing, and marketing fish for purposes of profit making combined with rapid technological innovation and market expansion at the turn of the twentieth century virtually devastated the fisheries. Efforts to conserve the fishery and rehabilitate it through licensing, regulating seasonal catches, regulating technologies, market efficiencies, and replenishing it by stocking have overwhelming lagged behind competitive private economic pressures to maximize catches. Indeed, some of the policies designed to shore up the fishery have incorporated supports for the most powerful fishing interests. The "tragedy of the common," in which private competitive use of common resources devastate the resource base, manifests the dilemmas in trying to adequately resolve issues through public policies aimed at controlling private market activities. As our discussion of Weber demonstrated, legal rationality founded on the public/private distinction has divergent principles from the public/private distinction that characterizes economic rationality. The public/private distinction becomes politically mobilized to support excessive short-term gains over longer-term collective needs.[4]

Although the recreation of the public/private distinction through the legal formulation of market activities and economic policy limits rational approaches to problem solving, it is also conceptualized as formative for social oppression. Feminist scholars have developed rigorous and substantive critiques of the public/private distinction. They have argued that the public/private distinction is fundamental to the subordination of women. The relegation of women to the private sphere of domesticity and the virtual identification of the public sphere with masculine virtues has been a defining feature of patriarchal domination (Olsen, 1983). Through the public/private distinction, women have been rendered into a condition of domestic bondage and personal dependency that is a condition for the more public exploitation of wage labor, in part because it is a condition for reproducing wage labor (Harding, 1981). Moreover, women have historically been denied any presence in the public arenas through occupational, professional, and educational interaction and identity formation. Their relegation to the private sphere has meant a denial of political and cultural life in which even their very biological fate has been subjected to discourses that have denied their participation.

The centrality of the public/private distinction for the oppression of women, as well as the need for overcoming it, has been broadened and rationalized by social development. The social transformation of the public/private distinction has lead to a transformation of "the power of men within families to the power of men through the state, facilitated by law and public policy" (Boris and Bordiglio, 1981: 70). During the nineteenth and early twentieth centuries, public policies and law brought a variety of social functions out of the family and extended rights to women and children. While this social transformation eroded the power of men in the private household, it led to the formation of "social patriarchy: the organization of hierarchical gender roles throughout society" (1981: 73). Increasingly, the public institutions of law and state policy created a gendered distinction between public and private spheres: Men participated in political and economic activities outside of the home while women were relegated to the domestic sphere as childbearers and rearers.

While the early legal form of this distinction rested on private rights to property and contract, after the Civil War there was greater state policy intervention into family relations. Family members were defined through their relations to the state rather than to the male head of the family. State policies and court decisions, however, increasingly defined women as incompetents in the ways of the world who required shelter, protection, and distance from harsh political and economic spheres of action. The family increasingly became defined through state labor and welfare policies in a manner that assumed that women would continue to be privatized: They are responsible for the domestic spheres of household management and child rearing, whatever other social roles they might assume. Consistent with our critical discussion of Durkheim's analysis in Chapter 6, the gendered distinction between public and private spheres has been a central feature of the social structure that is partially reproduced through law and state actions.

The gendered ordering of social life has been sustained not only by defining women in public law through terms consistent with private domesticity and men through terms consistent with public realms of work and politics, but also by the historical absence of regulation of the domestic sphere (Taub and Schneider, 1983: 121). Although marriage takes the legal form of a private contract, for example, contract law has historically not been available for enforcing the support obligations of husbands to wives and children during marriage. "A woman whose husband squanders or gives away assets during a marriage cannot even get an accounting" (1983: 121). Also, tort law, which deals with harms and injuries that individuals inflict on one another, has historically been unavailable for wives to use against husbands because of interspousal immunity.

Limitations on the intervention of law into the domestic sphere have largely been justified on grounds of a right to familial privacy. Family relations, unlike private business relations or other arenas of voluntary association, are deemed to have a virtual natural harmony that benefits from limited legal intervention. In effect, the world of private domesticity which has been taken to be central to the legal definition of women is a sphere that has minimal legal regulation. Indeed, even Supreme Court decisions that have had the effect of extending reproductive rights of women through rights to contraception and abortion have not been based on notions of rights to reproduction but on rights to privacy. Major aspects of family life are regarded as outside of the state's regulatory authority. This approach legitimates the view "that there are naturally separate private and public spheres of human existence" (Polan, 1983: 299). Just as the law has heightened women's dependence on men by limiting their participation in public spheres of work and politics, it has limited their contractual rights and tort remedies in the private sphere by defining it outside of state regulation.

These considerations suggest that the boundaries of the public/private distinction have become permeable as they have become increasingly socialized. Both persistent and newly established features of social action move between private and public spheres as social relations become more dense, technologized, and interdependent. Indeed, the public/private division appears increasingly more relativized, arbitrary, and defined through relations of power legitimated through claims based on social and biological necessity. The division is increasingly determined by social forces. Under these pressures, critics allege that in legal discourse, in economic policy making, and in the construction of gender, the distinction increasingly operates in ways that block rational and emancipatory action. The public/private distinction seems to be so deeply structured into legal discourses and social organization that it constitutes a necessary ideological mystification for ritualized, destructive, and oppressive social relations. At one and the same time, the public/private distinction is losing its coherence because it is dissolving into social processes rooted in social control, imperatives of societal survival and life itself, while it is continually recreated as a feature of legal discourse and as a principle of economic and gender organization of society.

These characterizations raise a dilemma: The incoherence of the public/private distinction occurs along with increases in societal power that make the individual and the private sphere a zone of surveillance, manipulation, and intensive technological control. Increased socialization recreates the public/private division in ways that undermine the integrity of the private sphere as grounds for autonomous action in public arenas, rendering it into a zone of potential legal regulation and state intervention. Yet, affirming the distinction supports irrational policies and oppressive gender relations. To support the continued decline of the public/private distinction enhances social processes that incorporate elements of private life into technologized intervention, manipulative interaction and symbolic processes, and statist control; to affirm the public/private distinction supports inadequate approaches to collective problems and oppressive patterns of social organization.

In the face of this dilemma, our reconstruction of the public/private distinction in the tradition of social theory is instructive. To be sure, there are major differences among the approaches to the public/private distinction that we reformulated in the writings of Marx, Durkheim, Weber, and Parsons. Moreover, to the extent that society is a confusion of public and private divisions, social theory has often reflected that confusion rather than resolved it. Yet once it is unpacked from sociological concepts that unwittingly conflate its terms, the division appears at different theoretical levels. Most importantly, the general tendency is for public and private elements to merge at the levels of social structure and macroinstitutions while the distinction holds at levels of action close to social agents.

Marx incorporated the public/private distinction in analyses rooted in commitments to a scientifically based and democratically accomplished socialist transformation of society. He formulated the public/private distinction through critiques of Hegelian philosophy and classical political economy, centering on the roles of the working class in the development of capitalist production and as an agency of social change. For Marx, the public/private distinction is fundamental for critiques of philosophy, political economy, and analyses of watershed events in state formation and law creation. As the social relations of production are articulated through particular historical social formations that distinguish between private and public spheres, the tendency is for these spheres to merge with the development of the forces of production. Marx's theory, rooted in working-class movements that aim at enhancing the production of wealth and the emancipation of workers, affirms the private and public rights of workers while attempting to go beyond the limits of the division at the level of the social relations that determine production. As in the case of legislative efforts to regulate the working day, the social relations of production are determined through broadening the public control of private property relations as a condition for enhancing the political autonomy and private lives of working people.

Durkheim theorized the public/private distinction through the categories of a professionalized sociological epistemology and method. His corporatist approach to knowledge and social structure constructs the public/private distinction as evolving in the state, law, morality, and social organization along with ever denser and more complex patterns of association. For Durkheim, the private and public spheres are functionally related in a hierarchical direction: Processes of societal survival determine the relations between public and private realms, giving public spheres such as law, the state, and science functional priority. The relative autonomy of the private sphere is a zone of individual freedom, partial knowledge, and innovation; it has major social importance as it supports the public spheres of the state, science, production, and law. The private sphere is an arena structured by broad social forces. It is a source of morality, innovation, and destabilization for society as a whole. The institutional arenas that are the context of everyday occupational life are afforded autonomy through public laws that make them self-regulating as the private rights of individuals are protected.

Weber formulated the public/private distinction from the methodological standpoint of liberal/legal individualism. He stressed the interactions among conflicting patterns of public rationality based on divergent premises of legal rationality, economic rationality, bureaucratic organization, and politics. The merging of these rationalities, because of their divergent premises, opens conceptual space for substantively different patterns of social organization rooted in value commitments. Moreover, existentially rooted value commitments are, in principle, incapable of being fully incorporated into the logics of public rationality. For Weber, these foundations of social action posed by the public/private distinction are central to the freedom of the individual, especially in an increasingly rationalized and interconnected world. They heighten the problem of agency by making the agent the locus of deep, irreducible subjective commitments that require publicly constituted knowledge and rationalized social order for their realization. This sets the stage for the dilemmas captured by "an ethics of responsibility" in political action.

For Parsons, the public/private distinction is rooted in critiques of utilitarian positivism that seek to overcome the reductionisms of both statist collectivism and market economism. The public/private division is at the core of voluntaristic action at personal levels of interaction and institutional processes that cannot be accounted for through technical, economic, and or political rationalities. The depth of the social character of public and private elements is demonstrated by Parsons's analysis of categories such as capital and investment that have a political as well as an economic content conditioned by relations to societal maintenance and enhancement. The very definition of economic, legal, and political categories are determined through societal processes and imperatives that erode dichotomous features of the public/private division. Yet the distinction is central to individual personality formation and the nondeterministic nature of values and choice as categories of social action. The private sphere and liberal notions of rights are basic to the formation of agents of social action.

Across their differences, these classical theoretical approaches share a core conceptual commitment: An adequate theory of social change and social action must relate but not confuse the analysis of the public/private distinction as an underlying structural condition with the public/private distinction as a category through which agents are formed and social action is accomplished. The public/private distinction, as an analytic category and a feature of social life, must be rooted in ongoing social relations. To be sure, sociological approaches blur the public/private distinction as its elements are socially transformed as conditions of action. Yet our reconstruction of these sociological approaches, consistent with current approaches to relations between structure and agency developed by Giddens (1979; 1984) and Bourdieu (1989), argues that social action and knowledge adequate for social action is in part a struggle against reducing humanity to its conditions, including the social conditions that transform the public/private division. The interpenetration of public and private elements at the level of structural relations is a condition for the reconstituting public and private features of action at the level of agency.

The blurring of the public/private distinction is a condition of action that results from social processes; at the same time, social action that is at least partially autonomous from its conditions requires the public/private distinction in some institutional and discursive forms that shape agents. As we have demonstrated, Marx's analysis of politics and law creation, Durkheim's analysis of differentiation and the social nature of law, Weber's formulation of will and rationality, and Parsons's differentiation between the personality system and the social system all share a dual approach to the public/private division: The public/private division is a feature of indeterminacy and freedom in the relations of social action and in the formation of social agents that interpenetrates with the structural processes that fuse public and private elements. Most particularly, the public/private distinction is formative for the constitution of social agents in their self-referential participation in social processes. It is a distinction through which power is mobilized, commitments are made, and associative bonds are formed and dissolved. Zones of privacy for social classes, individuals, and various associations are requisite for identity formation, reflexivity, value and interest formation, and organizational autonomy. The recognition, organization, legitimation, distribution, and protection of these relatively private zones is a feature of public discourse and freedom in action that must be reconstituted as underlying adaptive processes fuse public and private realms.

Legal scholars have developed parallel approaches to our sociological formulation of the public/private distinction. While critical of the public/private distinction as an ahistorical structural relation, they have recognized its importance at the level of social action and agency. Most centrally, they have formulated the public/private distinction as a framework for articulating conflicts in a manner that prepares them for resolutions based on applications of legal precedents and legal principles to particular cases by judges. From the standpoint of the sociology of the public/private division, law mediates institutional processes that have cross-cutting public and private elements while affirming the public/private division for social agents.

Arguing that the boundary between public and private "is a human construct that must be fought for and quarreled over," Louis Michael Seidman (1987: 1006) maintains that the public/private distinction is at the heart of three intersecting "dilemmas" (1987: 1007): relationships among universal and particular values, relationships among government intervention and libertarianism, and relationships among openness and secrecy. In ways reminiscent of Weber, Seidman argues that these dilemmas cannot be fully resolved or transcended; rather, they constitute objects of conflict that condition human agency and social action. The public/private distinction stands for dilemmas in social action that make legal authority necessary.

"Whole persons" are in positions of decision making that are shaped by dimensions of the public/private distinction (Seidman, 1987: 1024). In everyday life, we are ethically torn between particular values that demand our personal resources for those whom we share an interpersonal world and, especially, for those whom we love and live our lives with and to universal values that shape broader commitments rooted in cultural, historical, and societal values. When we try to solve problems through governmental intervention, we create laws from the standpoint of universal social values such as collective history, common identity, and equality that come in conflict with particular commitments. Such universal laws, moreover, require maximizing openness and limiting what can be held secret in the private sphere. Libertarianism, on the other hand, opens the likelihood of privatized oppression and inequality while it supports secrecy. From the standpoints of social actors who have different values rooted in varying combinations of particularism and universalism, there is no theoretical resolution to these problems, let alone practical resolution: Social action is constituted through these dimensions of the public/private distinction.

How, then, are the dilemmas posed by the public/private distinction to be mediated? Law and politics are joined in both posing issues in their public and private form and acting on them in ways that maintain that form while modifying it through novel combinations of elements. Thus, at the level of constitutional law, Seidman maintains that while there is no fully rational resolution to public/private dilemmas, judges, ideally embodying a reflective capacity for responsible action, are best suited to dealing with them:

> Only a judge who is sensitive to the contradictory demands of public and private values—who is caught between the desire to do "justice" to the particular, real litigant and the desire to formulate a general rule to maximize utility for the remaining faceless multitude—can be trusted to maintain the boundary between the two spheres without invading either. (1987: 1052)

This notion of law resting on judicial decisions, especially law that evolves through cases based on actual conflicts that require interpreting statutes made by legislators articulating universal interests and values, is the hallmark of a civil society composed of associations that are neither statist nor private. Law constitutes core relations through which the public/private division is recreated in agents of social action at the same time that it is being socialized at deeper structural levels. It is in this set of relations that we can analyze the public/private distinction in law as pivotal for mediating conflicting interests as the public/private division is more fully blended in social structure. Particular examples enable us to demonstrate the historically contingent nature of these relations and to critically interpret them.

The dispute over the explanatory adequacy of corporate liberalism in political sociology lends itself to a critical interpretation rooted in our formulation of the public/private distinction. The core claim of corporate liberalism, propounded by historians Gabriel Kolko (1964), James Weinstein (1968), David Noble (1977), and Martin Sklar (1988) is that roughly from the end of the nineteenth century through the early part of the twentieth century a variety of legal, occupational, administrative, and political changes were shaped by elites from the emerging corporate sector of capitalism to establish new patterns of power and social relations by rationalizing and expanding property and market relations. Fred Block (1987) and Theda Skocpol (1980) have argued against corporate liberalism as a version of instrumentalist state theory. They maintain that corporate liberalism has overestimated the extent to which big capitalists are class conscious and sustain a coherent policy approach. Rather than this approach, they maintain that both class conflicts within society and features of state autonomy, especially state managers, are more fruitful for explaining the nature of the state and state actions.

These critiques of corporate liberalism are problematic for several reasons: First, they do not adequately construct corporate liberalism as a form of institutionalized political action that shapes and defines issues independently from specific social agents.[5] Second, they do not attend to the importance of law for defining political issues and patterns of action through which divergent interests are mobilized and state power is exercised (Heydebrand, 1990). Third, and most central to our approach, they do not attend to the ways in which public and private elements were structurally combined in corporate liberalism and how the public/private distinction was reconstituted through law at the levels of economic and political action.

Martin Sklar's study of the formation of corporate liberalism is especially instructive on these issues (1988). It demonstrates how the interplay between case law and statutes reconstituted the public/private distinction from 1890 to 1916, a period of massive social change. This was a period that initiated the transformation of the United States to a modern industrial society. It was a time of massive technological innovation, great economic development, increased economic and regional interdependence, the concentration of financial power, and the reconstitution of society on the basis of the concentration of production through the legal and organizational form of the modern corporation.

Basic to this social transformation was the creation of new forms of property and market relations that enabled the deployment of vast amounts of investment capital and outlets for mass-produced goods. Property was going beyond its private proprietary form as local and regional market relations were becoming encompassed through national and international relations. These changes toward greater interdependency fed into wider arenas of public decision making and alternative proposals for public policy.

Even though negotiable securities—the premier property form of corporate capital—were relatively easily accepted and established in public life and in law, there was a much higher degree of conflict surrounding the role of private corporations in determining prices, conditions of sale, and control of the market. The issue of market power and the determination of markets became a nodal point for alternative political approaches that combined the state, law, and economic institutions through mixtures of public and private aspects.

Agrarian interests, small manufacturing businesses, and political and social groups associated with proprietary property and competitive capitalism sought to limit the power of large corporations through statutes that enforced strict market conditions. They sought to maximize the definitions of corporate power as illegal restraints of trade, favoring a private ordering of economic and social life by imposing strict definitions of legal and political equality through law. This approach constituted the most atomistically privatized policy to market regulation since it relied on the state and the courts solely for policing private actors on the market equally on the basis of strict legal codes that allowed minimal discretion.

At the other extreme, political leaders, government officials, state managers, and associated interests sought to maximize public control over corporations, transforming them into publicly accountable agencies. They favored such policies as federal licensing, governmental reviews of assets, capitalization and investment decisions, and governmental certification of contractual relations involving corporations, including pricing. In this statist policy approach, private corporations were explicitly defined as serving the public interest for politically defined purposes, much like public utilities. Political leaders representing the interests of society as a whole would direct economic activity through the agencies of quasi-private corporations. In between these extremes, and partially incorporating the logic of each, was the corporate liberal approach favored by most large corporations, associated government officials and, to a lesser degree, organized labor. This approach sought to leave it largely to corporations to determine market relations under a state system of regulative law, enforced through the courts on a case-by-case basis. This view heightened the notion of responsible, fiduciary agents within a publicly regulated sphere of economic action. This vision went beyond immediate calculations of profit and loss to include broad public responsibilities in social policy and economic relations.

This corporate liberal approach, combining organizational and social dimensions much more fully than either atomistically privatized or statist approaches, embodies a conceptual transformation of the public/private distinction. It reconceptualized the public/private division from a Weberian dichotomy of private proprietary capital embodying market rationality bounded by the political and administrative rationality of the state to a kind of Parsonsian institutional voluntarism that lacked the determinacy of Durkheim's corporatism. It sought to blend the liberty of powerful private actors with regulative functions of the state primarily through a public ordering that relied heavily on courts.

While the public and private dimensions of life were being increasingly linked through the massive development of the forces of production and expansion of the market, conflicts over the form that this change was to take at the level of policy and political action were set in motion by judicial interpretations of the Sherman Antitrust Act (1890). From 1890 to 1897, court decisions favored a common law interpretation of the Sherman Act. This judicial construction of the act gave considerable discretion to private corporations to regulate the market contractually. Corporations could engage in reasonable restraints of trade as long as they were not creating a monopoly by keeping out potential competitors and as long as their actions were consistent with the public interest.

In several decisions in 1897, the Supreme Court changed the common law construction to a construction that did not distinguish between reasonable and unreasonable restraints of trade. Maintaining that the Constitution gave Congress full power to regulate interstate commerce, the Court found that all restraints of trade involving the sale, transfer, and distribution of goods were illegal whether or not they were reasonable or unreasonable. This construction supported those groups that valued a purely competitive economy. At the same time, it provided an occasion for mobilizing corporate capitalists to restore the common law definition of the Sherman Act to enable corporate regulation of the market. Meanwhile, it enhanced the power of the executive branch of government to selectively use the Sherman Act and to brandish the power of government over interstate commerce.

The shift in judicial construction of the statute had complex consequences for action: It seemed to favor those who sought to maximize egalitarian private ordering on the logic of competition. It energized corporate interests that sought to maximize private ordering through common-law definitions of contract. It enhanced the power of the central government to engage in economic policy-making in the name of the Constitution and the public interest.

By 1911, the Court returned to a construction of the Sherman Act that distinguished between reasonable and unreasonable restraints of trade. This common-law-centered construction set the stage for the triumph of corporate liberalism. It provided an alternative to both overly economistic definitions of contractualism and overwhelming state intervention. It forged an arena of regulative policy that maintained the rule of law and private ordering of the market.

The example of corporate liberalism demonstrates the importance of law and historical contingencies for fusing public and private elements at the level of social structure and reformulating the distinction at the levels of agency, action orientations and politics. While structural changes deepened the interpenetration of public and private aspects of social life, there was also a reconstitution of separate public and private spheres at levels of agency and action. In addition, these structural changes and the reconstituted forms of action raise other issues from our approach to the reconstitution of the public/private division in social theory: In what ways are these changes progressive and/or regressive from the standpoints of social and political emancipation? Did they facilitate and/or hinder such emancipatory interests as enhanced material life, extended equality, extended democratic participation, and individual autonomy?

Corporate capitalism redefined the public/private distinctions in ways that dramatically developed the forces of production and rendered them controllable through public regulation due to the size and pattern of corporate enterprise. It also expanded market relations, heightened international orientations and interdependency. Moreover, it fostered, through the need for expertise and the formation of corporate and governmental bureaucracy, a fuller everyday rational orientation to the world. In these ways, corporate liberalism appears to be consistent with Marx's notion of a progressive transformation of the public/private dimensions of competitive capitalism.

Yet, there are clear regressive features of corporate liberalism. Its emergence rested on the exclusion of blacks and large segments of the working class from the public arenas of political discourse, electoral politics and institution building since these groups would have enhanced populist and socialist alternatives to corporate liberalism. In addition, it fostered an elite public sphere that facilitated technocratic decision making and expert regulation through administrative law (Alchon, 1985). Moreover, it furthered the commodification of everyday life, shaping zones that recreated a private sphere through corporate definitions of gender and an isolated, administered everyday life through advertising, patterns of domestic consumption, housework, and career. These progressive and regressive features of the corporate liberal transformation of the public/private division are historical conditions that shape contemporary social life.

Our reconstruction of classical social theory and our brief discussion of corporate liberalism maintain that legal formulations of the public/private distinction are central for transposing structural transformations into political issues and frameworks for shaping political actors and conditions of action. As this example demonstrates, however, the legal form through which the public/private division is recreated is itself constituted through social forces. Under prevailing conditions, legal discourse does not remain fixed in relation to its social conditions. Legal discourse formulates the public/private distinction as a framework for legal decision making and action under social conditions that lead to a breakdown of some of its most formal and rational features.

Constructing social order through universal laws that are applied equally to the actions of private actors becomes increasingly problematic as social relations become more dense, anonymous, and symbolically mediated, and as concentrations of financial resources and market power combine with legislative lawmaking. The public/private distinction in legal discourse is increasingly shaped by government interventions into social and economic relations that strive to stabilize social order and to deal with consequences of economic organization. Largely as a result of the importance of large corporations for the national economy and the capacities of large corporations to mobilize political pressures, the public/private division in law is pushed in particularistic, purposive directions. Whether viewed from perspectives of societal corporatism (Schmitter, 1979), postliberalism (Unger, 1976), advanced capitalism (Habermas, 1973), or postindustrialism (Bell, 1976), the public/private distinction in legal discourse shapes frameworks of action and decision making under conditions that require an increasing recognition that legal categories are rooted in societal changes that combine public and private institutions and discourses in purposive, goal-oriented directions that partially construct private interests. As such, inquiry should be increasingly directed toward developing a sociologically rooted, critical reconstruction of the public/private distinction in law that more fully realizes both the fusion of public/private elements structurally and the centrality of the distinction for the formation of agents of action.

One concrete direction for inquiry is the analysis of different legal forums. Legislative lawmaking, with its focus on mediating private interests by representatives using collective symbols and referents, is a core institutional location for the formation of agents and legal discourses that combine public and private in novel ways. In loan guarantee legislation aimed at bailing out specific corporations such as Lockheed (Turkel, 1981) and Chrysler (Turkel, 1982), in industrial policies that rely on privatization (Turkel and Lofquist, 1991), in new definitions of bankruptcy law (Delaney, 1992), and in the changing constellation of welfare policies (Gilbert and Gilbert, 1989), statutes are shaped through mixtures of public and private discourses and institutional responsibilities that cut across public/private divisions. In all of these instances, public purposes are articulated through accounting procedures, legislative oversight, and overlapping executive decision making among governmental and private institutions. They combine various limits on disclosure through confidentiality, market rationalities that assume motivations toward private gain, and structural interdependencies. In large part, the public power of the state maintains quasi-private forms of economic and familial relations to fulfill societal purposes.

In addition, other forums have emerged as the density of social relations has led to institutional innovations that supplement courts, administrative agencies, and legislative bodies for legal action and for dispute resolution. The expansion of mediation and arbitration as forums for dispute settlement, while subject to criticism for fostering inequalities of legal resources (Forer, 1984; Wertheimer, 1988), provides an arena that is more secret, less adversarial, and more open to shared determination of values and interests than the privatizing effects of litigation. Indeed, these forums of dispute settlement, because they require recognition and interaction among disputing parties, lead to individual and mutual recognition of needs as grounds for dispute resolution rather than articulating rights by judges or articulating interests by legislators (Silbey and Sarat, 1989: 490–98). They provide the institutional and discursive grounds for formulating needs and purposes of social agents in part because they are neither fully public nor fully private arenas. They facilitate a shared discourse of mutual recognition that mediates private identities, interests, and sources of conflict.

Mediation and arbitration are forums that allow for informal discourses that enable the formation of juridical subjects on the basis of mutuality and reflection that goes beyond purely privatized self-referencing based on publicly stipulated rights. In addition to analyzing forums of legal action, departures in legal theory provide substantive issues for analyzing the changing content of the public/private division at levels of structure and agency. Doctrinal challenges to the gendered public/private division that grounds the construction of constitutional rights raised by feminist legal scholars are crucial here. Nadine Taub and Elizabeth Schneider, while raising fundamental criticisms to how the public/private distinction has historically articulated male domination, have argued that there should be increasing legal regulation of the private domestic sphere (1983). Domestic relations should be articulated through public discourses and institutional changes that are infused with feminist perspectives and that facilitate the full participation of women. At the same time, they recognize the importance of delineating a private zone of self-determination, activity, and relationships that is personal and outside of collective determination (1983: 173–74).

In a similar vein, Christine Littleton has argued that the legal equality of women requires that the hierarchical relationship between the employment structure and the domestic sphere must be reworked in a way that gives equal legal footing to employment responsibilities and family responsibilities (1987: 1053). By equalizing the social importance of these spheres through law, the separations between them can be overcome in directions that bring men and women into a common social sphere of production and reproduction. These fusions of public and private zones in legal discourse would initiate conditions for the fuller exercise of self-reflection, identity formation and other nonlegal patterns of interaction, enabling people to more fully determine gender definitions and relations. The reordering of public/private elements in directions that overcome their structural segregation open up possibilities for deepening private dimensions of self-determination. Arguing through these same principles, Sylvia Law has sought to reformulate relations between masculine occupational spheres and feminine domestic spheres so that "the appropriate function of law is not to enforce a general vision of what men and women are really like but rather to respect each person's authority to define herself or himself, free from sex-defined legal constraints" (1984: 969). Here again, legal frameworks for determining private identity and the capacities of agents are rooted in a fuller interpenetration of public and private institutions. This, in turn, paves the way for fuller public participation and project formation.

These reformulations of the public/private distinction in legislative lawmaking, in alternative patterns of dispute settlement, and in feminist legal theory are bolstered by more general approaches in the sociology of law. This analytic direction seeks to identify underlying tendencies within, on the one hand, legal institutions and discourses, and, on the other hand, broader patterns of social change that lead from the relatively strict public/private division characteristic of formal rational legality to the more interrelated pattern of public and private elements characteristic of substantive legality. Phillipe Nonet and Philip Selznik's concept of "responsive law" (1978), for example, stresses internal changes in legal institutions and discourses that lead from formal rationality to a more purposive and participatory pattern of legality. Jürgen Habermas provides a critical alternative to administrative law in the form of institutions that facilitate communicative action (1986). Niklas Luhman argues that substantive dimensions of law emerge with integrative learning capacities that characterize complex societies (1986). Gunther Teubner's neoevolutionary approach to law stresses the formation of reflexive capacities and substantive rationality (1983). Joel Handler formulates law as source of "dialogic community" that shapes identity and collective projects (1988). These approaches infuse law with tendencies toward the formation of emancipatory purposes in part by recombining elements of social action across public and private differences. The relative autonomy of law, both institutionally and discursively, combines with social complexity and enhanced material capacities that reduce toil for maintaining life to provide for the emergence of a more socially reflexive, purposive legality.

Through these approaches, the public/private division becomes increasingly referential to processes of social development and to the potentials for institutional and individual recognition and will formation. As Michael Walzer argues in his radicalization of liberal social theory, the liberal "art of separation" is best viewed as efforts of human emancipation to create autonomous arenas of activity founded on equality and democratic participation (1984). These autonomous arenas of action combine public and private features. They are based on principles through which their projects can be publicly articulated, they are noncoercive, they fulfill particular interests and purposes, they are capable of confidentiality, secrecy or some other type of nondisclosure, and they are "in the hands" of their members (1984: 327). The autonomy of the individual, including that which is reflective, hidden, and private, renews its sources through a political economy and a political society that realize the public/private division as a feature of autonomous arenas of action.

The public/private division is a feature of the human condition. It becomes more pervasive, more differentiated, and associated with divergent historical tendencies as the human condition becomes more social. One tendency, a totalizing tendency, is for the public/private division to be an aspect of hierarchically organized social power that dominates people through the executive powers of the state, the corporation, and socialized patriarchy. Here the public/private division is extended, elaborated, and focused through technologized means of surveillance, manipulation, and intervention into hidden, particular spaces that are defined through organized power legitimated through appeals to necessity. Privacy, devalued as isolated visibility, and the public sphere are constituted through procedures of control. Here agency is reduced to an ideological representation of hierachical power. The other tendency, active and emancipatory, is for the public/private distinction to be extended by reflective social agents who create spheres of autonomous action justified through principles of participation and equality. Here the private sphere is deepened through public spheres of action that enable the recognition of a fundamental social principle: We are simultaneously socially made and participate in making ourselves and society as we deepen our private lives. The private is constituted through particular commitments, self-reflection in protected spaces while the public is constituted in open arenas of association based on principles of equality that establish grounds for forming and realizing qualitative projects. Politics and law are the discursive and institutional relations through which the public/private division is realized. At its best, social theory conceptualizes the totalizing tendency as a condition to be struggled against and the active, emancipatory tendency as a world to be struggled for.

## NOTES

1. Criminological studies are often formulated around the hidden and secretive motives, acts, and structures through which criminal activity is motivated and organized. See, for example, Donald Cressey's classic analysis of "nonshareable problems" as a central feature of embezzlement (1953) and William Chambliss's analysis of the systematic yet necessarily hidden nature of public corruption (1978).

2. For an insightful and provocative discussion of *1984* that evaluates it from a critical theory analysis of domination, see Douglas Kellner (1990). The effect of constant surveillance leads, in Irving Goffman's terms (1959), to the virtual absence of a back region where performances can be rehearsed and composed before they are accomplished. The distinction between private and public faces and interaction dissolves as individuals are always on guard. This renders it virtually impossible for individuals and institutions to engage in forming projects that result from deliberation and planning (Westin, 1967: 44–63). For an analysis of the intricacies of Fourth Amendment jurisprudence on rights to privacy, see Richard Wilkins (1987).

3. A watershed case that exemplifies this is *Marsh v. Alabama* (326 U.S. 501 [1946]). The Supreme Court held that the more the private owner of a town opened up his property for use by the general public, the more the town became subject to state regulation since it was engaged in a public function. While intermediate terms like *public function* may serve to resolve particular cases, these terms are difficult to maintain since they are grounded in disagreements over which differences are important in constructing them: which aspects of a situation are public and which are private are subject to interpretation and are controversial. See Leslie Friedman Goldstein for a discussion of the movement from state action doctrine to public sphere doctrine in Supreme Court interpretations of the Fourteenth Amendment (1977).

4. Charles Lindblom (1977) argues that the relative absence of political acrimony and the relative stability of politics in liberal democracies results from the fact that there are really two systems of power: the market economy and the state. Most of the actions that are decisive for everyday life are determined through market power, rendering politics more into an arena for drama and derision rather decisive action.

5. It is also important to consider that corporate liberalism was constructed by historians, chiefly to analyze a particular historical period. Yet sociologists have tended to use *corporate liberalism* to define a type of economic/state relations. While this is not in itself problematic, there must be a clear under-

standing of the historical meaning of the term. Ira Katznelson (1989) provides a valuable example of the importance of context for defining types by comparing the New Deal to the Great Society.

# Bibliography

Albrow, Martin. 1975. "Legal Positivism and Bourgeois Materialism: Max Weber's View of the Sociology of Law," *British Journal of Law and Society* 2: 14–31.

Alchon, Guy. 1985. *The Invisible Hand of Planning: Capitalism, Social Science, and the State in the 1920s*. Princeton, NJ: Princeton University Press.

Alexander, Jeffrey C. 1980. *Theoretical Logic in Sociology, Vol. I*. Berkeley: University of California Press.

_______. 1987. "The Dialectic of Individuation and Domination: Weber's Rationalization Theory and Beyond." In Sam Whimster and Scott Lash (eds.), *Max Weber, Rationality and Modernity*. Pp. 185–206. London: Allen & Unwin.

Annas, George. 1989. "Predicting the Future of Privacy in Pregnancy: How Medical Technology Affects the Legal Rights of Pregnant Women," *Nova Law Review* 13: 329–53.

Appelbaum, Richard P. 1978. "Marx's Theory of the Falling Rate of Profit," *American Sociological Review* 43: 67–80.

Arendt, Hannah. 1951. *The Origins of Totalitarianism*. New York: World Publishing.

_______. 1959. *The Human Condition*. New York: Doubleday.

_______. 1965. *Eichmann in Jerusalem*. New York: Viking.

Auerbach, Jerold S. 1983. *Justice Without Law?* New York: Oxford University Press.

Balbus, Isaac. 1977. "Commodity Form and Legal Form: An Essay on the 'Relative Autonomy' of Law," *Law and Society Review* 11: 571–88.

_______. 1982. *Marxism and Domination*. Princeton, NJ: Princeton University Press.

Baxi, Upendra. 1974. "Durkheim and Legal Evolution: Some Problems of Disproof," *Law and Society Review* 8: 645–51.

Bay, Christian. 1970. *The Structure of Freedom*. Stanford, CA: Stanford University Press.

_______. 1981. *Strategies of Political Emancipation*. Notre Dame, IN: University of Notre Dame Press.

Beirne, Piers. 1979. "Ideology and Rationality in Max Weber's Sociology of Law," *Research in Law and Sociology* 2: 103–31.

Bell, Daniel. 1976. *The Coming of Post-Industrial Society*. New York: Basic Books.

_______. 1978. *The Cultural Contradictions of Capitalism*. New York: Basic Books.

Bellah, Robert N., Richard K. Madsen, William M. Sullivan, Ann Swidler, and Steven M. Tipton. 1985. *Habits of the Heart*. New York: Harper and Row.

Bensman, Joseph, and R. Lillienfeld. 1979. *Between Public and Private*. New York: Free Press.

Berger, Peter, Brigitte Berger, and Hansfried Kellner. 1974. *The Homeless Mind*. New York: Vintage.

Berman, Marshall. 1970. *The Politics of Authenticity: Radical Individualism and the Emergence of Modern Society*. New York: Atheneum.

Bershady, Harold. 1973. *Ideology and Social Knowledge*. New York: John Wiley & Sons.

Bierstedt, Robert. 1981. *American Sociological Theory: A Critical History*. New York: Academic Press.

Bittner, Egon. 1973. "Objectivity and Realism in Sociology." In George Psathas (ed.), *Phenomenological Sociology: Issues and Applications*. Pp. 109–28. New York: John Wiley & Sons.

Block, Fred. 1987. *Revising State Theory*. Philadelphia, PA: Temple University Press.

Bologh, Roslyn Wallach. 1979. *Dialectical Phenomenology: Marx's Method*. London: Routledge & Kegan Paul.

Boris, Ann, and Jane Bordiglio. 1981. "The Social Transformation of Patriarchy." In Irene Diamond (ed.), *Women, Family and Public Policy*. Pp. 70–93. New York: Longman's.

Bottomore, Tom. 1981. " A Marxist Consideration of Durkheim," *Social Forces* 59: 902–17.

Bourdieu, Pierre. 1989. "Social Space and Symbolic Power," *Sociological Theory* 7: 14–25.

Bourricaud, Francois. 1981. *The Sociology of Talcott Parsons*. Translated by Arthur Goldhammer. Chicago, IL: University of Chicago Press.

Braverman, Harry, 1974. *Labor and Monopoly Capital*. New York: Monthly Review Press.

Bruun, H. H. 1972. *Science, Values and Politics in Max Weber's Methodology*. Copenhagen, Denmark: Munksgard.

Bryant, Christopher G. A. 1978. "Privacy, Privatization and Self-Determination." In J. B. Young (ed.), *Privacy*. Pp. 59–86. New York: John Wiley & Sons.
Chambliss, William J. 1978. *On the Take*. Bloomington: Indiana University Press.
_______. 1979. "On Lawmaking," *British Journal of Law and Society* 6: 149–71.
Christman, John, ed. 1989. *The Inner Citadel: Essays on Individual Autonomy*. New York: Oxford University Press.
Cicourel, Aaron. 1964. *Method and Measurement in Sociology*. New York: Free Press.
Collins, Randall. 1988. *Theoretical Sociology*. New York: Harcourt Brace Jovanovich.
Colomy, Paul B. 1986. "Recent Developments in the Functionalist Approach to Change," *Sociological Focus* 19: 139–58.
Cressey, Donald R. 1953. *Other People's Money*. Belmont, CA: Wadsworth Publishing.
Culler, Jonathan. 1982. *On Deconstruction: Theory and Criticism after Structuralism*. Ithaca, NY: Cornell University Press.
Delaney, Kevin J. 1992. *Strategic Bankruptcy*. Berkeley: University of California Press.
Domhoff, G. William. 1990. *The Power Elite and the State: How Policy Is Made in America*. New York: Aldine de Gruyter.
Dougherty, Charles J. 1985. "The Right to Begin Life with Sound Body and Sound Mind: Fetal Patients and Conflicts with Their Mothers," *University of Detroit Law Review* 63: 89–132.
Durkheim, Emile. 1958. *Professional Ethics and Civil Morals*. Translated by Cornelia Brookfield. Glencoe, IL: Free Press.
_______. 1961. *Moral Education*. Translated by Everett K. Wilson and Herman Schnurer. Glencoe, IL: Free Press.
_______. 1962. *Socialism*. Edited by Alvin W. Gouldner. New York: Collier Books.
_______. 1964a. *The Rules of Sociological Method*. Edited by George E. G. Catlin. Translated by Sarah A. Solovay and John H. Meuller. New York: Free Press.
_______. 1964b. *The Division of Labor in Society*. Translated by George Simpson. New York: Free Press.
_______. 1966. *Suicide*. Translated by John A. Spaulding and George Simpson. New York: Free Press.
_______. 1982. *The Rules of Sociological Method and Selected Texts on Sociology and its Method*. Edited by Steven Lukes. Translated by W. D. Halls. New York: Free Press.
Elias, Norbert. 1978. *The Civilizing Process*. Translated by Edmund Jephcott. New York: Urizen.
Elshtain, Jean Bethke. 1974. "Moral Woman and Immoral Man: A Consideration of the Public/Private Split and Its Political Ramifications," *Politics and Society* 4: 453–73.

Engels, Frederich. 1968. *The Condition of the Working Class in England.* Translated by W. O. Henderson and W. H. Chaloner. Stanford. CA: Stanford University Press.

Evans, Sara. 1980. *Personal Politics.* New York: Vintage.

Fenton, Steven. 1984. *Durkheim and Modern Sociology.* Cambridge: Cambridge University Press.

Flacks, Richard. 1988. *Making History: The Radical Tradition in American Life.* New York: Columbia University Press.

Flacks, Richard, and Gerald Turkel. 1978. "Radical Sociology: The Emergence of Neo-Marxian Perspectives in U.S. Sociology," *Annual Review of Sociology* 4: 193–238.

Forer, Lois. 1984. *Money and Justice.* New York: Norton.

Foucault, Michel. 1973. *The Birth of the Clinic.* Translated by A. M. Sheridan Smith. New York: Vintage.

_______. 1977. *Discipline and Punish.* Translated by Alan Sheridan. New York: Vintage.

_______. 1980. *Power/Knowledge: Selected Interviews and Other Writings.* Edited by Colin Gordon. New York: Pantheon.

Freud, Sigmund. 1961. *Civilization and Its Discontents.* New York: Norton.

Gane, Mike. 1983. "Durkheim: Woman as Outsider," *Economy and Society* 12: 220–70.

Garfinkle, Harold. 1967. *Studies in Ethnomethodology.* Englewood Cliffs, NJ: Prentice Hall.

Giddens, Anthony. 1972. "Introduction." In *Emile Durkheim: Selected Writings.* Cambridge: Cambridge University Press.

_______. 1979. *Central Problems in Social Theory.* Berkeley: University of California Press.

_______. 1984. *The Constitution of Society.* Berkeley: University of California Press.

_______. 1986. "Introduction." In *Durkheim on Politics and the State.* Edited by Anthony Giddens. Translated by W. D. Halls. Cambridge, England: Polity Press.

Gilbert, Neil, and Barbara Gilbert. 1989. *The Enabling State: Modern Welfare Capitalism in America.* New York: Oxford University Press.

Gitlin, Todd. 1987. *The Sixties: Years of Hope, Days of Rage.* New York: Bantam Books.

Goffman, Irving. 1959. *The Presentation of Self in Everyday Life.* New York: Doubleday.

_______. 1961. *Asylums.* New York: Doubleday.

Goldstein, Leslie Friedman. 1977. "Death and Transfiguration of the State Action Doctrine—*Moose Lodge v. Irvis* to *Runyon v. McCrary*," *Hastings Constitutional Law Quarterly* 4: 1–33.

Goldstein, Philip. 1990. *The Politics of Literary Theory: An Introduction to Marxist Criticism.* Tallahassee: Florida State University Press.

Gottlieb, Gideon. 1983. "Relationism: Legal Theory for a Relational Society," *University of Chicago Law Review* 50: 567–631.

Gouldner, Alvin. 1962. "Introduction." In Emile Durkheim, *Socialism.* New York: Collier.

_______. 1970. *The Coming Crisis of Western Sociology.* New York: Basic Books.

_______. 1976. *The Dialectic of Ideology and Technology.* New York: Seabury Press.

Habermas, Jürgen. 1970. *Toward a Rational Society.* Translated by Jeremy J. Shapiro. Boston: Beacon Press.

_______. 1971. *Knowledge and Human Interests.* Translated by Jeremy Shapiro. Boston: Beacon Press.

_______. 1973. *Theory and Practice.* Translated by John Viertel. Boston: Beacon Press.

_______. 1973. *Legitimation Crisis.* Translated by Thomas McCarthy. Boston: Beacon Press.

_______. 1986. "Law as Medium and Law as Institution." In Gunther Teubner (ed.), *Dilemmas of Law in the Welfare State.* New York: Walter de Gruyter.

_______. 1989. *The Structural Transformation of the Public Sphere.* Translated by Thomas Burger with the assistance of Frederick Lawrence. Cambridge: MIT Press.

Handler, Joel F. 1988. "Dependent People, the State, and the Modern/Postmodern Search for the Dialogic Community," *UCLA Law Review* 35: 999–1113.

Harding, Sandra. 1981. "What Is the Real Material Base of Patriarchy and Capital?" In L. Sargent (ed.), *Women and Revolution.* Boston: South End Press.

Harrington, Michael. 1972. *Socialism.* New York: Bantam Books.

_______. 1989. *Socialism: Past and Future.* New York: Arcade Publishing.

Hartsock, Nancy. 1985. *Money, Sex and Power.* Boston: Northeastern University Press.

Hawkins, M. J. 1977. "A Re-Examination of Durkheim's Theory of Human Nature," *Sociological Review* 25: 229–51.

Hayward, J. E. S. 1960. "Solidarist Syndicalism: Durkheim and Duguit, Part I," *Sociological Review* 18: 17–36.

_______. 1960. "Solidarist Syndicalism: Durkheim and Duguit, Part II," *Sociological Review* 18: 185–202.

Heydebrand, Wolf. 1990. "Government Litigation and National Policy Making: From Roosevelt to Reagan," *Law and Society Review* 24: 477–96.

Hill, Melvyn A. ed. 1979. *Hannah Arendt: The Recovery of the Public World.* New York: St. Martin's Press.

Hobsbawm, E. J. 1979. *The Age of Capital, 1848–1875.* New York: Mentor.

Hochschild, Arlie. 1983. *The Managed Heart: Commercialization of Human Feeling.* Berkeley: University of California Press.

_______. 1989. *The Second Shift: Working Parents and the Revolution at Home.* New York: Viking.

Horkheimer, Max. 1974. *Eclipse of Reason.* New York: Seabury Press.

Horowitz, Irving. 1982. "Socialization without Politicization: Emile Durkheim's Theory of the Modern State," *Political Theory* 11: 353–77.

Hunt, Alan. 1985. "The Ideology of Law: Advances and Problems in Recent Applications of the Concept of Ideology to the Analysis of Law," *Law and Society Review* 19: 11–37.

Johnson, Barbara. 1980. *The Critical Difference: Essay in the Contemporary Rhetoric of Reading.* Baltimore, MD: Johns Hopkins University Press.

Katznelson, Ira. 1989. "Was the Great Society a Lost Opportunity?" In Steve Fraser and Gary Gerstle (eds.), *The Rise and Fall of the New Deal Order, 1930–1980.* Pp. 185–211. Princeton, NJ: Princeton University Press.

Kaufman-Osborn, Timothy. 1986. "Emile Durkheim and the Science of Corporatism," *Political Theory* 14: 638–59.

Kellner, Douglas. 1990. "From *1984* to *One Dimensional Man*: Critical Reflections on Orwell and Marcuse," *Current Perspective in Social Theory* 10: 223–52.

Kennedy, Duncan. 1982. "The States of the Decline of the Public/Private Distinction," *University of Pennsylvania Law Review* 130: 1349–57.

Klare, Karl E. 1982. "The Public/Private Distinction in Labor Law," *University of Pennsylvania Law Review* 130: 1358–1422.

Kolko, Gabriel. 1964. *The Triumph of Conservatism.* New York: Free Press.

Kronman, Anthony. 1983. *Max Weber.* Stanford, CA: Stanford University Press.

Kuhn, Thomas. 1970. *The Structure of Scientific Revolutions.* Chicago: University of Chicago Press.

LaCapra, Dominick. 1972. *Emile Durkheim: Sociologist and Philosopher.* Ithaca, NY: Cornell University Press.

Lakatos, Imre. 1970. "Falsification and the Methodology of Scientific Research Programmes." In I. Lakatos and A. Musgrave (eds.), *Criticism and the Growth of Knowledge.* Pp. 91–196. London: Cambridge University Press.

Lasch, Christopher. 1979. *The Culture of Narcissism.* New York: Norton.

_______. 1984. *The Minimal Self.* New York: Norton.

Law, Sylvia A. 1984. "Rethinking Sex and the Constitution," *University of Pennsylvania Law Review* 132: 955–1040.

Lehmann, Jennifer M. 1990. "Durkheim's Response to Feminism: Prescriptions for Women," *Sociological Theory* 8: 163–87.

Lemert, Charles, and Garth Gillan. 1982. *Michel Foucault: Social Theory as Transgression.* New York: Columbia University Press.

Lindblom, Charles E. 1977. *Politics and Markets: The World's Political-Economic Systems.* New York: Basic Books.

Littleton, Christine A. 1987. "Equality and Feminist Legal Theory," *University of Pittsburgh Law Review* 48: 1043–59.

Lockwood, David. 1956. "Some Remarks on *The Social System*," *British Journal of Sociology* 7: 134–46.

Luhmann, Niklas. 1986. "The Self-Reproduction of Law and Its Limits." In Gunther Teubner (ed.), *Dilemmas of Law in the Welfare State*. New York: Walter de Gruyter.

Lukacs, Georg. 1971. *History and Class Consciousness*. Translated by Rodney Livingstone. London: Merlin Press.

Lukes, Steven. 1973. *Emile Durkheim*. New York: Penguin Books.

Macpherson, C. B. 1962. *The Political Theory of Possessive Individualism: Hobbes to Locke*. New York: Oxford University Press.

Marcuse, Herbert. 1941. *Reason and Revolution*. Boston: Beacon Press.

_______. 1964. *One Dimensional Man*. Boston: Beacon Press.

Marx, Karl. 1963. *The Eighteenth Brumaire of Louis Bonaparte*. New York: International Publishers.

_______. 1964. *The Economic and Philosophical Manuscripts of 1844*. New York: International Publishers.

_______. 1970. *The German Ideology*. New York: International Publishers.

_______. 1977. *Capital. Vol. I*. New York: Vintage.

_______. 1978a. "Contribution to the Critique of Hegel's Philosophy of Right." in Robert C. Tucker (ed.), *The Marx-Engels Reader*. New York: Norton.

_______. 1978b. "On the Jewish Question." In Robert C. Tucker (ed.), *The Marx-Engels Reader*. New York: Norton.

_______. 1978c. "The Manifesto of the Communist Party." In Robert C. Tucker (ed.), *The Marx-Engels Reader*. New York: Norton.

Mashaw, Jerry L. 1983. *Bureaucratic Justice: Managing Social Security Disability Claims*. New Haven, CT: Yale University Press.

Mayhew, Leon. 1982. "Introduction." In Leon Mayhew (ed.), *Talcott Parsons: On Institutions and Social Evolution*. Chicago: University of Chicago Press.

_______. 1984. "In Defense of Modernity: Talcott Parsons and the Utilitarian Tradition," *American Journal of Sociology* 89: 1273–1305.

McEvoy, Arthur. 1983. "Law, Public Policy, and Industrialization in the California Fisheries, 1900–1925," *Business History Review* 57: 494–521.

Merton, Robert K. 1934. "Durkheim's Division of Labor," *American Journal of Sociology* XL: 319–28.

Mestrovic, Stjepan G. 1988. *Emile Durkheim and the Reformation of Sociology*. Totowa, NJ: Rowman and Littlefield.

Miliband, Ralph. 1969. *The State in Capitalist Society*. New York: Basic Books.

Miller, James. 1987. *Democracy Is in the Streets: From Port Huron to the Siege of Chicago*. New York: Simon & Schuster.

Mills, C. Wright. 1956. *The Power Elite*. New York: Oxford University Press.

_______. 1959. *The Sociological Imagination*. New York: Oxford University Press.

_______. 1967. *Power, Politics and People: The Collected Essays of C. Wright Mills*. Edited by Irving Louis Horowitz. New York: Oxford University Press.

Mnookin, Robert H. 1982. "The Public/Private Dichotomy: Political Disagreement and Academic Reputation," *University of Pennsylvania Law Review* 130: 1429–40.

Mommsen, Wolfgang. 1987. "Personal Conduct and Societal Change." In Sam Whimster and Scott Lash (eds), *Max Weber, Rationality and Modernity*. Pp. 35–51. London: Allen and Unwin.

Mouffe, Chantal. 1990. "Radical Democracy or Liberal Democracy?" *Socialist Review* no. 2: 57–66.

Münch, Richard. 1982. "Talcott Parsons and the Theory of Action. II. The Continuity of the Development," *American Journal of Sociology* 87: 771–826.

Nicolaus, Martin. 1973. "Foreword." In Karl Marx *The Grundrisse*. Translated by Martin Nicolaus. New York: Penguin Books.

Nisbet, Robert A. 1965. *Emile Durkheim*. Englewood Cliffs, NJ: Prentice Hall.

_______ . 1966. *The Sociological Tradition*. New York: Basic Books.

Noble, David. 1977. *America by Design: Science, Technology, and the Rise of Corporate Capitalism*. New York: Knopf.

Nonet, Phillipe, and Philip Selznik. 1978. *Law and Society in Transition: Toward Responsive Law*. New York: Harper & Row.

O'Connor, James. 1973. *The Fiscal Crisis of the State*. New York: St. Martin's Press.

Ollman, Bertell. 1971. *Alienation: Marx's Conception of Man in Capitalist Society*. New York: Cambridge University Press.

Olson, Frances E. 1983. "The Family and the Market: A Study of Ideology and Legal Reform," *Harvard Law Review* 96: 1947–1578.

Palmer, J., and F. Pearce. 1983. "Legal Discourse and State Power: Foucault and the Juridical Relation," *International Journal of the Sociology of Law* 11: 361–83.

Parsons, Talcott. 1937–1968. *The Structure of Social Action, Vols. I and II*. New York: Free Press.

_______ . 1951. *The Social System*. Glencoe, IL: Free Press.

_______ . 1966. *Societies*. Englewood Cliffs, NJ: Prentice Hall.

_______ . 1977. *Evolution of Societies*. Englewood Cliffs, NJ: Prentice Hall.

_______ . 1982. "The Superego and the Theory of Social Systems." In Leon H. Mayhew (ed.), *Talcott Parsons: On Institutions and Social Evolution*. Chicago: University of Chicago Press.

_______ . 1982a. "The Hierarchy of Control." In *Talcott Parsons: On Institutions and Social Evolution*. Chicago: University of Chicago Press.

_______ . 1982b. "Evolutionary Universals in Society." In *Talcott Parsons: On Institutions and Social Evolution*. Chicago: University of Chicago Press.

Parsons, Talcott, and E. A. Shils. 1951. *Toward a General Theory of Action*. Cambridge, MA: Harvard University Press.

Parsons, Talcott, and Neil Smelser. 1956. *Economy and Society*. London: Routledge & Kegan Paul.

Pateman, Carole. 1987. "Feminist Critiques of the Public/Private Dichotomy." In Anne Phillips (ed.), *Feminism and Equality*. Oxford, UK: Basil Blackwell.

Polan, Diane. 1982. "Toward a Theory of Law and Patriarchy." In David Kairys (ed.) *The Politics of Law: A Progressive Critique*. New York: Pantheon.

Pope, Whitney. 1973. "Classic on Classic: Parsons' Interpretation of Durkheim," *American Sociological Review* 38: 399–415.

_______ . 1976. *Durkheim's 'Suicide': A Classic Analyzed*. Chicago: University of Chicago Press.

Pope, Whitney, Jere Cohen, and Lawrence E. Hazelrigg. 1975. "On the Divergence of Weber and Durkheim: A Critique of Parsons' Convergence Thesis," *American Sociological Review* 40: 417–427.

Poster, Mark. 1978. *Critical Theory of the Family*. New York: Seabury Press.

Poulantzas, Nicos. 1973. *Political Power and Social Classes*. Translated by Timothy O'Hagen. London: New Left Books.

Prager, Jeffrey. 1981. "Moral Integration and Political Inclusion: A Comparison of Durkheim's and Weber's Theory of Democracy," *Social Forces* 59: 918–50.

Riesman, David, with N. Glazer and R. Denney. 1950. *The Lonely Crowd*. New Haven, CT: Yale University Press.

Ritzer, George. 1988. *Sociological Theory*. New York: Alfred A. Knopf.

Roth, Guenther. 1979. "Charisma and Counterculture." In Guenther Roth and Wolfgang Schluchter (eds.), *Max Weber's Vision of History*. Pp. 119–37. Berkeley: University of California Press.

Rothchild-Whitt, Joyce. 1984. "Worker Ownership: Collective Response to an Elite-Generated Crisis," *Research in Social Movements, Conflict and Change* 6: 167–94.

Rybczynski, Witold. 1986. *Home: A Short History of an Idea*. New York: Viking Books.

Savage, Stephen P. 1981. *The Social Theories of Talcott Parsons: The Social Relations of Action*. New York: St. Martin's Press.

Schmitter, Phillipe C. 1979. "Still the Century of Corporatism?" In Phillipe C. Schmitter and Gerhard Lembruch (eds.), *Trends Toward Corporatist Intermediation*. Beverly Hills, CA: Sage.

Schmitter, Phillipe C., and Gerhard Lembruch. 1979. *Trends Toward Corporatist Intermediation*. Beverly Hills, CA: Sage.

Schroyer, Trent. 1973. *The Critique of Domination*. New York: George Braziller.

Schwartz, Richard. 1965. "Reply," *American Journal of Sociology* 70: 627–28.

_______ .1974. "Legal Evolution and the Durkheim Hypothesis: A Reply to Professor Baxi," *Law and Society Review* 8: 653–68.

Schwartz, Richard, and James Miller. 1964. "Legal Evolution and Societal Complexity," *American Journal of Sociology* 70: 159.

Sciulli, David. 1986. "Voluntaristic Action as a Distinct Concept: Theoretical Foundations of Societal Constitutionalism," *American Sociological Review* 51: 743–66.

_______. 1988. "Reconsidering Blumer's Corrective Against the Excesses of Functionalism," *Symbolic Interaction* 11: 69–84.

Seidman, Louis Michael. 1987. "Public Principle and Private Choice: The Uneasy Case for a Boundary Maintenance Theory of Constitutional Law," *Yale Law Journal* 96: 1006–72.

Seidman, Steven. 1983. *Liberalism and the Origins of European Social Theory*. Berkeley: University of California Press.

Sennett, Richard. 1977. *The Fall of Public Man*. New York: Alfred A. Knopf.

Sennett, Richard, and Jonathon Cobb. 1973. *The Hidden Injuries of Class*. New York: Vintage.

Shils, Edward. 1956. *The Torment of Secrecy*. New York: Heinemann.

Sica, Alan. 1988. *Weber, Irrationality and Social Order*. Berkeley: University of California Press.

Silbey, Susan, and Austin Sarat. 1989. "Dispute Processing in Law and Legal Scholarship: From Institutional Critique to the Reconstruction of the Juridical Subject," *Denver University Law Review* 66: 437–98.

Sklar, Martin J. 1988. *The Corporate Reconstruction of American Capitalism, 1890–1916: The Market, the Law, and Politics*. New York: Cambridge University Press.

Skocpol, Theda. 1980. "Political Response to Capitalist Crises: Neo–Marxist Theories of the State and the Case of the New Deal," *Politics and Society* 10: 155–201.

_______. 1990. "Fighting Poverty without Poverty Programs," *The American Prospect* no. 2: 58–70.

Smart, Carol. 1986. "Feminism and Law: Some Problems of Analysis and Strategy," *International Journal of the Sociology of Law* 14: 109–23.

Smith, Dorothy. 1974. "The Ideological Practice of Sociology," *Catalyst* 8: 39–54.

*Social Research* 44. 1977. Special Issue on Hannah Arendt.

Spitzer, Steven. 1975. "Punishment and Social Organization: A Study of Durkheim's Theory of Penal Evolution," *Law and Society Review* 9: 613–35.

_______. 1983. "Marxist Perspectives in the Sociology of Law," *Annual Review of Sociology* 9: 103–24.

Stone, Alan. 1985. "The Place of Law in the Marxian Structure-Superstructure Archetype," *Law and Society Review* 19: 39–67.

Stryker, Robin. 1989. "Limits on the Technocratization of the Law: The Elimination of the National Labor Relation Board's Division of Economic Research," *American Sociological Review* 54: 341–58.

Swidler, Ann. 1973. "The Concept of Rationality in the Work of Max Weber," *Sociological Inquiry* 43: 35–53.

"Symposium on the Public/Private Division." 1982. *University of Pennsylvania Law Review* 130.

Taub, Nadine, and Elizabeth M. Schneider. 1982. "Perspectives on Women's Subordination and the Role of Law." In David Kairys (ed.), *The Politics of Law: A Progressive Critique*. New York: Pantheon.

Taylor, Steve. 1982. *Durkheim and the Study of Suicide*. London: Macmillan Press.

Teubner, Gunther. ed. 1983. "Substantive and Reflexive Elements in Modern Law," *Law and Society Review* 17: 239–85.

Teubner, Gunther, ed. 1988. *Autopoietic Law: A New Approach to Law and Society*. New York: Walter de Gruyter.

Thompson, E. P. 1975. *Whigs and Hunters: The Origin of the Black Act*. New York: Pantheon.

_______. 1978. *The Poverty of Theory and Other Essays*. New York: Monthly Review Press.

Tiryakian, Edward A. 1962. *Sociologism and Existentialism*. Englewood Cliffs, NJ: Prentice Hall.

Toby, Jackson. 1977. "Introduction." In Talcott Parsons, *The Evolution of Societies*. Englewood Cliffs, NJ: Prentice Hall.

Trubek, David. 1972. "Max Weber on Law and the Rise of Capitalism," *Wisconsin Law Review* no. 3: 720–53.

Turkel, Gerald. 1979. "Testing Durkheim: Some Theoretical Considerations," *Law and Society Review* 13: 721–38.

_______. 1981. "Rational Law and Boundary Maintenance: Legitimating the 1971 Lockheed Loan Guarantee," *Law and Society Review* 15: 41–77.

_______. 1982. "Situated Corporatist Legitimacy: The 1980 Chrysler Loan Guarantee," *Research in Law, Deviance and Social Control* 4: 165–89.

_______. 1990. "Michel Foucault: Law, Power, and Knowledge," *Journal of Law and Society* 17: 1–24.

Turkel, Gerald, and William S. Lofquist. 1991. "Privatizing Nuclear Power and the Price-Anderson Act: Establishing Limits to Liability," *Studies in Law, Politics, and Society* 11: 137–63.

Turner, Bryan. 1981. *For Weber*. London: Routledge & Kegan Paul.

Udy, Stanley. 1965. "Dynamic Inferences from Static Data," *American Journal of Sociology* 70: 625–27.

Unger, Roberto M. 1976. *Law in Modern Society*. New York: Free Press.

Wallace, Michael, Larry J. Griffin, and Beth A. Rubin. 1989. "The Positional Power of American Labor, 1963–1977," *American Sociological Review* 54: 197–214.

Wallerstein, Immanuel. 1974. *The Modern World System, Vol. I*. New York: Academic Press.

Walzer, Michael. 1983. *Spheres of Justice*. New York: Basic Books.

_______. 1984. "Liberalism and the Art of Separation," *Political Theory* 12: 315–30.

Warner, R. Stephen. 1978. "Toward a Redefinition of Action Theory: Paying the Cognitive Element its Due," *American Journal of Sociology* 83: 1317–67.

Weber, Max. 1946. "Politics as a Vocation." In Hans Gerth and C. Wright Mills (eds.), *From Max Weber: Essays in Sociology*. New York: Oxford University Press.

_______ . 1949. *The Methodology of the Social Sciences*. Translated by Edward A. Shils and Henry A. Finch. New York: Free Press.

_______ . 1954. *Max Weber on Law in Economy and Society*. Edited and annotated by Max Rheinstein and translated by Edward Shils and Max Rheinstein. New York: Simon and Schuster.

_______ . 1958. *The Protestant Ethic and the Spirit of Capitalism*. Translated by Talcott Parsons. New York: Free Press.

_______ . 1968. *Economy and Society, Vol. I and II*. Edited by Guenther Roth and Claus Wittich. Berkeley: University of California Press.

Weinstein, James. 1968. *The Corporate Ideal in the Liberal State, 1900–1918*. Boston: Beacon Press.

Wellmer, Albrecht. 1971. *Critical Theory of Society*. Translated by John Cummings. New York: Herder and Herder.

Wertheimer, Alan. 1988. "The Equalization of Legal Resources," *Philosophy and Public Affairs* 17: 303–22.

Westin, Alan F. 1967. *Privacy and Freedom*. New York: Athenium.

Wilkins, Richard G. 1987. "Defining the 'Reasonable Expectation of Privacy': An Emerging Tripartite Analysis," *Vanderbilt Law Review* 40: 1077–129.

Wilson, William J. 1987. *The Truly Disadvantaged: The Inner City, The Underclass and Public Policy*. Chicago: University of Chicago Press.

Wimberley, Howard. 1973. "Legal Evolution: One Further Step," *American Journal of Sociology* 79: 78–83.

Winkler, J. T. 1976. "Corporatism," *European Journal of Sociology XVII: 104–27.*

Wolfe, Alan. 1987. "Is Sociology Dangerous?" *Tikkun* 1, no. 1: 96–101.

_______ . 1989. *Whose Keeper?* Berkeley: University of California Press.

Wood, Ellen Meiksins. 1981. "The Separation of the Economic and the Political in Capitalism," *New Left Review* 127: 66–89.

Wright, Erik Olin. 1978. *Class, Crisis and the State*. London: New Left Books.

Young-Bruehl, Elizabeth. 1982. *Hannah Arendt: For Love of the World*. New Haven, CT: Yale University Press.

# Index


Alexander, Jeffrey, 13, 145n
Annas, George, 2–3
Appelbaum, Richard P., 58n
Arendt, Hannah: on the bourgeoisie, 22–23; on careerism, 23–24; on Adolph Eichman, 23–24; on Greek antiquity and public/private division, 18–19; on the household and the political sphere, 20; on the household and the public/private division, 20; on imperialism, 22; on the labor process and the public/private division, 19–20; on Karl Marx, 41; on normalization in sociology, 109n; on the social realm and the public/private division, 19, 20; on totalitarianism, 21–24
autonomy, 36–37n

Balbus, Isaac, critique of Karl Marx, 42
Bell, Daniel, 8, 161, 198n
Bellah, Robert, et al., on the public/private division and individualism, 16
Bensman, Joseph, and R. Lillienfeld, on the public/private division and role theory, 16n.
Berger, Peter et al., 8; on self and personalized meaning, 32
Block, Fred, on the state and class power, 77n
Boris and Bordiglio, on the public/private division and social patriarchy, 220–21
Bottomore, Tom, on Marx and Durkheim, 96n
Bourricaud, François, 184n
Braverman, Harry, 165n
Bruun, H. H., 134, 136, 138
Bryant, Christopher, 37n

Chambliss, William J., 236n
Collins, Randall: on feminist issues, 109n
Colomy, Paul, 184n, 214n
contemporary left theory, 2
corporate liberalism, 227–31; 236n; and law, 229–31
corporatism: and law, 111–112; provisional definition, 111
Cressey, Donald R., 236n

Dougherty, Charles J., on fetal rights, 2
Durkheim, Emile, 14–15, 221, 223–24, 225; on altruistic suicide and masculinity, 107; on the anomic division of labor, 96; on anomic society and privatism, 95; on anomic suicide, 101; on anomie, 91; on anomie and markets, 95–96; on anomie and public consciousness, 101; on anomie and the collapse of public order, 101; on the autonomy of private individual, 84–85; on biology, 103; on communism, 121, 122; on corporate holism, 90; on corporate order and social health, 90; on corporatism, 120; on corporatist approach to public/private division, 82–85; on corporatist law, 111–13, 124; on corporatist reforms, 107–9; on democracy, 124; on division of labor and morality, 119–20; on economics, 88; on evolutionary approach to public/private division, 82; on fatalistic suicide and women, 107; on gender differences, 103–6; on gender differences in suicide, 102; on gender hierarchy and the public/private division, 100; on law and legality, 92, 112–14, 118–19, 123; and Marx, 81, 82, 115; on method and privatism, 99, 100–102; on method and the public sphere, 85–87, 88, 89; on moral solidarity and the public/private division, 91–95; on private property, 116; on private rights, 122, 123; on privatism and age segregation, 94; on privatism and occupational differences, 94; on professional ethics, 119–20; on property and contract, 115–17; on the public/private division and social functions, 117; on public rationality and knowledge, 124; on the public sphere, legal norms and crime, 118; on religion, 101–2; on schools and education, 108–9; on social facts, 87–88; on social facts and private consciousness, 89; on social pathologies and the public/private division, 83, 95, 96; on socialism, 120–21, 122; on societal survival, 92; on the state and legitimacy, 122–24; *Suicide*, 99; on suicide and egoism, 101; and utilitarianism, 121–22

Elias, Norbert, on strangers and public space, 37n

feminism, 220; legal theory, 234; on the public/private division and the oppression of women, 2
Foucault, Michel, 36n, 109n
Freud, Sigmund, 195–97

Gane, Mike, on Durkheim on gender, 109n
Garfinkle, Harold, 165n
Giddens, Anthony, 97n; on structuration, 144n
Goffman, Irving, 1, 7, 236n
Gouldner, Alvin: on altruism, 31; on family and property, 31

Habermas, Jürgen, 198n, 234; on mass democracy and economic concentration, 25; on legitimacy and the public/private division, 24–25; on positivism in Marx's theory, 41; on public sphere, 25; on public opinion, 25; on representation of interests, 24; on work and labor, 37n
Handler, Joel, 234

Harding, Sandra, 220
Hawkins, M. J., 109–10n
Hayward, J.E.S., 97n
Hobsbawm, E. J.: on home and the bourgeiosie, 37–38n; on production and private life, 37n
Hochchild, Arlie, 8
Hunt, Alan, on law and ideology, 77n

Kaufman-Osborne, Timothy, on corporatism in Durkheimian theory, 97n
Kennedy, Duncan, 219
Klare, Karl E., 3–5
Kronman, Anthony, 143, 156
Kuhn, Thomas, 13

labor law, 3–5
LaCapra, Dominick, 98n
Lakatos, Imre, 13
Lasch, Christopher: on narcissism, 33; on privatism and survivalism, 34; on survivalism and victimization, 35
Law, Sylvia, 234
law: and the domestic sphere, 221; and emancipatory purposes, 234; and political issues, 231; and the public/private division, 231
Lehmann, Jennifer M., on Durkheim on feminism and socialism, 109n
liberalism, 1–2; and Karl Marx, 41
Lindblom, Charles, 236n
Littleton, Christine, 233–34
Luhmann, Niklas, 234
Lukes, Steven: on corporatism, 97n

MacPherson, C. B., on "possessive individualism," 15n
Marcuse, Herbert, 36n, 58n
*Marsh v. Alabama*, 236
Marx, Karl, 14, 223, 225; on alienated labor and the public/private division, 47–52; on Louis Bonaparte, 68; on bourgeoisie and Bonapartism, 69–72; on bourgeois egoism, 71; on class, 51, 56–57; on class relations, 70; on Communists and the public sphere, 65–66; on democracy, 45; on democratic socialism, 42; on democratizing public life, 74; on egoism, 47, 51; on emancipated public sphere, 47; on family, 44; on the French Revolution of 1789, 68–69; on the French Revolution of 1848, 69; on human emancipation, 47; on labor and the public/private division, 43; on legal categories and the public/private division, 46; on the legal regulation of the working day, 72–77; on limits of political emancipation, 46–47; on method for reconstructing the public/private division, 42–43; on the lumpenproletariat, 71–72; on money, 52, 60; on private conditions of working class life, 74; on private individuals and class struggle, 73; on private property as active contradiction, 50; on private property and knowledge claims, 57–58; on private property as a legal category, 50; on the privatization of the senses, 51; on privatized power, 66; on property, 46, 50, 54–56, 66; on the public/private division and the division of labor, 54; on the public/private division in philosophy and in political economy, 43–49; on the public/private division, state theories, and law, 59, 61, 67; on the public sphere, 60–64, 70–72; on the state, 44; on

women and bourgeois marriage, 67
Mashaw, Jerry, 166n
Mayhew, Leon, 186, 213
McEvoy, Arthur, 219–20
Merton, Robert, 97n
Mestrovic, Stjepan, on egoism and anomie, 109n
Mills, C. Wright, 7
Mommsen, Wolfgang, 144n
Munch, Richard, 198

New Left, 16n
Nisbet, Robert, 9
Nonet, Phillipe, and Philip Selznik, 234

Olson, Frances E., 220

Parsons, Talcott, 15, 224–25; on agency and social action, 214; on alienation, 193–94; on autonomy, 186, 187; on capital, 205–6; on choice, 172–73; on conformity, 193; on contract, 205, 206; on cultural legitimacy, 209–10, 214; on culture, 199–201; on deviance, 194; on Emile Durkheim, 179–81, 208; on evolutionary universals, 210–11; on family, 212; on freedom, 213–14; on Sigmund Freud, 196; on functional requisites and the public sphere, 202–4; on fundamentalism, 212; on the hierarchy of control, 200–201; on the household, 204; on the individual/society relationship, 185–86, 193, 194–95; on kinship and culture, 209; on language, 209; on law and normative order, 212; on the liberal private sphere, 171; on liberal values, 213; on Alfred Marshall, economic theory, and the theory of action, 175–76; on mechanisms of personality formation, 193–95; on motivation, 188; on organizational complexity, 186; on ownership, 206–7; on Vilfred Pareto, 176–78; on pattern variables and the public/private division, 189–92; on personality and social system, 187–89; on the political sphere, 206, 207–8; on the private sphere, 214; on privatism, 189; on property, 206–7; on the public/private division, 169–71; on the public sphere, 211; on reductionism, 171; on resistant privatism, 194; on social evolution, 208–9; on the stability of the social system, 192–93; on the unit act, 171–72; on value integration, 171; on values, 173; on voluntaristic action, 174, 211; on Max Weber, 181–84
Parsons, Talcott, and Edward Shils, 198n
Parsons, Talcott, and Neil Smelser, 202–4
Pateman, Carole, on the public/private division in feminist theory, 109n
Patterson, Orlando, on slavery and public recognition, 36n
Polan, Diane, 222
politics and political legitimacy, 32–33
Poster, Mark, on parental nurturing, 33
pregnant women, and fetal rights, 2–3
property, 228
public/private division: contention in law, 2, 218–20, 226–27; and corporatism, 232; as a dilemma, 222–23; and legal forums, 232–33; and method, 37n; and political critique, 14; provisionally

defined, 2; and public interaction, 24; and social change, 217–18; and social development, 24; and social justice, 227, 235–36; in social processes, 225; and social transformation, 14; and tradition of social theory, 8–10

Riesman, David, on privatization, 37n
Roth, Guenther, 144n
Rothchild-Whitt, Joyce, 166n
Rybcinski, Witold, on privacy and the specialization of space, 38n

Savage, Stephen R., 12, 174, 202
Schmitter, Phillipe, on corporatism, 125n
Sciulli, David, 172, 174, 214n
Seidman, Louis Michael, 226–27
Seidman, Steven, on Karl Marx, 42
Sennett, Richard: on changes in the public realm, 25–32; on Karl Marx, 42; on narcissism, 33
Sennett, Richard and Jonathon Cobb, 5–7
Sherman Antitrust Act of 1890, 229–30
Shils, Edward, on privatization, 37n
Sica, Alan, 164
Sklar, Martin, on corporate liberalism, 228
Skocpol, Theda, 37n
Smart, Carol, 110n
social theory, 11–13
social transformatist approach to public/private division, 17–18
Stone, Alan, on base/superstructure division, 77
Stryker, Robin, 166n
Swidler, Ann, 144n

Taub, Nadine, and Elizabeth M. Schneider, 2, 221, 233
Teubner, Gunther, 234
Toby, Jackson, 212
Trubek, David, 152
Turkel, Gerald, 144n
Turner, Bryan, on comparing Karl Marx and Max Weber, 144n

Wallace, Michael et al., 166n
Wallerstein, Immanuel, 144n
Walzer, Michael, 166n, 235
Warner, R. Stephen, 184n

**About the Author**

GERALD TURKEL is Professor of Sociology at the University of Delaware, where he teaches courses in social theory and in law and society. His writings on social theory, law, politics, and political economy have appeared in *The Annual Review of Sociology*, *Contemporary Crises*, *International Journal for the Sociology of Law*, *Journal of Law and Society*, *Law and Society Review*, *Current Sociological Theory*, *Studies in Law, Politics, and Society*, and *Urban Life*. He is currently working on a book that develops critical approaches to law and society.

www.ingramcontent.com/pod-product-compliance
Ingram Content Group UK Ltd.
Pitfield, Milton Keynes, MK11 3LW, UK
UKHW020800290926
15470UKWH00003B/871

9 780275 941543